Front cover illustration of '.
K M DUNCAN

Front cover design
LEON THOMPSON

Rear cover photos of
HARRY MELLOR and PHIL WILDIN

MEMORIES OF TAPTON HOUSE SCHOOL

Compiled and published by Len Thompson
1 Orchard Gardens,
Cranleigh.
Surrey GU6 7LG
Email: spireqs@compuserve.com

Printed by
Designtime
4 Haydonleigh Drive
Haydonleigh
Swindon
Wilts SN2 3RX
1999

ISBN 0 9535084 1 2

BY THE SAME AUTHOR
Life Down t'Lane

Acknowledgements

First of all I would like to thank Her Grace the Duchess of Devonshire for being kind enough to write the foreword for this book. By doing so she has extended the link between Tapton House and Chatsworth, which has been in place for nearly two hundred years.

I am also very grateful to all those who have contributed to these Tapton House memories, to those who have supplied photographs, and to those who have helped in any way to produce this book.

I especially wish to thank Joan Riggott (nee Clarke), Bill and Pamela Kemp (nee Clark) and my daughter Julia for doing most of the word processing and to my old school chum Des Baker for reading the scripts.

A special mention for my cousins Delice and Stan Levenson for their guidance, support and enthusiasm for the project and to Marion Yeldham and my Aunty Eunice for carrying out research and cousin Roy Thompson for supplying photographs from his book *Chesterfield 1945-1995*.

I am also indebted to my son Leon for his help with the scanning of images, design and layout of the book.

My personal thanks and apologies also go to those who generously gave me their time and a memory for this book, but who have not been included because of the limit on time and number of pages.

Any discrepancy in any of the memories is entirely due to the passage of time.

Finally, a special word of gratitude to my wife Iris for her support during a very trying time when our 16-year-old dog Lucy was reaching the final phase of her life.

If any reader is still further interested in continuing the idea of Tapton House memories please send any additional articles to the author as a second edition may be published if there is sufficient interest. Also if anyone can provide the names of people in any of the photographs, we may be able to add their names at a later date if the book has a reprint.

Foreword

Perhaps the first link between Chatsworth and Tapton House was made when Joseph Paxton, gardener to the sixth Duke of Devonshire, met George Stephenson in the 1840s and helped him to create the conservatories of which he became so proud.

My own visit took place in June 1956, when I presented the prizes at Speech Day. I was impressed not only by the setting, for the presentations were made in the secluded gardens, but also by the easy-going and friendly atmosphere of the occasion.

Now the school has been closed for some years it is timely to gather together the thoughts and reminiscences of some of the people who taught and studied there.

It says much for those who established the school that the precepts of the original charter permeate the descriptions that former pupils give of their experiences at Tapton. Many contributors refer to the charismatic headmaster, Harry Mellor, who, together with his staff, created a particular ethos which endured for much of the school's life. The responsibility for the house and the park that was their playground seems to have been gladly assumed by the children, who show their love and respect for their splendid surroundings as well as appreciation for the education they received there.

The school no longer exists, Paxton's greenhouses have been demolished, but the spirit of Tapton's charter endures in the accounts of these former pupils and staff.

I am sure that all those associated with the school will enjoy reading this book, which will bring back many memories as well as the history of Tapton House.

The Duchess of Devonshire

Contents

Birthday   1999.
with lots of love Gilly & Cyril.

Lots of love on your Birthday
   from Patty & michael xxx

List of Illustrations

Introduction

Tapton House School was opened as a (co-ed) selective central school (academic - professional) in 1931 and was closed in 1991 after 60 years of education for the 6,000+ pupils who passed through its doors.

This book is a collection of the memories of more than 50 pupils and staff supported by suitable articles from The Taptonian magazines where appropriate. It results from a request by several Old Taptonians after they had read my autobiography *Life Down t'Lane*, which contained a chapter on Tapton House which I attended from 1949 to 1953.

I should like to start with a memory of my own. When I first went to Tapton House in 1949, after spending four years at Gilbert Heathcote primary (boys only), I was amazed at the large number of lovely looking girls that I came into contact with. My Mam's favourite photograph of me (which she placed in a silver photo frame) was taken with two girls, either side of me, under a cherry tree covered with blossom, on the lawn at the rear of the school. That same photo now takes pride of place in my memorabilia and records of those far-off days, which I now wish could be regained.

Readers may be interested to have an idea of how this labour of love has come to fruition: Once the seed was planted I wrote to the Derbyshire Times in October 1998 with a letter to the editor regarding plans for the book and received some encouraging responses.

In November I put the proposal to a meeting of OTs at the Winding Wheel in Chesterfield, where promises of contributions were made by a number of those present. I also visited the Chesterfield Library, Museum and Derbyshire County Council Records Office at Matlock several times to research background information of the history of Tapton House in case there was insufficient material to justify a book based purely on reminiscences. Fortunately my pessimism was misplaced and the project has borne fruit.

My aim was to have at least one contribution per year from school start to finish, and after mailshots to over 180 OTs and 30 OT couples who were subsequently married I almost succeeded; apart from the 1970s onwards. Just one year from the 30s and 40s is not represented, two years in the 1950s and three in the 1960s. Unfortunately, no responses from pupils attending after the early 70s have been received.

Additional written contributions and offers of photographs started coming in from December 1998. Either my own enquiries or tips from OTs, family and friends led to contact being made with teachers, pupils and others who had been associated with the school.

Once it became clear that there was going to be sufficient material to form the body of the book, work began transferring it to computer. This involved sending the text to one of my three WP assistants for digital conversion and spell checking. Each article was then sent to friends and family for editing and verification of accuracy wherever possible and final transfer to the production files. I was fortunate to contact some contributors via the Internet and that has made communications so much easier.

It was important to start by devising a filing system that would cope with tracking all of the communications with contributors and assistants to know who they were, when each article was received, when input to computer, spell checked, edited, supporting photographs received and scanned, relevant names and captions for the images etc. I keep a computerised alphabetical list of manuscript material in some form of chronology, and I file things under contributor and subject, cross-referenced where possible.

Photographs and illustrations then had to be scanned using my son Leon's computer equipment based in London and decisions made on which images would support each article. Unfortunately we came up against the fact that photographic film was extremely scarce during wartime and hence a gap of images in the book during that period.

Final activities included consultations with Leon on the size and format of the book together with decisions about typefaces and layout; how many pages, how many photographs and illustrations, what kind of book cover, which printer?

We carried out the publishing activities, did the entire design and layout, chapter and page headings and numbering. We selected the typeface and size of print, the positioning of the illustrations etc. The only thing we asked the printer to do was to print and bind the books from our manuscript, which was sent to them on computer disk.

So the book has taken some ten months to come to print. I hope you will agree it does our contributors justice and creates a realistic picture of what our school was like. You will see that the majority of the articles are in date order of the contributor's attendance at school with the exception of the first and last poems, which were thought appropriate for starting and finishing the book.

The book is dedicated to all the pupils and staff who are unfortunately unable to return to Tapton, to wander through the grounds, to sit in the Peace Gardens and reflect on the marvellous times we had in that wonderful part of Derbyshire. I am sure that even if they can no longer return physically, many of their spirits will be there. If you don't believe me just be there at 2.00 p.m. on 15 June (the anniversary of its opening) or mid-day on the last Saturday in June in any year (the day of the OTA picnic). You will see what I mean.

Len Thompson July 1999.

Tapton House Entrance Hall

Return to Tapton House School

Tom Jones 1944

Low whispers room to room disrupt your bounds.
Your voice, instilled with youth, is yearning still
With shrilling echoes smoothed in clear young sounds
Sweet lingering within the warmth they spill.
I come with memories - heretics in time.
They lay within me like forgotten seed,
To burst their life in flower, some to mime
A truth of past, and others to exceed.
Remembered joys are seen with sorrow's eyes,
And grief lies framed among the peace we sought.
We call into the past, and past replies
With mirror-like reversal of the thought.
I have not cried too long into this past
For time's mutations. Earth and moon are one
With universe, and though to shade they cast
Old faces, only imagery is gone.
Slow darkling years loomed suddenly away
And some returned, my school, to you. They lie
Upon your heart and wait the prospect day
Of my recalling, - lights of turned reply.

From Romans to Railways - and a little further

Malcolm R Handford - The Taptonian 1958

Reference to Tapton's past in all the usual works of local history are remarkably few, and the further we delve back the scarcer they become. Of late, however, much has been said and written concerning Tapton and its possible connections with the Romans.

Local tradition has it that on Tapton Castle Hill - the large earthen mound to the west of Tapton House - can be found the site of a Roman encampment. Near it the old Roman road from Derby to York was supposed to have run. The latter theory has now been largely discredited but the former still remains a vague possibility. It is possible that Chesterfield was a trading station under the Romans. The discovery of a few coins bearing the heads of long-dead Caesars lends weight to the theory that sons of Rome once occupied our modest mound - now clothing itself with trees - but hardly enough to warrant the assumption of its historical accuracy.

The Saxon name Chesterfield (meaning the field of the chester or castle) seems to imply that in Saxon times our ancient town was overlooked by the ramparts of a castle. Tapton Castle Hill (once called Windmill Hill) - now preserved by the Ministry of Works as an ancient monument - would, because of its commanding position, be an obvious choice of site for the erection of any fortification. Ford's *History of Chesterfield* (published in 1839) seems to regard this as an historical fact and talks of 'the ancient castle of which the foundation may even now be traced'. In the absence of other evidence to corroborate this statement, and bearing in mind that the particular book in question is riddled with inaccuracy, the possible existence of a castle on Tapton's doorstep (almost literally!) must, too, remain no more than an attractive theory.

Domesday Book - that inevitable resort of the local historian - provides the first recorded milestone in the course of Tapton's history. At the time of the great Domesday Survey (1086) Tappetune was one of six berwicks or hamlets of the Manor of Newebold (Newbold). Tapton thus came within the boundaries of the Worpentake of Scarredele (Scarsdale) and as such was the property of the king.

In the reign of King John (1199-1216) Tapton emerges as belonging to William de Briwere. Briwere, a noted royal favourite, had been granted Tapton along with the whole of Worpentake of Scarsdale by John, the king. It is next recorded as having passed into the possession of the Durrants, an old Chesterfield family.

The possibly Elizabethan stone Manor House of Tapton was partly demolished towards the end of the seventeenth century as a result of a misunderstanding which had arisen from a badly worded will. The remaining section with its stone roof, stout chimney stacks and mullioned windows can still be seen. It is in a well-preserved condition, though somewhat modernised in part, and is situated in a hollow some quarter of a mile to the S E of Tapton House.

But if Tapton Manor lays claim to distinction in the annals of antiquity it is Tapton House that attracts the tourist with an eye for a story.

The house is not of any great architectural importance, though its elegant proportions and many-windowed facade cannot fail to give pleasure to the sightseer. This handsome pile of mellow brick and stone rests - when free from its present inmates! - perhaps dreaming of the times when it would welcome carriages bringing guests instead of cars and teachers. Only with reluctance has it surrendered to those who thought - still think, I suppose - it more suitable to house a school than anything else.

Built towards the end of the eighteenth century, Tapton House stands proudly amidst a large rolling park and spacious gardens that are the pride of the men who plan and tend them.

About its early career there is still much opportunity for speculation. The first owner of Tapton House that we can record with complete certainty is Isaac Wilkinson. Wilkinson was a wealthy Chesterfield banker and it has been suggested that it was for him the house was built. On his death in 1831 he willed the house to a George Yeldham Ricketts who afterwards took the name of Wilkinson. This gentleman did not reside at Tapton and his visits appear to have been few. It is thought that Ricketts subsequently 'disposed of Tapton as part of a colliery lease'. The new owner was George Stephenson. It was the coal seams, discovered nearby, that first attracted him to Tapton and not the house.

But Stephenson soon realised the advantages of Tapton House as a residence and made it his home. The extensive gardens and the opportunity to indulge in his favourite hobby, horticulture, doubtless exerted no little influence. Extensive the gardens may have been, but they had been neglected and were much overgrown. Stephenson was determined to replan and set them. One of his first actions was to cut a woodland path to the S W of the House. The path, though much changed, is still in use today. It was 'Old George's' delight to challenge his guests to a race on the steep path and he was very disappointed if beaten!

In Grundy's *Pictures of the Past* we are told that Stephenson's 'one belief, save in steam and coal and iron was in these gardens of his'. He had many glass houses built (one of these may still be seen in the gardens behind the house) and he devoted much of his time to growing fruit of many varieties but especially peaches and pineapples. One of his distinguished friends was Sir Joseph Paxton (of Crystal Palace fame) who must have visited Tapton House more than once.

Stephenson's great love of animals and birds remained with him all his life, as is evident from the lengthy list of pets that he kept at Tapton. After reading a paper *On the Fallacies of the Rotary Engine* at Birmingham in the July of 1848 he suffered a severe attack of fever. The illness seemed to be passing when he had a sudden relapse and died on the 12 August 1848, at the age of sixty-seven. He was buried in the Church of Holy Trinity, where a simple 'G.S. 1848' marks his grave.

The next we hear of Tapton is as a boarding school run by two spinsters, the Misses Pocock and Walker. Little is known about the early progress of this venture except that it was here that Miss Violet Markham's mother received part of her education. Her initials and those of her sister are carved on a tree in the 'wilderness' behind the gardens. There appears to be no written reference to the later career of this school.

In her autobiography *Return Passage* (1953) Miss Violet Markham writes that 'Tapton had been unoccupied for some time and had fallen into considerable disrepair before my parents took possession of it'. Miss Markham's parents had previously lived at Brimington Hall, 'a Jacobean house within three miles of Chesterfield'. Her father, purchased Tapton House and he and his family moved to Tapton on New Year's Day, 1873. Tapton, happily, escaped most of the extreme bad taste of the Victorian era. Indeed, it is to Charles' wife, Rosa, that we owe the beauty of the old salon, or drawing room, which now houses the school library.

The family of Markham continued to live at Tapton for many decades, taking a great interest in Chesterfield affairs and winning the respect of the people of the borough. Miss Violet Markham, however, is known to a much wider public both as a writer of no mean ability and as an educationalist.

In 1925 Mr Charles P Markham gave Tapton House and its extensive grounds to the people of Chesterfield, suggesting that it might be used as a museum or some other public centre. A local museum collection was begun and housed for a time.

But here ends the story of the Tapton known to antiquity and the Tapton House which meant home to two noble families. Here, too, a story begins, the story of Tapton House, the school. However, it is not the present writer's intention to set down the history of that school. Perhaps someone else will take up his abandoned pen and pursue the story of Tapton ever further.

Memories of an Inaugural Scholar

Fred Goodwin 1931

The school was opened as a co-educational selective school at Easter 1931. I had been attending Gilbert Heathcote Junior Boys school on Whittington Moor for two years and took the county scholarship exam at the beginning of 1931. We were also asked to sit a test for Tapton House school and the results came through in March inviting me for an interview at the school accompanied by my parents.

My mother went with me and in the waiting room we sat next to Stuart Lawrence and his mother from Old Whittington. We both agreed to join the Tapton School provided we could move to the grammar school if we had won a county minor scholarship.

At the commencement of the term we were in the first-year class but there was certainly a second and third year class of older students and I am not sure how the selection operated for their students - was there an examination or just school selection? I don't know! Our first-year class had around thirty students equally divided - boys and girls. Our form mistress was Miss Griffiths Jones and she specialised in French and drama. The headmaster was Mr Mellor and the only other member of the staff I can remember was the games master, Mr Silcock.

During this summer term I learned I had been successful with a county minor scholarship to the Chesterfield Grammar School along with two others in the class, Stuart Lawrence and Jessie Hilson from New Whittington. Stuart went to Netherthorpe Grammar School and Jessie to the Chesterfield Girls' High School. This term at Tapton was a good introduction into grammar school education as we had a term of French and we were introduced to algebra in maths and to chemistry and physics in the laboratories.

The school was about four miles from our home, in Racecourse Road, Whittington Moor, so this meant a two-mile bus journey using scholars' tickets. These mauve tickets were 2s 6d for 50 and were purchased from the bus depot in Stonegravels. I used four per day. I caught the bus at the terminus in Racecourse Road to the terminus in Elder Way opposite the Co-op. I walked from there to the Staveley bus terminus below Stephenson Place and this bus took us to the bottom of the drive leading to Tapton House with a fair walk up to the school. When we arrived at school we had to change our shoes in the cloakroom into gym shoes (pumps as they were then called). The reason for this wasn't for comfort but to protect the polished wood floors in the Old House. I always remember in those days my crepe soles had a tendency to part from the uppers. There must have been a dining room at the school but I always took a packed lunch and whenever possible we used to eat this in the park - it was a very pleasant summer. There was a new assembly hall with a stage and we were introduced to drama lessons, although this wasn't my cup of tea!

Co-education was something new, apart from one year at the infants school on Whittington Moor; one term at Tapton wasn't long enough to test its possible success - but I think I was pleased to revert back to 'all boys' at the grammar school. I think it is fairly safe to say that Stuart Lawrence and myself were the first old boys of Tapton House School and Jessie Hilson the first old girl - leaving after three months.

An Old Taptonian Teacher

Harry Routledge - Geography (THS 1932 - 1972)

It seems strange to be writing about my life at Tapton, which extended to 40 years, with a break of three years in the middle for military service.

I like to think the family atmosphere which was prevalent made me stay there. This atmosphere was created by Harry Mellor, who had no family of his own, and came to regard the scholars and staff as his family, and how well it worked. We were privileged to work in lovely surroundings, I particularly in Room 1, the original dining room of the mansion with a beautiful William Morris wallpaper which was visited from time to time by visitors from the V and A.

Every day began with prayers and a hymn in the hall, and then on to work - and work it was - no disciplinary problems - pupils did as they were told, and everyone was happy. And then came the war, and most of those bright lads enlisted. Tragedy struck when very bright lads like Frank Checkley, Geoffrey Richards and Hugh Wolstenholme and 20 more failed to survive. These lads were all commemorated on a plaque, which stood in the hall.

Romance found its way into Tapton. Alice Smith, music, the first senior mistress married Jack Smith (English), Kath Clayton (PE) married Percy Heathcote (history) and in 1951 Hazel Hoole (domestic science) married me, H Routledge (geography). After their marriages, the first two left Tapton as it was the rule that married women were not employed by any education committee. Fortunately, the rule was changed during the war, as so many men were leaving for army service and failing to come back after it, so my wife continued her work at Tapton till 1957 when she left to await the birth of our son in 1958. In due time, romance caught up with the students, Bobby Wilson married Margaret Miles and Leonard Thompson married Eunice Causer, and no doubt there were many more.

One of the highlights of the year was Commemoration Day, 15 June, which was nearly always fine, and so we saw a number of superb plays, produced first by Harry Mellor, and later by Phil Wildin, in idyllic surroundings on the top lawn. How lovely it was, on those hot summer days, to wander round the grounds and to meet and talk to parents who had the welfare of their children at heart.

Money was short even in those days to buy necessary things for the school, so in order to help the situation, I opened the school tuck shop which operated from the domestic science window every break and lunch time. The pupils provided much needed cash, which bought necessities for the school, which were not provided by the education committee. It continued until 1972 when I left. It was steady extra work helped by my wife and Miss Pennington, but it enabled me to put back into Tapton some of what Tapton had given to me.

One must not forget that Tapton was originally a house - a home. The last person to occupy it as such was the celebrated Chesterfield industrialist, Charles Markham, who left it in the late 1920s to go to live at Ringwood. But the most outstanding occupant of Tapton was the celebrated George Stephenson, of railway fame, who was buried at Holy Trinity Church, and thus we always went there for our annual carol service, before breaking up for our Christmas holidays. After Mr Markham left, the council tried to make Tapton into a Stephenson museum. It was not a success as a museum, so the education committee took control of it and Tapton began as a school in 1931 and continued as such with great success until the early 1990s.

But all things come to an end, and so in 1972, I said goodbye to a happy working life, always remembering Tenax Propositi (Tenacious of Purpose), which the staff and pupils always adhered to and this contributed to a very happy and successful school.

Cherry Picking Disaster

Robert B Nightingale 1932 - 1935

I suppose many things happened during the time at school, but memories fade with the years. Three years was all my time spent at Tapton House. Economic necessity made leaving school on your fourteenth birthday imperative for the majority of children. However, I do recall one little episode.

Mr Percy Heathcote (Bandy), the history teacher, often arranged outings to historical sites in the locality. One such trip was to Creswell Crags. Entering the cave with flickering candles we crawled about on hands and knees, following Bandy's instructions to grub about in the sandy floor for old bones. Several minutes went by as fingers explored the fine sand; then a triumphant shout from someone. Shouted instructions from the teacher followed, telling the pupil to mark the exact location and not to move - other bones may be in the vicinity. The finder froze in position awaiting Mr Heathcote's arrival. He put a marker on the spot and took the bone from the pupil and gave it a thorough examination. As he bent it, it snapped, 'Oh dear! Someone has used this place as a lavatory.' 'Historical' laughter from the pupils.

A Series of Events at Tapton House School Year 1933.

Temptation: One cherry tree loaded with ripe cherries situated at the top of the park near the main house gates.

Results: Despite warnings by Tubby Mellor, four second-year pupils decided to thin out the crop.

Method: Two up the tree picking, two below collecting the falling fruit.

Security: Nil

Enemy: Head prefect John Godfrey rounds up the culprits and takes names.

Consequences: Signal sent to Room 8 stating that certain named offenders should report to the headmaster's study forthwith.

Punishments: Line up in front of headmaster's desk. Receive lecture on the evils of disobedience.

About turn, lean over and place hands on front edge of desk.

Ten strokes each from a 'foaming at the mouth' headmaster.

It was calculated afterwards that as the head caned, 1-2-3-4, - 3-2-1, - 2-3-4, etc, numbers 2 and 3 received more punishment than numbers 4 and 1. However, no complaint was lodged!

Always on the Outside

Smudger Smith 1932 - 1935

Describing a junior's view by the resultant old man is not easy. Not easy to remain unbiased but whatever I state I assure you, right now there is no malice towards anything or anyone but the truth as I remember it.

I reckon I just about scraped through as I was in the B stream at Tapton. My parents didn't want me to go, wanted me to go to the same elementary school as my brothers. But not me, I was the first kid in our street, as far as I know, to pass anything, so I wanted to go to Tapton. In retrospect I know why Mam and Dad didn't want me to go, they just couldn't afford it. We were on the dole! I think Dad got 22s per week and the rent for the two up and two down was 7s 6d so my Dad had to make a few coppers here and there.

My first knowledge of Tapton House was just before we sat our 11-plus exam. For that we had to go to a different school - I think I went to Boythorpe! I was at Derby Road Junior School. There was a competition of school choirs to be held in the Market Hall. Tapton House won it! I was in our school choir, we failed miserably because we had been taught to sing 'And the stormy Winds do blow'; whereas, apparently, when you are singing you pronounce it 'Wynds'.

I remember the Tapton House soloist. Nice lad! Much superior to me, in size and obviously in social scale. Wherever we met, which was seldom at Tapton, we got along nicely. He was a little superior but I liked him. He shall be nameless.

There is sufficient evidence to see why I had an inferior complex, big enough to fill the assembly hall. Of course, that couldn't be blamed on Tapton House, but nothing happened there to reassure me. Where other kids had their grey flannels and purple and black caps and ties, complete with blazer and leather satchels, I had patches on my trouser-bottom and darns in my cardigan - mostly all of which were hand-downs from all sorts of unlikely sources.

By sheer providence, just the same, I was seldom out of the top three in the elementary school and seldom out of the bottom three at Tapton. I was lucky enough to win a pen and pencil set in an essay competition so I turned-up at Tapton with my 6d cardboard case from Woolworth's containing my pencil set and a couple of sandwiches wrapped in newspaper. Can you really imagine it? I was licked before I even started! I was inferior! No doubt about it and it remained so until I left school and got a job at 7s 6d per 70-hour week. I feigned illness. I would be off school as much as seven weeks at a time and you don't need me to tell you the inevitable outcome of all that!

Now what do I tell you about the times that I was actually present! Obviously no one knew the real me and my circumstances. In other words most of the times I was living a big lie. In passing I must say that there was a girl in my class who was probably in the same predicament as me. She managed to have a school uniform etc and she managed to come in the top half of the results. I admired her for that! (Rooty, Mr Routledge, actually mentioned her when I met him almost forty years later).

The schoolmasters: As I remember Tubby Mellor, the two Routledge brothers, Mr Macara, Froggy Forsythe, Mr Silcock, Mr Dennison, Mr Smith, Mr Heathcote, Mr Charles (WAG) Middleton. Lady Teachers: Miss Clark, headmistress, Misses Vessy, Stanley, Walker, Clayton, Miss Sharkey, Miss Smith. Mr Smith had an irritating habit of shaking his right knee when he was standing to lecture the class. He married Miss Smith. I understand that Mr Heathcote and Miss Clayton married too. I believe they were both of farming stock. They were all great guys really but I was as remote from them as I am from the Queen today almost. I don't know why today's teachers moan about class sizes being as many as 30 pupils. I reckon we had about 30 in our classes - the only difference being that we all faced the teacher, not like today scattered every which way and practically uncontrollable.

I palled-up with 'Jinks' who lived about 3/4-mile nearer Chesterfield than me so I would call for him and together we would walk to school. We then walked from Birdholme to the Spire and then via Tapton Lane to the footbridge crossing the railway line and on into the zigzag woodland path leading to Tapton House. This time of the year I used to look in amazement at the flowers. We had no gardens at home and I marvelled watching the gardener tending the flowerbeds and mowing the lawns. I remember at autumn time, Mr Macara painting a scene, looking through the window of the art room, of the gardener burning brushwood.

We soon got together our gang: me and Jinks, Phippy and Thomas May and Graham. Mostly we ganged up; scoffed our sandwiches and off we went, sometimes not knowing what the time was and how far away from base we were. We would go away over past the playing fields to some big estate where there were ponds with wild fowl on. Someone said it belonged to Shentalls but I know not. Incidentally, can you believe I never had a cup of tea all the time I was at Tapton House?

I could go on writing a lot of twaddle about what we got up to like throwing at the conkers on the tree near the woodwork shop, when we were told not to throw at trees but I will tell of a few instances:

We are talking about the early 1930s. At that time our playground was a tarmac patch set amongst the trees bordered by the woodwork shop and dining hall. Latterly two brick buildings were built on it. Two Pope brothers played for Derbyshire county cricket; a younger brother, who would be about 16 or 17, was a pupil at Tapton and he was aspiring to be a bowler. Mr Smith would put one stump in the ground at the edge of the tarmac and would then face up to young Pope's bowling. You can imagine the speed at which the ball came off the tarmac. We younger ones would be fielding way behind the lone stump, and I admired Mr Smith as he had no protective pads or gloves, just dressed as he was when he took classes. Cricket - As we played wherever we could, with whatever we had, without any technical instruction, I suppose I can truthfully say that in my age group I was a pretty fair cricketer. The same applied to soccer too!

One thing I can never understand was: at sports form R versus forms A and B was the norm. While I admit that things worked out more or less evenly I couldn't see how academic achievement made one better at sport, here I reiterate, I hold nothing against any master (a little biased towards Tubby Mellor) but here's an incident where I consider the master was at fault - probably he never even considered it. There was one particular beech tree at the bottom of the park where the boys would chalk a wicket and practise during lunch hour. We half dozen rogues were coming back from scrounging eggs in the farm area near the railway footbridge. We charged into the park where the cricket was taking place. The captain of A and B was batting and he drove towards us. I picked up the ball and I was invited to bowl. I did, and clean bowled him.

I suppose, not surprisingly, I was in the cricket team at the next games period. Normally we rogues were dispatched away into the rough to more or less please ourselves. I had a good day! I went in halfway down the order and I got my eye in. They never looked like getting me out! Then Mr Silcock suggested they bring on the choir soloist whom I have mentioned earlier. After I had belted him all over the field Mr Silcock said something to him and he sent me a full tosser! I tried to straight bat it and was clean bowled. Accolades for the bowler, but not a mention for the bat. That may sound petty but that's the sort of favouritism which I had to suffer, which had a tremendous impact on a youngster. What Mr Silcock should have done was to advise me that the way to deal with a full toss was to belt it beyond the boundary. These incidents were not without good cause altogether! In later years I was to be in charge of men and I made sure the genuine underdog got all the assistance I could give without pandering to them.

Next comes Tubby Mellor, *'Let no one say it'* etc etc which I have never forgotten. I think it is very apt. 'The older pupils will know that I hate grumbling'. Under our breath we would say, 'but he never stops'. He would stand on the stage at morning assembly and say such things as, 'If you must bring sandwiches to school have them wrapped in a clean tea cloth. Don't wrap them in newspaper. The Chinese wrap their food in newspaper in the belief that the print comes off and the knowledge goes into the body through the food'. What did he know about that wee fellow down there on the floor who had his couple of sandwiches wrapped in second-hand newspaper because we couldn't afford a 1d for a daily paper. I so much would have liked to have met him later, but I never had the chance, and a good tete a tete would have given me pleasure. To his everlasting credit, on one occasion when I was off school in one of my blue funks, he sent me a jar of cod liver oil and malt. It was supposed to cure the itch, the palsy and gout etc, but I just couldn't take it; the fishy-ness revolted me. Nonetheless Mam doled it out and I dreaded it. I honestly don't think that any of the teachers ever even contemplated that the likes of me were in their midst.

And so to Tubby's masterpiece:

We were not allowed to use the wooden stairs (in later years pupils were). We had to use the stone stairs, the servants' stairs. At lunchtime, once we had come downstairs we were, under no circumstances, allowed back upstairs until the start of the afternoon periods. When the weather was really foul during lunchtime the girls would do country-dancing etc in the assembly hall - most of all the school would be standing around the wallbars watching. Now we half dozen rogues didn't go a lot on this, so we would sneak upstairs into our classroom and play a guessing game on the blackboard - you know the sort of thing put a dash for a letter until someone guessed, say, Tottenham Hotspur. We could hear the music playing and we were cocksure no one would come near us when suddenly the door opened and there stood a very surprised form teacher, Sally Walker. After the normal, 'What are you doing here?,' we were ordered, 'Report to Mr Mellor this instant'. Quaking in our shoes we trooped off - we entered the assembly hall just as a dance finished and Tubby was in the middle of the floor congratulating the girls when we half dozen approached him in single file and you only have one guess as to who was leading. He had a sickly smile on his face as he said, 'Yes?' I said, 'Please sir we have been upstairs.' That's all that was said. He drew back his right arm and with the flat of his hand he hit me across my left cheek - he must have been heard on the main road. Then he screamed, 'Get out of here.' That, in front of the whole school. We went down the passage into the toilets. I could sense the other five were just as mortified as I was - we hadn't time to have a pee before Tubby was on us again, berating us for being in the toilet - he ushered us right down to the cloak rooms and then went to his study. For him that was the end of that. For me untold humiliation. Now why were we not all taken to his study and given six of the best? We were all guilty and should have been equally punished, but the humiliation of being clouted like that in front of the whole assembly was mine alone.

Not so serious! I had no quibbles with the Routledge brothers. Music just didn't sink in. One lesson Jimmy called us out individually and asked us to play a chord. About the only chord I knew was the one he asked me to play. I must have had an elbow and arm in the correct position because he said, 'Well done Smith! I suppose if I offered to teach you during lunch-break, you would rather be off down the park!' Flippant probably, but at least it was a nice thing to say - lifted me a number of degrees!

Now, Rooty the geography! Sometimes, with the utmost of ease, we could get him talking about anything from nylon stockings to foxhunting rather than the lesson in hand. I well remember one such time we had got on to the subject of keeping chickens. He asked what one should do to stop a chicken flying over the fence? The answer he was looking for was, 'clip its wings'. Phipps caused an uproar when he said, 'Wring its neck.' As you know his room was on the ground floor. We were not allowed to wear shoes - must be plimsolls. Maybe same applied to you! If the last period was in his room we would change into our shoes, sneak into the classroom, then we were ready to blast-off at the last bell. This day he was too smart for us. As we went in he stood there checking each person's feet. He reached in, grabbed an earlobe between finger and thumb and dragged us out. We were given 50 lines each: I must not wear my shoes in class.

Footwear was often referred to as boots, boats, clogs, clompers and so on. I wasn't in on the plot but Graham and Monks hatched a little plot as they travelled home together to Brampton. When we were next in Rooty's class we had to produce our lines and would you believe, he checked every one. Graham and Monks lines contained boats, boots etc and when asked of course they said 'shoes'. Rooty even had the girls read out the lines. Result: those two had to rewrite their lines a hundred times!

One that tickled me happened in a class a couple of years later. At that time there were some cigarettes on the market called Kensitas. An extra 'four for your friends' were attached to a 20-packet . The slogan on everyone's lips was: 'No thanks, I'd rather have a Kensitas.' Apparently Miss Clayton was putting her class through a bit of Shakespeare. George Sergeant, a small fellow with a very alert brain was in the class - he was quite a character. Anyway, Miss Clayton asked, 'And what did Caesar say when Antony offered him the crown?' Up jumped Georgie with: 'No thanks, I'd rather have a Kensitas!' Now I can't vouch for the authenticity of that but it caused a laugh throughout the school.

Mr Charles Middleton. You know that anyone named Charles was nicknamed Wag. At that time there was a cowboy song on the go entitled *Wagon Wheels*. Mr Middleton used, occasionally, to ride to school on a large bicycle and when he passed us going to school the boys would start-up with a chorus of: WAG-ON WHEELS. More humiliation for me in that he accused me, one day, of, 'singing abusive words as he passed by last Thursday'. I said, 'I wasn't at school last Thursday', whereupon I got a vile dressing down as to how my stock excuse was that I was never at school, all of which was greeted with much hilarity by his favourite toadies in the class.

Mr Heathcote. He would be writing on the black board when someone would whisper to his/her mate. Round he would twist and 'wham', the chalk would come flying in the general direction of the culprit. Anyone could be on the receiving end! Another day, same situation, he would turn and simply stare toward the culprit. He wore those thick

16

pebble spectacles and his eyes bored through you. After a while, when the whole class were squirming in their seats, he would turn back to the blackboard without having uttered a sound.

Some years ago there was a quiz on television. The inquisitor said: 'There are five types of triangle', he named four and asked for the fifth. Could I hell as think of the name of the fifth one! When the answer came up 'Scalene' my wife thought I had gone crackers, here's why. Mr Charles Middleton! It was the last period of the day and I suppose we were on trigonometry. About quarter to four he said, 'I am going to ask you each a question. If you answer correctly, put your books away and go quietly.' Jinks and I sat together so it was imperative that we both answered correctly as we walked home together. My question came first and I answered correctly. I had the lid of my desk up putting my gear away when Charley boy pointed to a triangle and said, 'Wilkinson, what sort of a triangle is that?' and Jinks didn't know so I am whispering 'scalene', obviously too loudly because the booming voice said, 'Stay where you are Smith, and by the next class with me write out the word 'scalene' one thousand times.' I think the whole class sucked in breath. We were used to 25 lines - 50 lines maybe, but 1000, was about as much as any of us could count to. At his next class he opened his ledger and said, 'Ah! Smith, I see you owe me a little imposition.' I went out with my handful of scraps of paper and presented them. 'Are there a thousand lines here?' I said, 'Actually there are 1008, I miscounted.' 'In that case I will not bother to count them, I'll take your word for it.'

Notwithstanding the stories I have written I was and still am proud to state that I went to Tapton House.

However, about 35 years ago, I was passing on the main road and decided to swing in through the gates of Tapton Park. I had my two daughters with me, aged about 10 or 12. Naturally I was telling them about Tapton House - not what I have written herein - but a more illustrious side. I always taught my children 'tidiness'. If I went for a picnic, all litter was brought home. It was a school holiday period and so I drove round to what was our playground square. There were two brick buildings built on the tarmac where Pope and Mr Smith once practised cricket and where the inlaid tennis court was where Mr Dennison showed his prowess. He sure was good. Now Tubby Mellor went berserk if he found so much as a toffee paper - I don't know if he was dead or alive at that time. If he was dead he would have turned in his grave had he seen that mess. Maybe the two buildings were now the dining rooms; what a mess! I've seen tidier places in eastern slums. The whole area was littered - maybe wind-blown - but whatever, it revolted me. To further shatter my dream memories, the Conker tree near the toilet at the end of the woodwork shop had gone. My eldest daughter certainly wasn't impressed.

The next time I called to see the school was on impulse while I was passing. This time I was on my own, the gates were open and I drove in, parked and walked around to the cloakroom. Had I gone straight to the main doors, which were not for pupils in my day, I would have met the headmaster. However I missed him! In the cloakroom area I met a cleaning lady - she was about 25-30. I told her who I was and she said that she was an ex-pupil too. She said she would see if there were any teachers still around and sure enough she came back with some young fellow. He it was who told me I had just missed the headmaster. He showed me around. I was surprised to be told the pupils were now allowed to use the wooden stairway - didn't seem a good idea to me. In the foyer outside Rooty's geography room was a plaque to the memory of ex-pupils who had fallen during the war - it saddened me to remember faces. One name wasn't on there and I told the young teacher. He said he would enquire about it. When I met Rooty he enlightened me; this fellow was in the RAF and instead of taking demob, he stayed in the RAF. A gang of them, RAF and WAAFS, were on a flight to America - all were lost. This lad's name was Frank Dauncey. A nicer fellow never stepped into Tapton House. He was an officer and a gentleman from 12 years of age. Apparently Frank preferred to stay in the RAF as opposed to going into the family business.

I got Rooty's phone number from the young teacher and I got a note from the headmaster but I can't remember his name. When I went to see Rooty I got the impression that Rooty didn't go a lot on him. Incidentally I was under the impression that Rooty's wife was the cookery teacher. Miss Sharkey was cookery in my time, but she also taught my sister at the school on the Moor all those years before.

And so to the finale. I am pleased I went to Tapton. I learned a lot, but not the French verbs, algebra, trig etc. I learned more French in Indo-China than ever entered my befuddled brain at Tapton. I was one of the lucky ones in the army in that I met all manner of blokes - the ones like Frank Dauncey, who were public school boys and knew their stuff, taught me enough trigonometry, scratching in the dust with a stick, to enable me to glean enough to get by in gunnery. I am telling you all this codswallop because the last thing I want you to do is to get the impression that this old man is anything like the boy I have depicted. I have never written this much before since my 1008 lines but in my present predicament it has kept me alert. In the meantime I will carry on trying to be philanthropic in the knowledge that 'What you give, you save.'

P S. I was in the Royal Artillery in the far east. No Matter! I was a gunner - all ranks of the RA are gunner. Routy was 72 and I was 60, so it was the year 1981. I happened to be in Chesterfield and acquired his phone number. I rang him; although he couldn't remember me, he invited me over. Eventually I found his place and he was awaiting me. When I was 12 and he was 24 he was able to grab us by the earlobe and politely tell us where we were misbehaving. Now the age difference didn't have the same meaning so, with a nice glass of sherry, we started yarning. He never really placed me after 50 years, but it was surprising the people he could remember after a little prompting from me. After an hour or so and a drop more sherry (hic!) I had to take my departure but not before he had said, 'See that television? I can tell you anything you wish to know about it! And yet if so much as one screw fell out I would have to send for a mechanic to replace it.' He carried on, 'Of course, I was called into the army. I knew the radar system back to front and I went all round the British coastline teaching the artillery about radar.' He paused for another sip of sherry, then he said, 'Of course you know, those gunners were such a thick lot.' I was still chuckling when I got to the Baslow area.

A Little Learning

Roy Hartley 1933 - 1937

Near the end of 1952, a 21st birthday dinner was held at the Portland Hotel. There were upwards of 50 people crammed into the dining room to hear speeches from the chief guest, Violet Markham, accompanied by Alderman Cropper, who had been invaluable in persuading the borough council to open Tapton House in 1931 to selected students from the Chesterfield district catchment area, to form the first grammar school to be open to all, of both sexes, who passed the first ever 11-plus examination.

It was originally designated a central selective school, but in essence it was more elite than either Chesterfield Boys Grammar or St Helena High School for Girls, because both these were largely fee-paying grammar schools, having money as the chief criterion, rather than academic ability. After the 1945 general election, of course, it soon came about that the eleven plus became the only means of entry to all three grammar schools, but for over fifteen years, Tapton stood proudly alone.

I entered form 1 Remove in 1933, having passed my 11-plus at ten years of age, along with six others from Gilbert Heathcote Junior School, and I vividly recall being overawed by Tubby Mellor, as he delivered his time-honoured homily, *'Let no one say, and say it to your shame, that all was beauty here before you came'*.

Although I had been admitted into the top stream, along with almost forty others who had excelled in the selection exams, I had no illusions about my future at Tapton, for Dad had never concealed his hostility to the academic system, and made it obvious that I would have to leave school at the earliest time possible, to take up any job, in any factory, to make a contribution to the family income.

His attitude did not make me resentful because times were hard in the 1930s, with most families having a struggle to keep their heads above water. He was just one of many holding similar opinions. He, as well as my mother, felt they could not afford the luxury of allowing a long-term benefit for me to take precedence over their short-term financial strictures.

I started off well enough, coming top in my first French exam with 96% and third in Latin, but my initial euphoria soon turned to dismay when I realised that I was competing with students in 1R who were all at least as bright as I was. In my junior school, it had always been so easy to stay at the top without even trying; now I found that at Tapton I had to work very hard, both in class and at home, just to stay in touch with my stream.

This was never going to work, neither for me, nor my family. Mother and Dad were going to be of no help to me in any academic aims, so I very soon allowed myself to take the easy way out of the dilemma by freewheeling at school - just doing enough to drift along in a modest position in the form. This self-generated release from pressure brought with it a not unexpected bonus; more free time to do things more amenable, like soccer, cricket and swimming in the new open-air pool at Stand Road. Life was proving to be very agreeable in my new found Nirvana.

Then disaster struck; my cosy new world crumbled around me in the twinkling of an eye when I fractured my left tibia on the school soccer pitch and the games master - popular Frank Silcock, who was also an excellent Latin teacher, took me in his car to the hospital, waited until my leg had been encased in plaster from ankle to hip before taking me home, to begin an enforced three months' absence from Tapton.

On my return to school I discovered that Mr Mellor, in his wisdom, had decided that I could not possibly expect to catch up with the rest of my R form, so he had me transferred to the slightly less demanding regime of the A stream, where I could ease myself back in without undue difficulty.

This suited me very well, for I had already found the ease of freewheeling much to my taste. To complement the physiotherapy which was being applied to restore mobility to my leg, my mother had been persuaded to buy me a new bicycle - only a Wigfall's Royal, bought on hire purchase, and this gave even more scope to exploit my new stress-free lifestyle at school, for I was able to 'play wag' on days of particularly boring lessons, to go riding around the countryside instead. On one such day, I rode to Bolsover Castle - in those days a totally unguarded ruin, and ate my sandwich lunch there before continuing on into Nottinghamshire, finally reaching the tiny village of Laxted, where, according to our history master, Bandy Heathcote, the old Saxon practice of husbandry was still carried out, with plots of common land allocated to villagers and being rotated over a strict routine of one year fallow, one year corn and one year of other crops. My conscience was mostly untroubled, but any slight misgivings I may have had were justified to myself on the dubious grounds of putting my history lessons to practical use.

A few incidents offered light relief, owing nothing to my own inspiration. On one sunny afternoon, we were having a music lesson from Jimmy Routledge - brother to the geography master - when he somewhat bad-temperedly sent out Barry Hulley for talking in class. Some minutes later he was looking out of the window, in the middle of a rather boring lecture, when he suddenly stopped and flung the window open with fury in his face. 'Hulley, what do you think you are doing?' Barry must have been a bit on the deaf side, for he smiled back to Jimmy, waved to him and ambled off in the direction of the tennis courts. To Jimmy's everlasting credit, he saw the funny side of the situation and laughed it off - not something he was prone to do normally.

On another occasion, Jimmy's brother, Harry Routledge, was striding along the hall toward his geography room, when a female prefect of ample proportions came sprinting round the corner, barging into him with such force that he was knocked backwards on to the floor, in an undignified heap. The two unwitting combatants thereupon engaged in an argument, watched happily by not a few bystanding pupils. She must have bowled Harry over, well and truly, for soon afterwards it was strongly rumoured that their original hostility became friendship.

Unrelated memories connected with Tapton come drifting back, haphazardly: -

Predictably, my parents took me away from school when I was in the fourth form, to work in a factory, but as soon as I was sixteen I decided to escape from the utter tedium of the daily grind at the works, by enlisting in the army. With the war just around the corner, it seemed an interesting thing to do.

Some time later, when I was in the Libyan desert, I was pleasantly surprised to receive a letter from GKJ Hoffman, who had been my English teacher in form 3A. He had given me some encouragement at the time, when I had made a somewhat puerile attempt to produce a form newsletter. It didn't last very long, but it was an interesting experience. Some time after the war was over, I became acquainted with the brother of GKJ and I was surprised to learn from him that Kenneth Hoffman had run away with one of his female pupils.

I went to see Tubby Mellor after my early release from the army and he was very helpful with advice on how I could compensate for my broken education and the profession I could then aim for.

Another opportunity occurred to meet again some of my former teachers, when we, the OTA, combined with the school to organise the 21st anniversary celebrations in 1952. Among others, I was reunited with Miss Stanley, my onetime form mistress, who had since left to become headmistress in another school. I had a long and interesting discussion with her over a cup of tea in the then new dining room. Miss Stanley had always seemed kind but perceptive in the old days - unlike Miss Vessey, the voluptuous art mistress, who had always seemed to be rather bitchy towards me, possibly because I was hopeless at the subject. It was strongly rumoured around the school that she had more than a little romantic interest in Mr Macara, who combined art tuition with metalwork instruction. Other female staff I came in contact with in my time at school included the Misses Clarke and Walker (French) and Miss Clayton, a strapping, kindly young woman who was the girls' gym mistress, but also took our form for scripture.

Of the male staff, apart from Mr Hoffman, whom I mentioned earlier, I had particular regard for Mr Wilkins (maths), Mr C Middleton (English), Mr Heathcote (history), the Messrs Dennison and 'Foggy' Fawcett (science) and of course, Mr Frank Silcock, who doubled Latin with PT and games.   Others I came in contact with were Harry Routledge (geography) and his brother 'Jimmy' (music), also Mr Smith (maths), who taught well, but at the same time, seemed somewhat distracted by his wife's obsession with rehearsing and putting on the Shakespearean plays. For some reason I had hated my geography lessons and I found music a strangely frustrating subject, because although I enjoyed being in the school choir - especially the outings to the churches at Rowsley and Bakewell, where Jimmy was the organist - I could not get on at all with music theory, but Jimmy tolerated me reasonably enough because of my enthusiasm for singing.

I will not bore you with a complete list of my classmates, though I remember them all. Some are particularly vivid, however. Of the males there were Arthur Revill, Walter Shaw, Alec Fanders, Beresford, Musson, Grainger, Redfern, Bush and Hulley. There was also, briefly, brilliant Harold Taylor from Whittington Moor, who for some strange reason was driven to suicide, hanging himself with a lavatory chain at his home. A few of the girls also stand out, naturally. Among these were lovely and gentle Muriel Pears, Oriel Brailsford, Nancy Blakemore, Edith Marshall, vivacious Peggy Sullivan and glamorous, gorgeous, blonde Betty Radford. I recall responding to an invitation to go along to see the last two performing in an amateur Christmas pantomime at a village hall at Sheepbridge. I do not remember much about the show, but I do know they both looked very attractive.

One final recollection also involved Betty Radford. After my medical discharge from the army, I had married my first wife and had gone to the Co-op Hall in Elder Way to a dance there, and in one of the lady's privilege waltzes, I was amazed to see Betty approaching me, asking me to take her on the floor.   I had not seen her since schooldays, but the intervening years had been very good to her, for she had become an exceedingly beautiful young woman. She was a divine dancer and I was beginning to enjoy myself enormously, so I asked her for another dance a bit later on - a quickstep this time - but just as we were gliding along around the floor we were rudely interrupted by my wife's female friend, who danced me around the floor to where my wife was sitting, rather forlorn. I was furious that my dream of delightful dalliance had been shattered by the pair of them, but in retrospect, I had no real regrets, for my lovely wife was a treasure and it was right that she should not have been hurt to satisfy my ego.

Now, I am married again, very happily, to a cousin of my first wife, who shares my love for music and literature, which was undoubtedly fostered during my too-short time at Tapton. Jimmy Routledge, by way of Offenbach and Strauss, led me on to an appreciation of Beethoven, Mozart and many other composers, so you may see why I disagree with Alexander Pope when he said: 'A little learning is a dangerous thing', but I disagree. For me, the little learning I acquired at Tapton helped to open my eyes and ears to many wonderful aspects of life.

Memories of A Really Old Taptonian

David Durward 1935 - 1939

Let's start with a typical Monday morning in the early 1930s. Pupils would assemble in the school hall - new entrants like myself sitting on the floor at the front and so on, with the senior pupils behind us in orderly rows. The staff would be standing at various vantage points around the Hall. This followed a short prayer and a welcoming hymn, which went: - 'Those returning - those returning- make more faithful than before.'

The headmaster (Tubby Mellor) would then address the school from the stage and bring us all up to date with events concerning us and education in general. Warming to his work Tubby would then tell us that although we might have joined the school as sows' ears we would surely leave as silk purses. He also made it clear that we must strive to be gentlemen and gentlewomen. Then, depending on the season, he would warn us that we must wait for conkers to fall from the trees and not throw various items to bring them down. Leave it to Mother Nature. While on the subject of Tapton and its park, he would often quote: - *Let no one say and to your shame, that all was beauty here before you came.*

Then to our classes and feeling rather overawed as our teachers swished in wearing their scholastic gowns - I never saw any mortarboards though. So there we were each day, doing the three Rs and with French and Latin thrown in for free.

Another fond memory was that Tapton, having previously been the home of the Stephensons and one of the great houses, had numerous stairs and nicely curved banisters - ideal for sliding down in preference to walking down. This hilarious, not to say dangerous, practice was soon altered and to this day we can see the spiky brass inserts at intervals on the handrails to deter would-be sliders.

Tapton, in the 1930s, was rather isolated in transport terms and I believe was among the first to provide hot meals at lunchtime (for payment of course). Tubby also organised a variety of lunchtime activities independent of the weather. To name but a few: Le Cercle Francais, The Historical Society, lunchtime debates, and a hastily rigged badminton court.

As most of us oldies know, Tapton had and has a wonderful woodland, and thousands of daffodils were eventually supplied and planted by voluntary effort. We would often walk down the woodland path to the railway bridge and tracks, which ran alongside Brimington Road. Our favourite train was The Devonian which passed regularly at about 12.30 noon to stop at nearby Chesterfield station. A small hut at the base of the bridge served as a tuck shop.

Much of this happy time has faded away and the war took its toll of many young Taptonians, but Tapton goes on forever though its function has changed markedly.

FLOREAT TAPTONA!   TENAX PROPOSITI!

A Youthful Memory

Norman Hoddle 1936 - 1937

By accident of date of birth and the vagaries of an educational system, I was selected at 10 years 11 months to attend the new school at Tapton House. I met the celebrated Tubby Mellor in the first few days of September 1936. The memory of that first meeting is as vivid now as it was then. A man of ample figure, a large welcoming smile and a distinct air of authority. For myself, the product of a kind gentle home, I was not street-wise, not addicted to either hard work or education. In brief, soft, foolish and immature. I lived on the other side of Chesterfield from Tapton; I felt a long way from home and had no understanding of the nature of the establishment I had joined.

My natural complacency and ignorance were rapidly dispelled and within a few days I was discovering, and being involved in, a new and exciting experience - house rules, slippers, timetables, conduct, school uniform, homework, gymnasium, woodwork, house points, Grace Clark, French, the Art Room, scouts, Miss Stanley, first aid, library, the staircase - You Cannot Use - on pain of death! And the staircase you Must Use, important people, like Prefects and above all The School - motto Tenax Propositi. The list in my memory goes on but outside I discovered even greater joys. The woodland and the mystery of exploration along those dark paths. Magic!

However, above all the most outstanding impressions were the staff. I remember them as firm but understanding, kind and caring without exception. I can remember to this day - sixty three years on - the names of all those who taught me in 1936 and some who did not. The subjects and lessons they taught, their appearance, their mannerisms, and not to be repeated, their nicknames.

The experience of joining Tapton House School made a profound impression on me. On reflection, and with hindsight, I must say they were an incredible staff under the direction of an outstanding headmaster. I felt I belonged and was proud of my new status: 'I went to Tapton.'

Unfortunately, the story now changes. Because of my age, the system and some parental influences, I was a retake, and in September 1937, I found myself at another school in Chesterfield - an all-boys establishment. My experience was quite the contrary to my previous experience at Tapton. It was with relief that I left school at 16. Any success I may have achieved in later life, and certainly my attitude as a teacher, I can only attribute to my earlier training at Tapton School. It was at Tapton that I experienced true education. I neither understood nor appreciated this until I became a student again at St. John's, York, in 1945.

I can only hope that I was as successful a teacher as those who taught me at Tapton in 1936.

Day One, On the Fringes and Precautions

Tom Jones 1936 - 1940

Day One

A solidly built boy plodded thoughtfully towards the bus stop. He seemed apprehensive and occasionally touched his nearly new school cap as if to reassure himself that it was still there. A battered old satchel, seemingly an unfamiliar item to him, bumped heavily at his side. That was me, on my way to my first day at Tapton House School. It was September of 1936.

A three-halfpenny bus ride brought me to the park gate where I joined a noisy crowd of fellow pupils. Strangely, no one was walking up the driveway to the school. All chose to climb up the steep, grassy slope. Well, who was I to be different?

At the top of the rise grew a very large tree; its leaves still green and shining in the morning sunshine. Beyond lay a gently sloping playground, rapidly filling up with a mass of boys and girls, some already in small groups, watching and laughing. Very conscious of my old grey jacket and short grey trousers, I was certainly relieved to see that many of the youngsters were not wearing the prescribed black blazer. It seemed that families other than my own had a financial problem. All the girls wore regulation white blouse and black gym slip but, although most had chosen white ankle socks, a few had opted for long black stockings. All looked very attractive but remote to someone who had just served four years in a (rough) boys' junior school.

A tall, darkly moustached teacher blew his whistle to summon 'the new lot'. Checking off names on his list he despatched us in groups down the steps to the cloakrooms. Here we took possession of empty pegs on the iron rails, hung up satchels and slipper bags, then put on slippers to replace our outdoor shoes. This was apparently some kind of essential ritual.

Returning to the playground, clutching pencil, ruler and leaky fountain pen, I found that the pupils (except for the newcomers) were ordered in lines, one line of boys and one of girls for each class. There were several teachers in attendance now; some looking a bit harassed. One after another the lines trailed off down the stone steps and were swallowed up by the building.

The first-year children were now divided into three groups, given a name 1A, 1B or 1R, assigned to a waiting teacher, and escorted to their form rooms. The quiet Miss Muir was my form teacher. She led us via a steep stone staircase to a classroom on the first floor.

Desks were allocated, registers marked, dinner money collected and blank timetables filled in with much explanation. Assurances were given that the seven-day week system did not mean that we had to turn up for lessons on Saturday and Sunday. We were pleased about that but concerned over how we would know what day it was.

Inside each desk we found a dog-eared dictionary, a Bible and an atlas, together with pencil, ruler and a few sheets of paper. As instructed, we carefully inscribed our name inside the cover of each book and promised to care for it. It was pleasurable to mark our new ownership. One boy enjoyed it so much he went on to inscribe his name on the top of his wooden desk. This brought a sharp rebuke from Miss Muir, but we noted that he wasn't caned for the misdemeanour. He would certainly have been given at least two strokes on each hand at my old junior school. I never saw a cane at Tapton except for the one in the head's study, and was impressed by the staff's ability to maintain a reasonable discipline by the use of words, tone of voice - and lines.

After break we climbed an extra flight of stairs (much more fun this time as we were

26

able to push and pull a little) to a different room and a different teacher. Mr Davey welcomed us, chatted a little, gave us a writing book and an English grammar textbook. We did some written work and then, suddenly, it was lunchtime.

Appetising aromas came from the kitchen adjoining the dining room, but, being one of the packed lunch section, I ate my jam sandwiches and biscuit in thoughtful silence. After lunch, the playground seemed to be the most popular place to be. The older boys played peggy or ran about aimlessly always shouting and showing off. Most of the girls sat on the low walls or on benches. A few sat on the grass, under the trees, whispering and giggling.

The afternoon provided different rooms, different teachers, more books and more instructions. Miss Clarke introduced us to French and wrote the language phonetically on the blackboard. Very strange. We enjoyed making some funny sounds and learned how to say good morning, how are you, very well thank you, yes, no and goodbye. Mr Heathcote questioned us to find out what we knew about history. He was obviously rather disappointed but gave us some books anyway.

When the buzzer sounded we returned to our form room where Miss Muir was waiting for us. She carefully counted us and expressed pleasure that no one had been lost. Actually it was a near thing. During the lesson changeovers some members of our class had strayed into the wrong room or been caught up in a tide of children going in the opposite direction. I unloaded the newly acquired books into my desk. It was filling up very nicely now, but we hoped we would not be expected to carry everything home each evening. Miss Muir gave us some more information which we dutifully copied from the blackboard. She discussed problems and rules (there seemed to be a lot of these) and told us that in the morning, after assembly in the hall, work would start in earnest. For homework that night, we were to take home our exercise books and back them neatly with brown wrapping paper or 'discreet' wallpaper. (I didn't think we had any of that.) We were then to print our names, subject and class number on the front, and refrain from adding any 'unsuitable' decorations.

I made my way home, having met two potential friends and one potential enemy, which seemed reasonable odds. An interesting day. Not quite what I expected but worth going back to school in the morning.

On The Fringes

Just before the war came along to spoil things, Tapton House was a haven of relaxation, pleasure and, occasionally, adventure. At least, it could be, if it was just after lunch, if the weather was agreeable, and if one kept clear of the playground. The school grounds were generous in space if not in privacy, and it was usually easy enough to find a quiet spot somewhere under the trees.

Facing the school gates, but across the main road into Chesterfield, was a splendid little shop which sold many things, especially sweets. I remember it well even though my pocket money was only about sixpence per week even if I had behaved tolerably well and not broken anything. In those days there was very little traffic on the road so we were allowed to frequent this childhood cornucopia and spend a few precious pennies (or halfpennies!).

I can't remember any ice cream, but I think there were some watery ice lollies available. The lady in charge had great expertise in transforming a small square of white paper into a cone-shaped bag, screwed up at the bottom and open at the top. Into the bag she would load a pennyworth of chocolate drops, wine gums, aniseed balls, sherbet (with a little straw to suck up the delicious powder), jelly babies or whatever. Broken toffee, my own favourite, or liquorice sticks were popular and lasted a long time. Dolly mixtures were generally despised. The shop lady had infinite patience - and she needed it.

A little further down the road was the 'skull and crossbones' corner, where, so it was rumoured, many motorists, unable to make the right angled turn, had plunged off the road, down the steep bank and into the canal, there to drown horribly. I never saw any of these exciting incidents (though I lived in eager anticipation). However, there must have been some reason for the strikingly grisly skull and crossbones sign erected by the local council.

The canal itself ran parallel to the river. The only means of access at this point was to climb over or through a wooden fence and go very carefully down the bank. The fence was, to young teenagers, more of a challenge than an obstacle. The bank, however, was a deterrent, being steep, slippery and seemingly alive with brambles determined to grab any trespassers.

On the southern edge of the school was the golf course. Forbidden territory - although it was not uncommon for a first-year boy to sneak through the cluster of trees beyond the lawns, make a short drop on to the links, then make a quick search through scrub and long grass for any lost golf balls. I did it myself on one occasion. Unfortunately, all I found was a yellowing ball so scarred and misshapen the owner must have been quite happily resigned to losing it.

Along the far edge of the lawns was a line of trees upon which many a heart shape and initials had been carved. Guilty again - and no excuse, because I was in the third year at the time, although perhaps a little distracted emotionally. Those trees have now been removed or have managed to conceal the misdeeds of our youth.

A little further on, near the start of the drive, was a steeply sloping hillside, dotted with trees through which wriggled stony semi-footpaths. Unfriendly bushes and brambles tried to fill all available space. Even in the summertime this was a dark and vaguely threatening place. As a first-year pupil I was thrilled by stories of winter battles in the snow with invading hordes of youths from the grammar school. After seeing the wooded slopes in the winter I soon realised that it would be quite impossible to throw snowballs up or downhill through that tangle of trees. Rather disappointing. I would have made a good schoolboy dream, come true.

At the bottom of the slope was a recognisable footpath, which skirted the golf course and led towards the town via a remarkably ugly bridge. We found this a very useful short cut over the railway line and emerging on the main road only a few hundred yards from town. The bridge itself was a magnet to young trainspotters. (I am told that many famous express trains, including Mallard, passed along this line.) Collecting names and numbers held no appeal to me, but it was exciting to stand on the bridge as the train rushed underneath churning out great clouds of lovely dark, smelly smoke. By the second year, of course, this was less thrilling - and my mother became very inquisitive about how I managed to get my clothes so dirty at school.

To the north of the school a large gently sloping field, dotted with assorted trees, led to Paxton Road. The inevitable wooden fence was intended as a barrier, too high to vault but pleasurably high enough to climb over or through. Usually the girls filtered through the spaces with as much modesty as possible but young boys were less inhibited. There was no real path as this was not a recognised means of access to the school. However, the field was much used as a short cut to the bus stop and to Lockoford Lane. Beyond the fence it was safe to secrete one's cap in the satchel and become a normal individual boy again.

Precautions

Just a reminder that in the September of 1939 we were suddenly at war with Germany, and Tapton House School was, however unlikely, a possible target for enemy bombers. Precautions had to be taken. One lunchtime, feeling unusually benevolent, I helped Mr Heathcote protect the windows of our form room - I think it was Room 12. We used huge rolls of brown, gummed paper tape and a wet sponge. (Fortunately no licking was required). It was quite good fun on the whole and, by the time we had reached the last window, we were becoming reasonably competent. Looking at the result it didn't seem to me that this would be of much use in stopping bombs - more a gesture to raise morale in the school. Actually the effect was rather depressing. Cutting out so much of the daylight meant having the electric lights switched on for most of the time - and this was before the days of fluorescent lighting. Our trellis work of brown tape had little artistic merit - and also made it more difficult, without opening the window, to look down at the girls relaxing or frolicking on the garden benches below. Many boys grumbled about this.

One day we found buckets filled with sand or water standing around, presenting a hazard to everyone, but an unexpected opportunity for the more mischievous youngsters, (girls equally culpable with boys). I strongly suspect the caretaker was responsible for the removal of most of these buckets after a few days and offering as replacement some large, heavy, red cylinders which looked as dangerous as bombs. Perhaps wisely, they were firmly strapped in corners.

The day came when we had an emergency evacuation practice. No one wanted to be last out of the building so it became quite exciting when the alarm was sounded. Indeed, there was occasional chaos, largely because too many children in descent tried to use the splendid wide wooden staircase normally forbidden to them. Those using the narrow, and poorly lit, stone stairway had additional problems. It didn't help when a few forgetful children attempted to struggle upwards and go back for treasured possessions and even for gas masks! (Luckily most of us had not bothered bringing to school these 'essential' war time items, squashed into their flimsy cardboard boxes. Their novelty had long ago been exploited. Now they were just an encumbrance, much too bulky to stuff into our satchels. However, a few, in fancy waterproof fabric covered boxes, were carried as accessories). At last everyone, hopefully, was outside.

All too soon an excited mass of children noisily returned to the building. It was all over. No one seemed to be injured, although there were many complaints, and surprisingly no one was lost, so it must have been regarded as a success. Whatever the reason, we didn't have another practice that year. Perhaps the cold, unpleasant weather had something to do with it.

1936

Jean Briddon 1936 - 1940

Today is the day I am taken to George Stephenson's house to be interviewed by a Mr Mellor to see if I could be selected for a place in the school. My mother and I enter the gates at the bottom of the drive and walk up the roadway between the trees to the inner gates, and then through the main door, the door of Tapton House. As we enter there are about four children and parents waiting to be interviewed. We sit and wait, my heart was beating fast, my eyes wander around. Then there it was, this imposing polished staircase which was to remain vivid in my memories through the years. Suddenly I am drawn out of my dreams as my name was being called; we enter Mr Mellor's study.

The room was light, with a French window at the far end, and seated in the middle at a kneehole desk was this fairly plump man. He asked us to be seated; I was so scared. I do not remember what happened during the interview only when we were about to leave Mr Mellor turned to me and said, 'If you were painting a ship which coat of paint would you put on first?' I swallowed and quietly said, 'The first.' Mr Mellor said, 'No the second, the first is the primer.' My heart sank, I didn't know the answer, and I felt sure I wouldn't be chosen. It was a sad day but within a few days I was told I had been selected and had a place at Tapton House School; it was in the B class but it didn't matter, I would work hard. The main thing we had to learn was that plimsolls must always be worn indoors at all times. We were never allowed to use the main staircase, we had to use the stone maids' stairs. Woe betide anyone who didn't change from shoes to plimsolls before starting their day at school.

At 8.00 in the morning we started our walk to school. Firstly into town, along Brimington Road, over the railway bridge then up the woodland path to school. It was cold but it was a healthy life. Year followed year in this pattern.

We started our first term in September when we could wander around the grounds and gather new nuts, as we went shuffling our way through thick carpets of autumn leaves, then sitting in the sunken garden to eat our sandwiches for lunch. As winter approached we went indoors to have our lunch at the dining room on wooden tables and forms, served by a Mrs Skidmore.

Each period we moved into different rooms. We had a number of teachers - Mr Clarke (Nobby) music, Mr Geography Routledge, Mr History Routledge, Miss Muir, Miss Wildin. When it was cold and we had to crowd around the one radiator at the end of the classroom. We had an ink monitor to fill the inkwells. We had to dip our pointed nib pens into these, and they squeaked when we wrote, sometimes splattering the ink over the paper. If we got a 'J' nib the writing flowed much easier.

During the picnic season people visited the park and left litter all over the grass. Mr Mellor was strict about this and after the weekend on Monday morning we had to go round the front park and pick this up.

September 1939 The war came, we felt safe and happy during our school days, but we now had to carry a gas mask as well as our satchels. After many exams and much hard work we left school to follow our vocation. But my memories were those of a large house with many beautiful rooms and my dream staircase.

Fifty-five years had passed and I was invited to the last open day before the house closed as a school. A thrill grew inside me as I went through the main door and registered my name on the scholars' list. Everywhere was so small and dark my memories of rooms bright and large with laughter and happy feet moving around. My magnificent polished staircase - where was it?

These were not my memories. Like myself age had taken its toll but my memories stay clear and bright as strong as my love for Tapton House.

Remember, Remember, I'll Always Remember

George Tagg 1936 - 1940

Who do I remember at Tapton House School in the late 1930s? A lad called Roy Godfrey and myself were the only two boys from Gilbert Heathcote School to go to Tapton in 1936. There was another lad who came later, I think his name was Arthur Ford.

Among the teachers, well we all remember Mr Tubby Mellor; Mr Silcock, who taught maths, Latin and sport went on to be headmaster at Newbold Green School. Mr Wilkins - maths; Mr Heathcote - history; Mr Nobby Clarke - music; Mr Dennison who was also scoutmaster; Mr JKG Hoffman; Mr Fawcett - woodwork and chemistry; Mr Macara - art and metalwork. Oh yes, and Mr Harry Routledge - geography. This was one of my best subjects. If I didn't come in the first three in geography exams I was disappointed. There used to be a bit of a notice board just inside the geog room and Mr Mellor would put up postcards from around the world, sent by his brother who was in the Merchant navy. I think this stuck with me over the years and my interest in geography probably was something to do with my decision to follow in his footsteps. Harry had a brother, John, also a teacher at Tapton; he left fairly early in my stay. Now he was strict. There was also a Mr Davey. I remember him for his demon bowling during the annual masters v pupils cricket match.

On then to the lady teachers. Miss Clark taught French, as did Miss Wood. Who can forget Miss Phil Wildin? She died only in 1998 aged 90! I well remember her coming to the school. Don't remember any other lady teachers' names.

Who do I remember amongst the boys? Well there was Arthur Keen who I saw again a few months ago. Fred Smelt, the Salmon brothers, the Barnes brothers. Joe Spence, whose father was something to do with Chesterfield football club, Ken Randon, Cyril Thorneycroft, Derek Newton - now could he throw a cricket ball. Billy Whittaker who went on to play for Chesterfield and Middlesbrough. Alan Musson. You may know of Frank Dauncey. His family had a horticultural business in town. He was a RAF pilot during the war and later a civil airline pilot flying converted bombers. His aircraft went down in the Bermuda triangle and as far as I know has never been found.

Among the girls were Vera Hoole, Jean Briddon who I see quite occasionally, Jean Harle, Nora Sowerby and Cissie Foulkes. Now couldn't she sing; what a powerful voice.

One thing that I've never forgotten was something that Mr Mellor taught us. It was *'Let no one say it and say it to your shame that all was beauty here before you came'.*

One Remove; Two Remove; Three Remove; Four

Doug Morris 1937-1941

The summer holiday of 1937 was, I recall, a glorious one with the days spent playing cricket and marred only by the thought that, come September, my two best friends and I would part company. They were off to the grammar school whilst I went to Tapton. As a parting gift during our last game of cricket, my best friend sent down a dodgy in-swinger, which neatly removed the tubercular gland - the cause of my illness - from my neck. This had a twofold effect: one, a lifetime disaffection for all team sports but at the same time providing me with one of the most useful pieces of equipment to be found in an 11-year-old boy's pocket, a hospital Doctor's Note. Armed with this and a large bandage holding some thick black tar and iodine ointment to the hole in my neck I arrived at my new school in September 1937.

The note, which announced to the staff that I had to attend hospital on three mornings one week and two the next until further notice plus the evidence around my neck, gained me immediate sympathy from staff and seniors alike, and I exploited it to the full. Alan Musson, who I think, was Markham House captain at the time, always turned a blind eye when I frequently turned up late for assembly. Vivian Handforth and Jessie Yule, two of the senior girls; appeared as if by magic if I seemed to be getting the worst of a schoolboy tussle. The sympathy also extended to my academic prowess, as despite my poor showing in attendance and term exams, I was never 'back squadded' and stayed in the Remove for my first three years. I chickened out of 4SC and went into 4E but left at the age of fourteen to avoid sitting the East Midlands exam.

Not that I disliked school. I enjoyed English with JKG Hoffman, coped reasonably well in maths and geometry with Swiller Wilkins and Frank Silcock. I never missed science or woodwork with Sniff Fawcett or metalwork with Mac Macara. Geography under Harry Routledge; music with Nobby Clarke and history with Bandy Heathcote were not so appealing and my well thumbed note came in for some heavy use. The female staff were just as brilliant as the men, and Misses Clark, Wildin, Wood, Phoenix, Spot Stanley and Titty Clayton under the expert and disciplined headship of Tubby Mellor provided a team very hard to beat and would, today, put any Ofsted reject school back on track in two days flat.

The seniors of my first two years were a very active, attractive lot with some good footballers like Bill Whittaker, Dinah Harrison, Cyril Thorneycroft and Joe Spence, whose father played for Chesterfield, among them. There were also some delightfully attractive girls: Nancy Paul, Betty Ford, the Sambrooks, Norrie Blankley and a ravishing blonde, I think her name was Betty Radford. She had been spotted one day snogging on the woodland path with Frank Dauncey and was the object of most of the male juniors' lustful fantasies.

The 1937 intake (see register) had its fair share of characters. Alan Vickers, who was in the Scouts with me, was the first person I knew who could do 'wheelies' on his bike, long before the term and mountain bikes were invented. He became a pilot in the RAF attached, I believe, to the Queen's Flight. Don Robertshaw who had brothers and sisters, all musical, at the school, gained some distinction in the Indian army. Joe Smedley, who was envied because he had a part-time job on the dodgem cars on a fairground. Jeff Hughes, probably the first war casualty, of our year, killed in a flying accident as an ATC cadet at the age of 14 or 15. Trevor Swann and Lawrence Gainey, who were my particular chums, helped cover for me when I played 'wag' from school.

The most infamous character, however, was Melvin Fardell. He really deserves a book on his own, for his exploits were legion. When my daughter was small, she refused to go to sleep unless I told her a Fardell story. One of his exploits was to smash a lot of plant pots (no one knew why he did it) in the conservatory and he was chased all over the school by a most irate Tubby. This included running up and down the wooden staff stairs. We marvelled at Fardy's audacity as we were only allowed on these sacrosanct stairs on Commemoration Day. He once put a little Demon firework in a wasps' nest, which resulted in about forty pupils being treated for stings by Miss Muir who dabbed copious applications of 'blue bag' to faces and legs. The place looked as though a new plague had descended. He threatened a member of staff with a spanner, sank a small boat in the canal and was always in some form of trouble. His most memorable one, I think, was when he packed some calcium carbide into an inkwell, rammed down with blotting paper, in Room 1. It exploded just after the detention period had started at 1 o'clock and spattered the beautiful ceiling and everyone in the room, including Mr Routledge, with best blue school ink. I exaggerate slightly here but the thought is worth savouring.

1939 brought the war years and school life was interrupted. Air raid shelters were dug, fire watching duties and First Aid classes started. Male staff disappeared, seemingly overnight, into the army, navy and air force where they all served with courage and distinction.

My proclivity for playing truant (and I herewith stake my claim for the record over 1,

2 and 3 years) was the cause of some frustration during this period. I was on one of my illicit forays in the Barrow Hill area and rounded a corner to be faced by two men in overalls shouting, 'Get down, get down'. They disappeared beneath their lorry and I scrambled under the nearest hedge as a solitary Heinkel 111 loosed off a few rounds in our general direction. It was exciting and frightening, but I daren't brag about it as I was more frightened that Tubby would find out I was playing truant.

There were very few bad apples in the educational barrel that was Tapton House School in the late 1930s and early 1940s and I look back with affection on those days and cherish the friendships made there. Quite a few of my old friends, now in their seventies, are still around and I can say with certainty that, due to Tubbys' influence, there will not be an unintelligent, ill-mannered litter lout amongst the lot of them.

There are hundreds of stories of Tapton lurking in fast declining brain cells and I hope that there have been sufficient to enable a reasonable book to be compiled. Thank you, Len Thompson, for stirring my memory and giving me the impetus and opportunity to put a few disjointed thoughts on paper.

A lot of Tenax Propositi to the association.

Schooldays in Peace and War

Joan Norman 1937 - 1941

I started at Tapton House in September 1937, it then being a central selective school. After junior school it was rather bewildering for the first few days. Instead of having one teacher for all subjects we had a different teacher and room for each lesson. This was totally alien to me. We now had a form room and form teacher and all books not needed in the current lesson were kept in our own desk.

We found it very funny that we all had to wear plimsolls and always used the back stairs; only the teachers and prefects could use the main staircase. It did not take us long to find our way around and settle down to school life, which I found very enjoyable. We were so lucky to have such dedicated teachers who took interest in our out of school activities as well as school work and one or more was always willing to wind up the gramophone in the school hall on rainy days at dinnertime. One of the records played was *Ten Cents a Dance* to which we did the polyglide. I hear it occasionally on the radio and I am immediately taken back in time.

Our form mistress in year one was Miss Wood who, in 1938 married a French army officer and unfortunately had to spend the war years in occupied France. The other teachers I remember were the headmaster Mr Mellor (Tubby); he was a very good one (even if you trembled in your shoes if he sent for you).

Mr Clarke (music)	Mr Hoffman (English, maths, history)
Mr Routledge (geography)	Mr Stewart (maths)
Mr Davey (English)	Mr Silcock (Latin, maths)
Mr Pearson (maths)	Mr Fawcett (woodwork)
Miss Muir (cookery, domestic science)	Miss Clarke
Miss Stanley (science, girls)	Miss Clayton PE (She married Mr Heathcote
our history master),	Miss Wood, our French teacher.

What wonderful school grounds we had, the carpet of daffodils in the woods and park in spring and the beautiful gardens in summer. What a lovely setting for the Commemoration Day play, and the choir entertaining parents and friends. On this day when the cups and prizes were given out. How proud we were if our schoolhouse won cups; there was great rivalry to get credit marks for your house, these being Cavendish, Hardwick, Markham and Stephenson. Mr Clarke was proud of his choir and one of the favourite selections we used to sing was the music from *Merrie England.*

Christmas, apart from end of term exams, was a very enjoyable time. In the weeks before Christmas, under the direction of Miss Muir, the girls made Christmas cakes for the parties. We had three parties, year one the first night, year two the next night then years three four and five the night after. We could take our best dresses to change into and had games and dancing, then finished with presents, which we had bought each other; they were all put under the tree which stood on the stage. We also had two dances; year one and two held theirs on a Saturday afternoon. Years three four and five in the Chesterfield Co-operative ballroom; this was in the evening of course and we wore long dresses (our first) and all the male teachers in evening dress. We thought we were really posh; remember this was the late 1930s. Before we broke up for the holidays Mr Clarke would take the choir singing to some of the big houses around the school; we really enjoyed the cake and hot mince pies we were given.

With the coming of war things changed, the RAF seeing Mr Pearson, Mr Silcock and Mr Routledge. Mr Hoffman and Mr Stewart went in the army and Mr Davey in the navy. During the long summer holiday in 1940 the school stayed open and if anyone wished to go they could, not to do lessons but play games etc. and it says something about the school the number of pupils who turned up. Of course the teachers were there to supervise. It was a sad occasion when Mr Mellor announced that an old pupil had been killed in the war and we were encouraged to write to any we knew.

With the shortage of food, the powers that be in the Food Ministry suggested that nettles would be a good source of greens so consequently, one cookery lesson, our form sallied forth with baskets and scissors to collect as many nettles as we could. They were taken to the kitchen, cooked and served up at dinner; luckily they were never served again as nobody ate them. The dinners cost us 6d in the old money 4d for the first course and 2d for the pudding.

I had to say goodbye to Tapton in 1941 having made many friends during my years there.

Memories From The Early War Years

Joyce Marsden 1938 - 1942

My first sight of Tapton House was when I went with my mother for the interview with Mr Mellor. How very different it all seemed from our junior schools; how glamorous even to be entering something that looked like the boarding schools in our schoolgirl novels. All I remember of the interview, however, was that while telling us that there was a school special bus that ran each morning from Stephenson Place to the school, Mr Mellor urged me not to take the bus, but that all pupils should walk from town unless it was very wet. I learned later of course that he never walked anywhere, but at the start of term, proudly clad in my new blazer with its bright new badge, my new gymslip, the black velour hat with school colours on the band, and clutching my new hide satchel - a present from an indulgent grandmother, and the best that the Stephenson Arcade could supply. I did as I was told and walked down Tapton Lane and along Brimington Road to the railway bridge.

But horrors! The steps were old and very worn so there were big gaps between them and I felt I might slip between or at least drop the precious satchel down on to the railway line. The bridge was long, too, as it spanned a main line and the roaring steam trains puffed dirty black smoke and steam at us, and whistled shrilly as they approached the station.

For a whole year I hated that bridge but in August 1939, during the school holidays the entire bridge was re-planked, and although gaps still remained, they were not nearly so large as before. I wonder how many other pupils hated that bridge as much as I did though twice a day for four years I continued to walk this route.

The school however, never disappointed and through a first year spent settling in to our perceived levels in forms 1R, 1A or 1B, making new friends, as well as jostling for position on the porch radiators in cold weather, most of us changed from being a disparate mob of uncertain little junior school intakes to being real Taptonians.

Apart from the all powerful, and somewhat intimidating headmaster, Mr H Mellor, there was Mr Silcock who taught maths and Latin very well, and tall, thin Mr Davey who taught us some English; the same Mr Davey, I hear, who was wont to fall asleep in later classes but who overcame boredom with us by volunteering to join the navy at the outbreak of war. Mr Hoffman (GKJ) also taught English to those of us in the Remove forms and wrote poetry, some of which was published, and then there was Bandy Heathcote, our history master; a big burly man with thick pebble spectacles. He had a special interest in pre-history and helped his father at Creswell Crags and later at Birchover where they had a small Stone Age Museum. I had always loved history but having just done a term on the Stone Age at Old Road Junior School, another year of woolly mammoths, sabre-toothed tigers and flint axes did not exactly fire me with enthusiasm. Later we missed much of importance in our history and I felt it a wasted year because the gaps have remained.

Another tall, elegant master was Mr Routledge whose domain was the splendid Room 1. He taught us geography until our school certificate year when he disappeared into the forces, but I particularly remember him finding me talking in class, and instead of getting the expected reprimand he said, 'In our next lesson, as Miss Marsden likes talking so much, she will give us a lecture on badgers.' Then turning to me again, 'Meanwhile you will leave the room and prepare your lecture.' Why badgers I wondered. However I thought I had better do something about it, especially as at the next lesson he had not forgotten and I had to deliver my talk.

Miss Phil Wildin, a rather elegant figure with a boyish Eton crop hairstyle and smarter clothes than most of the others, was there to teach art rather than the English at which she later excelled. From the first week we realised that she was a PERSONALITY.

The Scottish Miss Agnes Muir taught cookery and domestic science and spent one whole lesson demonstrating what she called 'scooring pooder'. I often wonder how many of her ex-pupils ever bothered to make their own Vim afterwards. She also taught us to make beeswax polish. Later when she left to supervise cooking in the ATS she was replaced by Miss Isabel Carmichael, and Miss Mackrill arrived to teach crafts and some needlework.

I still have a conscience about our pretty French teacher, the delightful Miss Flora Wood, because in our first year we didn't give her an easy time, yet she continued to smile and treat us as if we were model pupils. Perhaps her good temper was influenced by the fact that at the end of July 1939 she was to marry a French army officer. In the next year she produced twins but was caught in the fall of France and remained there. Unfortunately that was the last we heard of her, but I hope that her life was happy afterwards.

The untidy, chalk-covered figure with the battered trilby hat who taught music throughout the school was Mr Nobby Clarke, and Froggie Fawcett was the master who drilled physics and chemistry into the boys, while Mr Macara took them for art and metalwork. The girls meanwhile, had separate classes in chemistry and biology with Miss Stanley (Spot to her family and friends from early childhood, not, I hasten to add, because of her complexion but I think from an unlikely diminutive of her name Charlotte.) There were always Charlotte Stanleys in her family, who were descended from the Earls of Derby. Not that Miss Stanley ever mentioned this herself, but in a quiet way she had a commanding presence - fixing us with her bright blue eyes in such a penetrating gaze that she could quell the noisiest rebel. Some years later she became head of a large comprehensive near Sutton Coldfield.

When the men began to be called to the forces in 1940 there were some changes of course - Mr Davey and Mr Hoffman going early, but Miss Woodall and Miss Pennington arrived, and in September 1941 the slightly Rabelaisian Dorothy Lowe. What a picture she would have made in an earlier century. As it was she took over the role of chauffeuse to her old friend Miss Wildin and once out of class usually had a cigarette dangling from her lips, though her main function was to teach geography for the school certificate form in place of Mr Routledge. She had never prepared pupils for SC before and somehow managed to teach us a great deal of unnecessary details so that when we sat the exam we opened our papers and looked at each other with dismay. Describing a route on the Ordnance Survey map was easy, but the rest was unintelligible to most of us and few passed. I had got through her trial exam and, having failed the real thing, was never quite forgiven by Dorothy so that years later when we met socially, she often reminded me of my failure. Behind her mock anger, her sarcasm, and the habit of calling a spade a spade, she had a surprisingly soft heart and a passion for grand opera, which could reduce her to tears. I liked old Dorothy.

In Mr. Mellor's years as Head he operated a seven-day timetable, its purpose being, I suppose, to include as wide a curriculum as possible. It may have seem complicated but we soon got used to it and there was the added advantage of never having a particular day related to our most unfavourite lesson. Instead of working the five days Monday to Friday, the timetable continued to the next Monday and Tuesday then started again on the Wednesday and finished on the Friday of the following week. Simple really!

Throughout my time there, Mr Mellor always filled in when teachers were away or not replaced immediately and I think he really enjoyed teaching more than anything else. In the two years I took French after Miss Wood left we had no fewer than eleven different teachers and consequently didn't do well, but I will never forget Tubby's vivid portrayal of a French climber who had fallen down a crevasse and the occasion when he pulled out his white handkerchief from his top pocket, and putting it over his left arm dashed around our desks playing the waiter and urging us to order drinks and food. There was no need to call for attention in Tubby's classes. He would even take cookery classes for the girls, though some years later he confessed to me that he didn't know the first thing about cooking, and he solved the problem of what to teach in the odd domestic science lesson by sending us off with buckets and mops to clean the school. The only thing he jibbed at was physical training, as he didn't care for exercise very much, but like many short, fat men, he was a good ballroom dancer and often helped the gym mistress on wet lunchtimes to teach us to dance the military two-step to the tune of *Blaze Away*, the schottische, the veleta, the St Bernard's waltz and the quickstep as well as various Scottish dances.

The lesson he excelled in was Latin, which he taught for school certificate, and for which he promised every child a credit. He got them too, though I wasn't prepared to spend every lunchtime from 1pm to 1.45 in extra Latin, and lazily gave up. He really wanted to teach Greek, too, as he said that Latin and Greek should be the basis for our English lessons, but whether the syllabus was already too overcrowded or whether the education committee thought it too elitist I don't know. But he did teach scripture for school cert, and although there was only one lesson every ten days, again all the students got a credit - except one, bespectacled, middle-aged looking Granny Green was the only one who wanted to go into the church as a career and he failed completely because he got too interested in the questions and never finished the paper.

Tubby ruled the school strictly but fairly, though we dreaded being sent to him for some misdemeanour and on the very few occasions when he heard bad language being spoken his punishment was to take the offender to the school cloakroom and make him (always a him) wash out his mouth with carbolic soap. He occasionally used the cane but most punishments consisted of hundreds of lines and being made to report to Room 1 on a daily basis for extra French or Latin lessons.

Indoors he insisted we all wear soft plimsolls to keep down the noise and maintained that sailors wore them on deck without coming to any harm. In those days, and probably later too, we seemed to change rooms for almost every lesson, hauling piles of books around with us. He had a favourite phrase, brought out regularly in assembly after a spate of untidiness, and one which I have often thought of quoting since, *'Let no one say, and say it to your shame, that all was beauty here before you came'*. With our huge grounds and park and children bringing packed lunches it was no doubt a necessary precaution.

Mr and Mrs Mellor had no children of their own but he protested that he had had hundreds and remembered every one of them.. The school was certainly his life, and although I don't think he had any independent means, he bought thousands of daffodil bulbs every year to plant down the drive. The school's resources were few, being financed meagrely by the local authority, so, as he believed in a good all-round education in the arts, he paid for theatre companies to come for two or three days at a time to perform Shakespeare, Bridie, Shaw etc on the sunken lawn. We were the first school in the country to have the well-known Pilgrim Players with E Martin Browne performing TS Eliot's *Murder In The Cathedral*, and the Shakespeare plays were usually performed by an intrepid group of ladies, under the direction of Miss Nancy Hewins MA. These amazing ladies, whose base was in the Cotswolds, toured the country districts, performing Shakespeare and Sheridan in schools and village halls wherever they could get bookings. Their large van not only carried costumes and some basic scenery and props, but they apparently slept and ate in it too, accompanied by three little Belgian griffons called Peaseblossom, Cobweb and Mustardseed, who appeared as extras. In wartime they had little petrol, so changed to a horse and covered wagon. This must have presented even more problems, because, it has to be remembered, that as a precaution against helping an invading enemy, all the sign posts had been removed - even railway names were eliminated - and their journeys on country roads in the blackout must have been very confusing. Added to this they had to carry emergency ration books, unlike the rest of us who had to register with a regular supplier, and shops were not always willing to provide for strangers. Despite this they cheerfully carried on, though one actress, Henrietta Trend, was already quite old and Miss Hewkins herself was past middle age. The working conditions were like those of the earliest travelling companies - perhaps worse than in Shakespeare's day, and though the standard was not perhaps what one would expect at Stratford they knew how to speak verse and gave very competent performances even in the male parts. It was exciting to see Shakespeare acted before we studied the texts, and I, for one, never lost the taste for it. I don't think anyone has written their story, though I heard a few years ago that someone was asking for information. I would dearly love to read a full account.

Drama was on the school syllabus for all forms even in the 1930s, which, I think was most unusual. We read and performed one-act plays (and everyone must remember *The Crimson Coconut*), and did exercises in mime, movement and improvisation. We were also encouraged to write and perform as well as costume and stage manage our own plays, so that a few friends and myself put on a lunchtime entertainment in aid of the mayor's Spitfire Fund in 1941, and costumed it from an exciting trunk outside the boy prefects' room. We charged 3d entry fee in the gym and quite a number of the staff as well as children turned up to support us although it was probably not very good.

Sports facilities were very poor and everyone remembers the tennis courts which sloped down the hill and sideways, so that tennis, netball and stoolball were punctuated by pauses while someone chased the balls down the park. Hockey for girls and soccer for the boys was played two fields away on an equally uneven site - a field rented from a farmer which still retained the old ridge and furrows of medieval England, so that in wet weather we ran through rain-filled furrows, trying to miss the cowpats, or dropped our scarves in them as we slid on frost and ice.

I had finished my first-year, and we were approaching the end of the school holidays when war was declared and we were told not to return for another two weeks while plans were made for our safety. These didn't go very far because when we returned, clutching our newly provided gas masks in their square cardboard boxes. 'Child, where is your gas mask?' 'Sorry sir, I forgot to bring it' 'Then go straight home and fetch it' It didn't matter that most of us lived four or five miles away. When we returned, the only precaution against air attack was a criss-cross of sticky tape stuck on all the Georgian window panes, and an exercise to see how quickly we could leave the building if the siren sounded. There were no air raid shelters at all and we were supposed to take shelter in an old stone barn near the entrance to the woodland path, which admittedly had thick walls but wouldn't hold a quarter of the school. Alternatively there was a ha-ha which dropped from the lawns outside Mr Mellor's study to the golf course below them, but it gave no cover at all, though only a little over 100 yards away was a prime target - the main line railway. In the event, though stray bombs fell in the area at night - one killing a cow in our already bumpy hockey field, the alarm only sounded once while we were in class - or was it the siren? Nobody was quite sure, so we filed out on a hot summer day, crouched in our ditch and waited. masters marched up and down in tin hats and still no enemy aircraft approached. Then someone thought of phoning the report centre, only to find that nothing was known of aircraft or siren. We discovered later that a certain lorry, climbing up our long drive, had a peculiar engine note, and this was our siren. Still, it made a welcome break and a spot of excitement.

At Christmas we still had our parties - shared with all our year, and the cakes made in cookery lessons. There was still a large Christmas tree holding simple presents from our school friends in addition to which Tubby provided a useful present - e.g. socks, black gym stockings, gloves and scarves, for every child whose father was serving in the forces. It was a kind gesture because anyone below officer rank had very little pay indeed. The disciplinarian had a heart of gold!

On a later occasion in 1942, Eddie Radford and myself were asked by a teacher to impersonate the French mayor and mayoress of Deauville for an auction in aid of Friends of France. I wore Miss Charmichael's fur coat and Miss Jackson's Parisian hat, and while I don't expect that anyone was taken in, we enjoyed ourselves immensely with our heavy French accents and managed to contribute a magnificent £3.12.6 to the fund. That amount was a week's average wage in 1942.

Wartime rationing became worse, and with only one egg allowed per week (sometimes only dried egg powder) the sandwich lunch became difficult, though we could warm up baked beans or Marmite in the domestic science room. However more of us took advantage of the two course cooked meal provided for 2s 6d per week (12 pence). A menu was posted up on a Monday morning and I learned to avoid the days when Mrs Skidmore, the school cook, was serving fried potatoes as these were always very hard and lumpy and very greasy. Another speciality of hers was cabbage, so overcooked and wet, that it was only edible if one was very hungry, and then it had to be swallowed very quickly without tasting. But her real piece de resistance came later in the war when she made nettle 'splodge'. She could be seen searching the perimeter of the golf course for nettles - not the fresh young ones that could have been nutritious - but any old nettle of ancient lineage, which she dropped into gallons of boiling water, and served half an hour later in a great disgusting mess. For years afterwards the memory put me off spinach too. We did enjoy the puddings though - even thick tapioca which was inevitably called frog spawn - but there was spotted dick, jam roly-poly, treacle tart, bread and butter pudding, and best of all, Savoy Creams. These never had any real cream in them, but had three sponge fingers sticking upwards and stuck together with a synthetic and jam. I don't think any ice cream was available in wartime - certainly not at school, but it may be that it could not be made at that time.

The only unpleasant aspect of school lunches was the fact that we queued in the narrow corridor between the dining room and the boys' lavatories, and the smell was far from salubrious. The girls' lavatories weren't much better ventilated either, and I trained myself over the years not to use them; leaving home at 8.15 and not returning until 5pm was quite a feat of endurance but I managed most of the time.

Ignoring the effluvia that arose from the corridor, one could look at the school magazine, *The Rocket*, so called of course in memory of George Stephenson. I wonder if it retained its format throughout the life of the school. Certainly in my day it was composed of single sheets of copy - poems, accounts of school journeys, essays on hobbies, cartoons and caricatures - all spread out in a glass case on the wall of the corridor. I don't think that there was a set time for a new edition but it changed whenever there was enough material to put in.

Between late 1938 and 1942 there were few school trips for obvious reasons. One to Snowdon at Easter 1939 I'm told was spent in pouring rain and a week in Belgium in August 1939 which was too expensive for my parents to afford, and I think there was one to Whipsnade too, and a few days at the Leam Hall YHA near Grindleford. But the only day trip I remember going on was a very cold Ascension Day spent in Castleton. Later, in 1941 I went on a week's camp with Miss Wildin and Miss Stanley, plus Miss Lowe on occasion (this was the week before she joined the staff) at what I think was called the Guides Hut at Darley Dale. This was fun, but by the end of the week I felt quite ill - not really surprising as we washed and brushed our teeth in the stream outside which we also used as a lavatory! One incident stands out - some time after lights out, when we were still talking and the staff were beginning to be a little irritated, there was a scuffle in the boys' room and sounds of someone climbing through the window. When Miss Wildin demanded to know what was going on, a hesitant voice (Dick Stafford) said with some diplomacy, 'I'm afraid expediency had to obey natural necessity'.

Does anyone remember the school tuck shop across from the bottom, of the park?

There was always a queue there at lunchtime until sweet rationing put an end to it, and also ended the so-called canteen held in the girl prefects' room in the morning break. Here we could buy ha'penny bars of Cadbury's Milk and biscuits. Those of us who walked from town also had to pass Willett's sweet shop at the bottom of Tapton Lane and this was well patronised until rationing and coupons stopped us. There were 2oz Cadbury bars filled with various flavoured creams for 2d - that's less than 1p.

A happier memory is of an encounter in the early part of the war when my parents, myself and small brother were on a train journey - me wearing my school blazer and Panama hat. Opposite sat a handsome young pilot (whether sergeant or officer I don't recall). Suddenly the train stopped at an unidentified station and we were told to get out without any further explanation, though this frequently happened in wartime. The pilot held the door for us and smiling at me said, 'Tubby wouldn't allow this would he.' Later I saw his photograph on the notice board near the domestic science room, kept for Old Taptonians in the services, and I think his name was Draycott.

The winter of 1940 came in with a vengeance and was not helped by the complete blackout for our journey home. It was reported that the snow was deeper than at any time since the year of Waterloo, and sometimes the main-road buses ceased to run. Having walked the two miles into town we usually found that the School Special was not running either and the walk over the railway bridge and up the woodland path was an exhausting scramble to say the least. On the way back at night we found it easier to sit on our satchels and toboggan down the zig-zag paths, though I finished up in hospital after a fall on a glassy slide that had been made at the bottom. I hadn't broken any bones but had somersaulted on to my face and in the great graze that covered one cheek managed to get some germ into it on my way home and it all ended in erysipelas.

From time to time the male staff disappeared into the forces and Miss Muir (of the 'scooring pooder') had felt the call of the ATS and volunteered at the outbreak to take charge of cooking. One has to give credit to the staff when one realised what disruption was made by the war. Not only were teachers being changed frequently but on top of teaching and marking they also had fire-watching duties. Every night of the week there had to be at least two staff ready to put out incendiary bombs and the rota was usually either two men or three ladies who could bed down in the staff dining room beside the kitchen and take turns to patrol the school, including the roof. At least, they usually got time for planning lessons and marking homework while on duty but I think that some of the lady staff also did duty at the central Report Centre.

Summer came with the rhododendrons and by June it was Commemoration Day. The school choir sang under the direction of Mr Clarke (standing always as he played the piano) and one of the high spots was always the solos sung by Joan Booth. I particularly remember *The Pipes Of Pan* with all its trills but Joan had a phenomenal voice for a young schoolgirl and later became a singing teacher I think. She also married Bert Hopkinson (?) the best male voice amongst the pupils. Although there was little contact in class between the sexes it was amazing how many old pupils married each other, which must say something about the school.

I was always rather disappointed that the school plays were produced by Mr Mellor to include as many pupils as possible, because they usually ended in pageant-like entertainment instead of 'proper' plays. Being mad about the theatre I would have been happy to have tackled Shakespeare but had to be content with being an angel or a Greek goddess most of the time. In desperation a friend and myself tried another tack - why not put on a play instead of the usual Wednesday morning homily from Mr Mellor at assembly. He had gone through all the letters of our school motto as subject matter, had encouraged the musically inclined to sing or play their instruments, and must have been running out of subjects for the weekly sermon so he accepted the suggestion with alacrity. We next had to persuade our form master, Mr Routledge, to produce the play if we found a suitable one. 'Suitable' seemed to be biblical as it would be rehearsed during the daily scripture session and as he wasn't over enthusiastic about the lesson he too accepted the suggestion and we rehearsed *The Passover*, put it on a few weeks later on a Wednesday morning, and so made sure of parts in the next Commem play.

In our fourth year school certificate reared its head and in those pre-O Level days we had to pass in English language and five other subjects or fail altogether. Earlier, maths and a foreign language had been compulsory too, but it also meant that we could give up subjects we disliked and have many periods left over for private study. In good weather we sat on the lawns to read in small groups or wandered off on our own and I'm surprised that we were fairly disciplined in this, although my particular friend and myself always made sure that we had a sketch book with us, and when being challenged for being half way up a tree could say that we were drawing action sketches.

In the biology class Miss Stanley decided that we needed to study the alimentary canal of the rabbit, being vaguely near to that of a human, and to this end she tried to buy a live rabbit. Unfortunately, they were in desperately short supply with meat rationing in place, but at last she located a beautiful pet rabbit which its owner could no longer look after. When she got it the pre-Easter exams loomed, so she had to keep it at home and feed it every day and by the time of the operation had grown very fond of the animal. However, not being one to shirk a duty she chloroformed the poor thing and we carefully dissected it and measured its lengthy intestine across the benches. History does not record if the rest of the animal was cooked and eaten. I hope it was. One pleasant aspect of Miss Stanley's classes was that occasionally we would be led across the golf course and down to the ponds to look for caddis worms. This was a great opportunity to 'rescue' golf balls with our fishing nets though I doubt that anyone made any money from them.

One of the subjects I did for school cert was art, and while Miss Wildin took illustration (with action figure drawing) and still life (with only pencils and charcoal available in wartime) we also studied the history of painting with Mr Mellor. Few schools taught this at the time and it was another aspect of Tubby's determination to teach us subjects that would be of great use and pleasure to us afterwards.

In literature classes we were to study Conrad's *Four Tales*, Tennyson's *Idylls of the King* and Shakespeare's *Midsummer Night's Dream* and though we were happy to be doing The Dream, my particular friend, Barbara Harper, and I wanted to do *Hamlet* - then only available for Higher School Certificate. So we studied this in our spare time with library books and learned all the great soliloquies which we declaimed at lunchtimes in the copse. It's surprising that Miss Wildin got such good results from her English classes because we spent so much time privately reading plays and as there were 36 in class there couldn't be much individual attention. In earlier classes there were as many as 40.

I was never lucky enough to be made a prefect and envied the girls their lovely shared study, but it was decided that the school library on the top floor was underused, and I was made the first school librarian. I now not only had the key to the library which Barbara and I could use for private study when the weather wasn't good enough outside, but the biggest prize of all - I could use the lovely central staircase too, and on every occasion swept down the elegant stairs trailing my imaginary farthingale or swinging my cloak round the newel posts from floor to floor. It's a pity that my elevation was so near the end of my schooling, because having passed school cert there was really nowhere to go. There were not enough teachers to have a fifth and sixth form so if we wanted to go further we were given the opportunity to transfer to the girls' high school or the grammar school, though the former was a whole year behind us. After Tapton only one girl opted for the high school as she wanted to teach and none of the boys transferred. The feeling was that nothing would be as good again though it inevitably cut short our education. Most of us tried to get jobs immediately and until that happened we went up into the fifth form located in George Stephenson's last bedroom. All Mr Mellor could offer us was a course in shorthand and typing, some bookkeeping and current affairs - all taught of course by the one and only Tubby. Those pupils who had been in 4b and not encouraged to take SC had already done a year of this course, but few of us lasted more than a few weeks before getting jobs, however unsuitable to our particular interests. On my last day I 'borrowed' a key from the head's study and when all was quiet after school, unlocked the door to the roof and stood gazing over the gardens and the park until a roar up the stairs for 'Prefect' made me realise that my shadow had been cast over the glass dome. Whether Mr Mellor had seen it or not I never knew but there were no repercussions and I had achieved a four-year ambition.

What was more important was that I had spent four years at a happy school, in glorious surroundings, and had the privilege of being taught by two brilliant teachers - Mr Mellor and Miss Wildin - whose dedication and communicative skills encouraged and expanded my interests for years to come. What more could one ask except perhaps another two years at Tapton House!

Many Memories

Kathleen Barber 1938 - 1941

I attended Tapton House School from September 1938 until December 1941 - following in the footsteps of my eldest sister Betty Stanforth (Barber), who was there in 1931 when the school opened. Unfortunately I do not have any school photographs - I don't think many were taken during the war years, but I do have many memories. One very clear memory of Tapton House is of Mr Mellor, or Tubby, as we affectionately called him, standing each morning on the hall platform taking school assembly, and Wednesday morning, as I recall, was the day he delivered a short sermon. He had two pet subjects, the school motto, Tenax Propositi, and litter. The one that stays in my mind is the one about litter and how at the end of his homily he would stand there, hands at shoulder height clasping his gown, his voice reverberating round the hall as he said, *'Let no one say and say it to your shame that all was beauty before you came.'* I heard that many times in my years at Tapton.

I also remember Commemoration Day plays, especially taking part (a very small part) in the 1939 production. The name of the play eludes me but I know it was written by L du Garde Peach, and I, along with Joyce White, Margaret Butler, Geof Keen and three or four other classmates (afraid I cannot bring names to mind), dressed as toy soldiers in red and white shiny material and had to inch our way across the big lawn (stage) to the strains of *Marche Militaire*. As Miss Wildin and Mr Mellor were perfectionists we had to practise this many times! One of the 'soldiers' had to fall over and at dress rehearsal his braces snapped - we could hardly contain our giggles but as the saying goes, 'It was alright on the night.'

I also remember Joan Booth singing to the School on many occasions including her part in *The Mikado* - another Commemoration Day presentation. In fact my friend Doreen Bambroffe (Heath) reminded me that she had sung in the chorus and we both had a laugh about in choral class (Nobby) Mr Clarke had us practising *Behold the Lord High Executioner* until we almost knew it backwards.

We then recalled hearing the wail of the sirens and going to the air raid shelters which were somewhere near the Markham burial ground, and again Joan Booth sang to us as we waited for the sound of the all-clear.

There are so many memories - Miss Wood trying to teach us phonetic French; Mr Silcock, Latin and algebra; Mr Heathcote all about the Romans and the Stone Age; Miss Wildin - art etc. Subjects in those days, so unfamiliar to most of us straight from junior school.

Then the teachers began to leave as they were called to join H M Forces - Messrs Dennison, Silcock, Harry Routledge, Davey and Pearson, and by the time they returned I had left school.

There was something special about attending Tapton House School, something indefinable about being an Old Taptonian. Perhaps Jim, the husband of my friend Marian Bryan (Greaves) summed it up when he once said to me, 'You Taptonians always stick together.'

The Dark Days of War

Pamela J Birks 1939 - 1943

Unfortunately my school years were during the war 1939-43 so life was really very mundane and restricted. I clearly remember the heavy snow and how we used to sledge down the park on our school satchels, which of course, my parents were not too happy about. Also having to eat boiled nettles as part of our school dinners, but things could have been far worse. Looking back they were happy years - well, as happy as they could be in those dark days.

A Special Souvenir

Betty Moore 1939 - 1943

I started Tapton the week after the war started and met my husband there, when I was 15. He was a prefect and they often had to stand at the top of the stone stairs to see that we came up them quietly. I used to cheekily say, 'Hello Hall', until he must have noticed me, as the next Christmas he had put a present under the school tree for me. We had a very happy life together until he died six years ago. I miss him very much. When he made his speech at our ruby wedding, he said, 'You have all heard the story that Betty ran after me at school. Well after a while I succumbed.'

Mr Mellor was the headmaster and was very strict and his nickname was Tubby. No one ever walked on the grass and there was never any litter about. He was always quoting, *'Let no one say it and say it to your shame that all was beauty before you came.'*

I suggest you ask Vic Brocklehurst about when one of the boys nearly blew himself up and Vic, my Ted and some other boys went to visit him and all of them brought a bit of shirt back with them as a souvenir.

Commemoration Day Celebrations 1932 - A Midsummer Night's Dream

Back row, left to right: R Boam, M Ford, E Clarke, B Mayfield, G Tinsley, O Hayes,
N Higginbotham, D Moore, C Eyre.
Second row: B Lander, G Ward, E Holmes, W Share, H Draycott, J Godfrey, R Parton,
J Hudman, G Stobbs, D Handford. Seated: W Bunting, D Briddon, H Bingham,
E Hawkins, M Marshall, J Baggaley, B Horne.

Commemoration Day 1934 - The Prince who was a Pauper

Pupils 1935 including front row second from left: Fred Taylor and Mr F Silcock

Staff members 1935

Back row, left to right: John Macara, Harry Routledge, Jack Smith, Ron Wilkins, John Routledge, Charlie Middleton, Frank Silcock. Front row: Clifford Fawcett, Marjorie Vessey, Edith Davidge, Grace Clark, Harry Mellor, Constance Walker, Kathleen Clayton, Charlotte Stanley, Norman Denison.

Form1A 1937

Back row, left to right: Pud Shaw, Lewis Bullock, Jeff Hughes, Raynor Peyton, Ernest Bargh, Frank Cherry, Doug Roe, Derek Edge, Frank Clark, Jack Bunting, Reg Barnes. Second row: Jean Crossley, Mary Saxton, ?, Betty Wilde, Ruth Dore, Mary Tiplady, Joyce Walker, Joan Shaw, Joyce Baker. Third row: Dorothy Bannister, Barbara Bradley, Margaret Twelves, Barbara Marsh, Hilda Clarke, Miss Wood, Maureen Coogan, Jean Cooke, Joan Norman, Bernice Graham, Betty Doram. Front row: John Pilkington, John Smith, John Redfern, Ron Marsden, Tony Jervis, David Robert, Tony Marshall, Jim Crocker.

Form1R 1937

Back row, left to right: Roy Norton, Derek Parsons, Joe Smedley, Eric Goodwin, Lawrence Gainey, Soapy Hudson, Dennis Wigston, Keith Parkin, Derek Higginbottom, Geoff Salmon, Arthur Hudson, Alan Francis. Middle row: Doug Morris, Alan Vickers, Nora Clarke, Dorothy Holmes, Iris Brailsford, Jean Lowrie, June Bowden, Doreen Bowler, Marion Wetton, Dorothy Hodgeson, Olive Heath, Trevor Swann, George Pud Webster, Donald Robertshaw. Front row: Jack Cartwright, Ida Webber, ?, Mary Taberner, Audrey Sambrook, Queenie Knightley, JKG Hoffman (form master), Pat Holmes, ?, Sylvia Cooper, Joan Hunt, Gordon Watson, Reg Smith.

Students watching tree being planted 1939

Front row, left to right: John Cumberland, Auriel Sambrook, Muriel Kirk, Betty Sanders, Kathleen Turner, Jean Hughes, Barbara Harber, Dorothy Smith, Mavis Herring, Irene Cox.

The Wrath of Miss Lowe

Doreen Housley 1940 - 1943

I suppose we were about the first intake to use the new air raid shelters. These were situated outside the then school boundaries, under a wall to the south side of the school. They were dark, dank and dismal, and, if you were unfortunate enough to find yourself near to the more sexually aware boys, fraught with trouble.

Commemoration Days were very hectic. We all gathered on the sunken lawn and the dignitaries sat on chairs on the upper pathway. One year, Miss Wildin auditioned two girls to dance *The Sugar Plum Fairy*. My family was very poor and there was no money. My mother could not have afforded to buy the costume and shoes needed, so I had the daunting task of going and telling Miss Wildin that I didn't want to take part. Looking back, I always seemed to be learning something for Miss Wildin; *Cautionary Tales*, verses from the Bible. I was the Queen of Hearts in *Alice In Wonderland* and had to shout, 'Off with his/her head' very much in the style of Miss Wildin. She frightened us all, I think, with a healthy fear. Getting to know her in later life, I often wondered why I was so afraid. She commanded respect and got it, as also did Mr Mellor. I was never naughty enough to be sent to the hallowed place, the headmaster's study.

I did, however, invoke the wrath of Miss D Lowe, the geography teacher. When we had internal exams, we sat next to a class from a different year, doing a different exam. We were doing geography, they were attempting maths. No one was allowed to talk. However, the girl next to me whispered a question and I just shook my head. Unfortunately the teacher in charge saw the movement, assumed I had answered a question and promptly removed my paper. When we were eventually given the results, Miss Lowe had me standing in front of the class and, in her stentorian voice, harangued me for breaking the rules. No explanations were allowed. I was the lowest of the low. I felt very aggrieved by the whole affair. My father was not pleased with me when he read my report.

Mr Clarke, who taught Latin, history and music, was an untidy figure in a battered trilby and raincoat, but I have never come across anyone who could play the piano, standing up, as well as he could. I remember needlework with Miss Mackerel. We all had to make a pair of navy blue knickers, with gusset. Those knickers would have fitted Tessie O'Shea. They were huge. I don't even remember wearing them. We also had to knit. A scarf was the obvious starting point. I'm ashamed to say mine 'got lost' in my drawer at home. It was long after I left school that I disposed of it. Miss Woodall I remember with affection. She taught us history and we loved her. She told us that she was a friend of the actress Cicely Courtneidge. But we all tried hard for Miss Woodall.

Miss Pennington, who taught French, was quite different. She could not control the class and the boys ran rings round her. Consequently, very little work was done. Mr Moorhouse, Mickey to all, taught maths. He was a crack shot with a piece of chalk and woe betide anyone who let their attention wander. He also had the nasty habit of keeping a ruler up his sleeve and, as he walked about checking a pupil's work, some unfortunate child got their knuckles rapped quite regularly. Uniform, even in wartime, was strictly adhered to. Woe betide any child seen in Chesterfield in uniform without a cap or hat. This was Miss Wildin's department and a summons to the women's staffroom on the top floor filled one with trepidation.

The school, placed as it was, was a lovely place to spend a few years. The grounds were, and still are, delightful and, after I married, I spent over 50 years living in the Tapton area and enjoyed the gardens and woods of Tapton House with my children.

My Amateur Dramatics Beginnings

Mavis Hill 1940 - 1944

I have tried to set down some of my memories of my years at Tapton House School, which with hindsight, seem very uneventful.

Academically I did very little; I suppose you could say I was an underachiever. Most of my qualifications I earned going to evening classes at the technical college. I did leave, however, with some happy memories of spending my school days in such beautiful surroundings. I especially remember when the daffodils were in bloom in such profusion. Sometimes these were mutilated or trampled underfoot which gave Mr Mellor the opportunity to say, as he did every year, *'Let no one say and say it to your shame, that all was beauty here before you came'*.

We had productions by travelling players when seven or eight well upholstered ladies would arrive in a van and on one occasion performed Julius Caesar with great gusto. One group I remember performed *As You Like It* on the top lawn with the players appearing appropriately from the shrubbery - halcyon days indeed.

Performing in the Commemoration Day productions, again on the top lawn, weather permitting, whetted my appetite for amateur drama, a hobby I enjoy to this day.

I was at Tapton House during the war years, which curtailed many activities. But I do remember the Christmas parties with a huge Christmas tree in the assembly hall and each year having its own party with sandwiches and cakes and games, in which the staff used to join us; even Mr Mellor used to participate.

Passing Muster

Sheila Burgess 1940 - 1944

In 1940 I arrived in Chesterfield, my mother's home. Our family home was in Seaford, Sussex where my father and his brothers ran the family building business and where I attended a convent. Father had been called up before war was declared and we had already followed him first to Cardiff and then he was posted to RAF Sealand, near Chester, which was nearer to Chesterfield than to Sussex. So began a succession of digs, first with relatives and later at Walton and Brampton. Then one day I was told we were going to Tapton House for an interview, to behave myself and if I was lucky I might go to school there. I went into Mr Mellor's study (he had been called out of retirement to become headmaster again) where I was questioned by this dignified elderly gentleman. He said that though I was not up to Tapton's standards (a convent education laid too much emphasis on ladylike pursuits like needlework and deportment) he would take me on a term's trial and if I passed muster I could stay. Threatened with dire penalties if I misbehaved I duly became a pupil at this remarkable school. At the time I didn't realise how lucky I was. School was school wherever it was and this one had boys as well. Being the eldest of numerous cousins and having only one little sister, boys were an unknown quantity, but I looked forward to getting to know them better, much better. Eric Fearn and Colin Cautrell, where are you now? And whatever happened to Dennis Brocklehurst who did my maths homework while I did his English. We were only found out when exams came and we both had awful low marks. Obviously you will have realised, dear reader, that I was allowed to stay on. Perhaps it was Tapton's contribution to the war effort, but it was my good luck too. Apart from a good old fashioned education we learnt to obey rules (sometimes), put up with teasing, dealing with boys, and accept discipline. Even school dinners weren't too bad at 2s 6d a week, I think it was, and we had all those glorious grounds at our disposal. Who remembers what was it called: Open Day? Founders Day? or something in the summer when the teachers sat above us on the sunken lawn and Margery Hopkinson appeared from behind the rhododendron bushes as the Sugar Plum Fairy. cookery lessons in our blue caps and aprons learning to make Russian fish pie. Do Russians really eat such things? Congregating at the bottom of the back stairs learning to dance, Irene Marsh and I doing the foxtrot while someone sang *Skylark*. Hearing it always reminds me of her. Incidentally we lesser mortals were not allowed down the graceful front stairs, only teachers and prefects, unless it was a dare of course. If you got caught, it was some detention or other: I had so many I can't remember what they all were. At least we weren't caught when some of the boys tied me to a tree in the park. Luckily I escaped just in time for afternoon school. I was caught passing a note to Eric Fearn by the head mistress, Miss Wildin, and subjected to a scathing speech on 'unseemly behaviour'. I didn't think it was, but that's besides the point. In the fourth year playing hooky to go to the Regal and when the lights went up there were at least half our class puffing away on their Woodbines. One could go on in this nostalgic mood indefinitely but in retrospect I am grateful I had the chance to go to Tapton, and although I returned south in 1944, it brings back many happy memories and I'm sorry it is no more.

Inky Little Urchin

Peter Ashley 1940 - 1945

'Twas not my privilege to be captain of the First XI; top of the batting and bowling averages; male lead in that shortest of Shakespeare's plays, performer in satirical sketches sending up the Nazi leaders, nor one of the more precocious youths who would join a girl in the dark recesses of the cellars for some lessons in basic human anatomy.

I, a seedy, inky little urchin (although most of us must have looked seedy in those days of soap rationing and clothing coupons; quicker growing children received extra coupons!) spent roughly 1,000 days between September 1940 and August 1945 doing my best to avoid the baleful gaze of various underpaid and overworked teachers, who, either on account of age, or physical impairment, had managed to escape the attention of His Majesty's recruiting officers. (Towards the end of the war, staff came and went with alarming rapidity - apart from a nucleus of stalwart souls).

Therefore, my ability to retain a low profile means, alas, that I have no compendium of shocking stories, creepy characters, frightful facts or amusing anecdotes with which to titillate our eager readers. Any sparse recollections I may have would be almost certainly libellous against others or detrimental to myself.

One image I do remember is of a group of itinerant thespians who made at least two visits to Tapton during the early 1940s. A most curious bunch as you may imagine, they arrived in a battered and ancient Rolls-Royce with all their props strapped on the roof. I recall one performance, *Tobias and the Angel*, given in the garden. The angel made his appearance by walking atop the wall which separated the kitchen garden section. What an entrance!

I certainly have no memories (Wilcox style) of a pupil-beating psychopathic headmaster, although it occasionally fell to him to administer physical chastisement, as was the practice of those times.

Harry Mellor was a polymath. During the later years of the war he frequently took classes caused by staff absences. He would hurry into a classroom, usually several minutes late and enquire as to the content of the last lesson. Whatever the subject, he would, off the cuff, give a lecture superior to that of the teacher whose speciality it was. In maths, I recall several occasions when he would pace around the room firing off twenty quite taxing mental arithmetic sums and later write the answers on the blackboard for us to self-mark; all memorised without any notes whatsoever. He spoke French more fluently than the French teacher and taught us Latin and such esoteric subjects as double entry bookkeeping and shorthand.

A devout individual, who read from the Bible every night before retiring, his education at the end of the 19th century would have been demanding and rigorous.

Having said that, he never bothered to clean more of his car (a Singer) than he could reach by hand. The centre of his car roof appeared not to have been cleaned since the car left the showroom.

Prefect

Roy Houghton 1942 -1947

I was a fifth former at Tapton in 1946-47 along with such people as Gordon Ison, Brian Quartermaine, Gerald Presswood, Margaret Ford, Mary Smith and Esme Noble, to mention just a few of my form colleagues.

Esme Noble was a vivacious and bubbly girl with a crowning mop of ginger hair. I was a boy prefect and at the end of one particular schoolday, after copying down the homework from the blackboard in our formroom, I went up to the boy prefects' room on the next floor to collect my books and satchel. On arriving there, I was surprised to see (the late) Derek Moore, a form mate and fellow prefect, with a paintbrush in his hand and applying a sickly looking sort of yellow paint to the walls.

'Thought the place wanted brightening up a bit,' said Derek. I thought the window ought to be opened a bit to let some fresh air in so I lifted up the sash window and, looking down, saw directly below me the red hair of Esme's head poking through our form room window. I was about to utter some immature boyish comment to her when a better idea came to mind. I had noticed a bottle of water on the windowsill beside me, so quickly removing the top from the bottle I emptied the contents out of the window and scored a direct hit on the ginger haired target below. I was about to tell Derek (still painting) how I had cleverly put one over a female element of our form when I heard, and getting ever closer and louder, the clatter of speeding leather soled soles on the bare wooden treads of the flight of stairs leading up to the boy prefect room. In burst Esme. 'What have you poured on my head Roy Houghton? She enquired with great volume. 'And where has all the turps gone out of that bottle in the window sill?' enquired a puzzled looking Derek Moore. 'My scalp's beginning to smart' cried a by now anguished-looking Esme. Realisation of the cause of Esme's predicament dawned on all three of us at the same time. There was a mad rush down to the porch (cloakroom) and Esme's head was unceremoniously pushed under the cold water tap. After a three-minute rinse a bedraggled looking Esme announced that her head wasn't smarting anymore. I said I was very sorry and Derek loudly wondered who was going to pay tuppence for some more turps. If a postscript is required for this story it is that come the following morn we were all friends once more - that is until Derek mentioned his tuppence again. I rather optimistically suggested that as Esme had been the recipient of the turps then perhaps she would like to pay - but Esme found this suggestion not at all to her amusement. I got a good handbagging and finished up with only a penny change from a threepenny bit that was supposed to keep me in biscuits for the rest of the week.

Those Were the Days That Were!

Joan Clarke 1943 - 1947

Probably we all tend to remember the things we like to remember and forget the things we prefer to forget!

The first thing about Tapton, which I love to remember, is having heard that I had passed the scholarship to go there. It was wartime - coupons, and finding coupons for uniform was quite difficult - can't really remember how everyone got around the problem. I was thrilled when my mother knew someone whose daughter was leaving Tapton and had a blazer for sale and so I could have that superb piece of kit - a blazer - second hand or not; it was wonderful. Mother was an excellent seamstress so we managed to rustle up the gym slip; the shoes they were a problem but Granny came up with a black pair of hers, pointed toes and button straps - they would be fairly 'in' now, but I still squirm about the ridicule and the rude comments made. However I did have another pride of possession and that was acquiring and wearing a purple/black Tapton tie. I had made it.

The first-year, I seem to remember, was quite hard. I had left most of my old peers and friends behind at Old Road School; at Tapton we had to stand in crocodile lines of class for roll call on the cold tarmac yard, all weathers, before going to assembly and having a hymn and morning prayers by Tubby Mellor. I can still visualise him saying, O Lord our heavenly Father, who hast safely brought us to the beginning of this day, that all our doings may be ordered by Thy governance, to do always that is righteous in Thy sight; rather than the modern version given today in Church of 'to guide us to do always what is right in your eyes'; It's like trying to update Shakespeare! Tubby really ingrained lasting things in our memory. One of the lasting things also was not to be brought before him for discipline and have to wait in trepidation outside his study.

I can still visualise Phil Wildin gliding down the posh staff and prefects' staircase with its wonderful glass dome at the top, Phil usually wearing trousers, something unheard of those days except for women in the forces, and her hallmark - vivid red lipstick. We, the students, had to use the back staircase, the banisters studded with brass knobs to stop sliding down the three floors; to do so would have either ruptured one's virginity, or neutered the male masculinity.

Nobby Clarke who used to take us for music - our music slot was usually before mid-morning break. Each week he used to say, 'We will now have a break to partake of the extract of udder.' How I hated those little bottles of milk we were supposed to drink, often going sour in the summer. I understand why I like something stronger these days. Mrs Berrisford, the kitchen cook - we were always wanting to know if it would be mince for lunch - the gourmet meal of the week; other dishes were at times to be avoided at all costs, particularly salads with the occasional wee creatures lurking in the lettuce.

Miss Lowe, the geography mistress, short cropped hair, usually in a dark grey pin stripe costume - we were frightened to death of her - but one day her pink boned stays jutted above the waistline of her skirt and we all wanted to laugh but just didn't dare until we came out of class. Must say I was really chuffed when she stopped me in the schoolyard and told me I had come top in the geography exam and she went on to say that she didn't think I had it in me.

Of thinking how glamorous Isobel Carmichael, the domestic science teacher was - can remember an army officer coming to collect her after school, and we were all oh and ah. Not so glamorous was the occasion when I let one of the cast iron saucepans boil dry in the domestic science class and the smell of burnt cabbage pervaded the whole kitchen - couldn't do anything much more exciting than vegetables and fruit in those days as parents weren't prepared to let us experiment with meagre wartime rations.

Lunchtimes we often went down to the railway line placed coins on the track and waited for the express train to run over them and then collect the flattened coins. One of the highlights of the year was when it snowed and we would bring our sledges to school and stay on after class until dusk just sledging down that superb hill, across the drive and a huge drop down into what was then referred to as the potato field - as potatoes were grown there during war time.

By this time I lived in the Highfields area, so often walked to school over the canal, the railway bridge and up the hill through the woods to Tapton House. On this circuit I went with Alan Savage, Pat O'Donnell, Tony Cable and then met Margaret Connelly down Wharf Lane - we weren't all in the same forms but we all got on very well. We had a year when we had a lot of snow and afterwards it resulted in severe flooding; the canal was impassable so we had a very long walk round. Strangely enough in those days it wasn't an excuse for missing classes, merely for finding another route of getting there. By the fourth form, we also collected Lennie Lennon, PE teacher, recently demobbed out of the RAF, and who was living on our route to Tapton. Oh how I loved to walk up the drive to school with him as all the girls thought he was ace.

Still can remember the occasion when I annoyed that infamous ginger headed boy, renowned for his prowess as a footballer - he treated the girls in the same way he would treat the opposing football team. He also used to play against us at hockey, it was equality all the way. I'm sure Eric, or 'Ecca', to give him his nickname, won't remember that he stuffed my head up one of the chimneys in one of the classrooms after I called him ginner - I came down like Sooty; I never called him ginner again!! I did meet him again fairly recently and he's the perfect gentleman - perhaps because he is now going slightly grey.

And the fourth form - the joy of having some authority and of growing up - the Christmas party when we stayed on at school, brought our mufti gear and changed in the art room - a very elegant room which was located on the ground floor in the Old House, next to Tubby Mellor's study - it had magnificent decorative mirrors. The fourth and fifth form school dance being held at the Co-operative ballroom, all eyeing each other up and down as we looked so different out of uniform, and seeing who looked the best. Dior hadn't yet arrived on the scene. The boys could dance then - even the Maxina, as dancing was part of the curriculum for all.

At that time Mademoiselle Schialle arrived. Unfortunately my French has never been very good but that is probably justice. Our class frequently had poor Miss Pennington, our French teacher, in tears; she just couldn't cope with us. Mlle. Schialle arrived from France, young and with a wonderful accent, superb clog type shoes, chic clothes and a twinkle in her eye - we all tried to emulate her. This also coincided with the arrival of Joyce shoes from America. If any of the girls came in a pair of these we were all really envious - two or three of the older girls visited Burtonwood to see the GIs and they used to show us their shoes, lovely wedged heel jobs in either yellow or red and nylon stockings with seams, sometimes black seams - we all wanted to know how they had got them.

Came the day to say goodbye to Tapton; had just finished my school certificate. I was most upset, but I was told by my parents that if I didn't want to be a teacher I would have to leave to help earn some money, father only recently arriving home from the army. Protest was of no avail - it would be so different now. The strange thing is that several decades later I have been teaching and of all things IT (word-processing). I'm indebted to the education and the discipline and the wider horizons of mixing at an early age with the other sex. There are many happy memories of Tapton.

I Failed Tapton

Cliff Greaves 1943-46

I went on to Tapton House via Edmund Street Infants and Gilbert Heathcote Junior Boys' School. In the last year one took the 11-plus exam which determined one's route into secondary education. Soon after taking the test the letter arrived informing Mum and Dad that I had got a place at Tapton House - the school which my elder sister had gone to earlier.

Looking back, well over fifty years, the first days at Tapton House were a profound culture shock for someone like me coming from an area/home which was depressed in terms of educational opportunity. Not only that - going to school now entailed wearing a school uniform, catching the school special bus at the bottom of Whittington Hill, doing set homework every night, dealing with school prefects and most important - mixing with children from more advantaged areas of town, such as Walton, Ashgate and Holymoorside. One began to realise that not everyone's Dad worked down the pit or at Sheepbridge Works. In terms of the school curriculum I had to get involved with all the additions to it which school life at Tapton entailed. From the elementary concepts of tables, long division and decimals I was now pitched into Latin, French, English literature and language, algebra, geometry, physics and chemistry. All this gave me a sense of pride at the beginning, that is, until the newness wore off and I had to get down to some real hard work of assimilation. Another very important factor was the very close proximity of girls - Tapton being a co-educational school. From the very beginning of our school life at Tapton we were expected to sit next to the opposite sex. This didn't cause me any major problems apart from the odd adolescent crush one experienced with certain female members of the class. Relationships with the opposite sex were encouraged since dancing was available at lunch time. I enjoyed this aspect of school life for at lunch times in the hall and under the control of a lady teacher and with music provided by a gramophone we learnt the veleta, waltz and progressive barn dance etc. All this was a good way of making friends and was a foundation for my later dancing career at the Bradbury Hall, the Co-op and later at The 'Vic' dance where I met my wife, who was educated not at Tapton, but at Chesterfield Girls' High School.

Early experiences at Tapton brought me down to earth with a bang. At Gilbert's I had been a pupil of some importance (or so I thought) - I had been a house captain and a monitor and these positions had entailed certain duties and privileges. As a year-oner at Tapton these considerations meant for nothing. Now one felt very small in the company of much bigger lads in the fourth and fifth forms. This was all the more apparent at morning assembly, since year-oners went into the hall first and assembled at the front. The second year followed and so on until all the school had assembled, with the eldest pupils at the back, who, to my eyes looked very mature indeed.

Coming from a home where living conditions were certainly cramped, schooling at Tapton was an uplifting experience. The place was really a large mansion set in a parkland of mature trees, extensive lawns and rose beds. In fact as the crow flies it was very near the centre of Chesterfield but up at Tapton there was fresh air and space. It also had a very real historical feel to it. There were many references to George Stephenson, who had lived and died there and many rooms were laid out in the classical style. The entrance hall had a mosaic floor, most rooms had ornate fireplaces and ceilings and the art room had two supporting fluted columns with Corinthian capitals. Both the main entrance hall and the main wooden staircase were out of bounds to pupils except on Commemoration Day, which was the day the school celebrated the original school opening on 15 June 1931.

Commemoration Day was an enjoyable, colourful experience in which parents and friends were encouraged to take part. The graduate members of staff wore their university gowns and hoods and usually some very distinguished visitor made a speech. I either sang in the school choir or took part in some dramatic production.

When I think of Tapton, I inevitably think of people I knew there - both pupils and staff. As I write their names come flooding back into the memory. In my year I remember Joe Blissett, Joan Clarke, Peter Rodgers, Michael Globe, Arthur Wood, Geoff Watson, Enid Slaney, Betty Ward, Jean Finney, Alan Innes, Brian Quartermaine, Patricia Batteson, May Broughton, Jean Goodwin, Clinton Keeling, Jean Harding, Josie Bower, Bill Hallowes, Ted Bradbury, Roy Buxton, Eric Twelves, Phil Rudkin, Pat Smith, Iris Lowe, Harold Hartshorn, Bill Ward, Stuart Gadsby and George Williamson. Sadly some of the people are with us no more.

Clinton Keeling I remember very well. He'd come to Chesterfield from down South and arrived at Tapton via Highfield Hall School where he was a pal of Joe Blissett. Clinton had one great passionate interest - anything to do with insects, reptiles and animals. In Year one, our teacher Miss Woodall, invited anyone out of the class to give a talk on any subject they were interested in. Clinton gave a very interesting talk on stick insects and he brought some along to show us. At a later date he invited me to his home to show me his collection of mice, reptiles and stick insects and even then one could see that he was very informed on this aspect of his hobby. When he left school I lost touch with him but I know that he had his own private zoo near Chesterfield and I later learned that he had been made a Fellow of the Zoological Society. The last I heard of him was a couple of years ago when he was being interviewed by Peter Snow on BBC2's Newsnight over some dispute at London Zoo.

Bill Hallowes and I were pals at Gilbert Heathcote's; he came from Avenue Road off Whittington Moor so we used to see much of each other. Even then it was obvious that Bill had been blessed with a good brain but, perhaps just as important, his parents recognised the value of a good education. I think Bill wanted to leave school at the age of fourteen but his parents had the good sense to make him stay on to do his school certificate. In the senior forms he realised his early promise and went on to university to read chemistry. Later he was awarded a doctorate. Part of Bill's career involved a teaching spell at Chesterfield Grammar School where the pupils knew him as Doc Hallowes. It is ironical that as a young lad Bill was not considered suitable for a grammar school education, yet as a man he obtained a teaching post there.

I was at Tapton under the regime of Tubby Mellor - the headmaster who had been there from the school's beginning. Many pupils who got to know him better and longer than I did would testify to his wonderful teaching abilities, since he taught the older pupils who were staying on for the school certificate examination. Regrettably, I only experienced his vicious brutal streak - a defect which other pupils also experienced from time to time. He had warned us about throwing snowballs near the school and soon after this caught me with snow in my hands. He gave me six very painful strokes with the cane. On another occasion he caught me and Alan Innes larking about on the school stage. Alan saw him coming but Mr Mellor caught me with his clenched fist which knocked me from one side of the stage to the other and gave me a nose bleed. I never could respect Mr Mellor after those two incidents. After I had left school I bumped into him occasionally at the Civic Theatre but he never acknowledged that he knew me.

One thing Mr Mellor was very keen on was that Taptonians should have a reverence for their surroundings. Pupils were not allowed to walk on the lawns and the dropping of litter was almost a hanging offence. An acceptance of this aspect of the school's ethos was pursued with rigorous efficiency. After all this time I still get inwardly agitated when I see some people throw down litter in the streets and if I see litter near my home it's almost a compulsion for me to go out and put it in the bin.

Apart from the two painful incidents related above my memories of Tubby Mellor relate mainly to his role in morning assembly. The school would be assembled in the hall, then Mr Mellor MA would enter to a pronounced hush, the importance of the occasion marked by his black academic gown which he always wore for assembly. He would then lead the short morning service after giving out any notices, reprimands, or congratulations for any sporting or academic success. Then he would finish always with the same prayer - a prayer which, even now, transports me back to early mornings at Tapton House School. It was and is as follows:

Lord keep us all the day long of this troublesome life,
Until the shades lengthen,
The evening comes,
The busy world is hushed,
The fever of life is over,
And our work is done.
Then Lord in thy mercy
Grant us a safe lodging,
A Holy Rest
And peace at the last.

There were other members of staff who I had great respect for. One of these was Norman (Nobby) Clarke, a practising Christian who lived his Christianity seven-days a week. Mr Clarke took us for music but I really got to know and appreciate him through my involvement with the school choir in the Commemoration Day event, the Christmas carol service and sometimes at some local concert. Nobby could be a little eccentric at times and he could lose his temper, but on those occasions when he thought he had hurt a pupil's feeling he always found some way of saying sorry. I loved to hear him play the piano and he was the one who introduced me to the joy of music. He had a very great influence on the school for the good and I salute his memory. He died in 1974 at the age of 71.

Phil Wildin specialised in English and drama. She wasn't one of my regular teachers but on those occasions when she took my class it was always a most enjoyable experience. She loved her subject and she had the ability to enthuse her pupils likewise. She also had very high standards, due no doubt, to herself being a very accomplished actress. I remember once a travelling group of actors came to school to give a performance of *Macbeth* in the school hall. The following morning Miss Wildin asked the pupils who had seen the play to put their hands up. Then she said, 'Well I want you all to try and banish that production from your memory!' She told us that it was an awful production and Shakespeare could be much more exciting than that. When I think of Miss Wildin I remember her as a person with great personal style and flair. The way she dressed, the way she moved, the way she held a cigarette; she used a very bright red lipstick which perfectly complemented her dark hair - all these things imparted an air of glamour and charisma. In any group of people Phil Wildin stood out. She was a very attractive person. I think of her as Tapton House's very own Miss Jean Brodie.

When I think of Phil Wildin I automatically think of Miss Lowe - known affectionately as Ma Lowe, or in my day Old Lass Lowe. Phil Wildin and Miss Dorothy Lowe were very good friends and always together socially. Miss Lowe taught geography in Room 1. I liked Miss Lowe very much and although she had a very pronounced deep throated bark, this was very much worse than her bite. When Miss Lowe was in full voice she could be heard all over the school. One of my very strong memories of her was when she frequently acted as teacher monitor in charge of the dining room. Soon after we had all started to tuck into our school dinner, Miss Lowe would stride through the dining room and bellow, 'Nothing to be left, Nothing to be left.' This saying has become a family joke in our household since, in a kind of genuflexion to her memory at family dinner parties, I too shout, As Old Lass Lowe used to say at Tapton - Nothing to be left, Nothing to be left! The rest of the family think I'm a bit doolally on these occasions but I get a laugh out of it. Miss Lowe was certainly a very strong character and her lessons were always enjoyable and filled with incident. I remember her telling us of the time when she was driving through the night with Miss Wildin. They were going on holiday, and on that particular night the weather turned misty and foggy such that visibility was not very good and they had to slow down to a crawl. Then she said, 'I thought I must be dreaming'. Out of the mist and fog the car headlights picked up the huge backside of an elephant obviously on its lumbering way from one circus location to another. Both Miss Lowe and the class rocked with laughter as she told us this tale.

Ronnie James - an Old Taptonian who was in the year above me - told me that when he was at Tapton Miss Lowe used to borrow fags off him and Ron said, 'I never got them back.' Mention Miss Lowe to an Old Taptonian of my generation and I guarantee the first reaction will be a smile.

Mrs Lloyd was my English teacher. Her husband was Canon Lewis Lloyd, who was a local vicar. Mrs Lloyd was a refined, cultured lady and I liked her very much. I didn't realise it at the time but it was she who triggered in me a liking for and interest in Shakespeare and the grandeur of the English language. For Mrs Lloyd we had to learn the chorus opening lines to *Henry V.* This was a chore at the time but to this day I can still recite it.

'O for a Muse of fire, that would ascend

The brightest heaven of invention!

A kingdom for a stage, princes to act,

And monarchs to behold the swelling scene!
Then should the warlike Harry, like himself,
Assume the port of Mars; and at his heels,

Leash'd in like hounds, should famine, sword and fire,

Crouch for employment.   ....

My wife and I see most of the productions at The Royal Shakespeare Theatre/Swan Theatre at Stratford and I often think of Mrs Lloyd on these occasions.

For three years Miss Pennington laboured to teach me the rudiments of French with little success. At that stage in life I hadn't yet learned that education demanded dedication, application and hard work. I never did knuckle down to learn all those irregular verbs so in this subject I was groping in the dark! I wasn't one of Miss Penningtons star pupils but I had a great respect for her. I remember submitting some homework after copying it from a more able pupil. The work came back marked 10/10 and 'Very Good - if your own work'!

Other teachers whom I remember with gratitude were Mr Haddock and Mr (Mickey) Moorehouse for maths, Miss Woodall who did her best to impart her enthusiasm for history, Miss Stanley who specialised in biology, Mr Macara for woodwork, and Miss Isobel Carmichael who taught cookery and domestic science to the girls and who acted as nurse in the sick room. Mickey Moorhouse had a sadistic streak. He had a habit of twisting the short hairs on the back of one's neck as he looked over your shoulders at your maths work book. I remember him looking over my book one day as he exclaimed, 'O Greaves, it does grieve me to see you putting down such nonsense.' Twist, twist!

Although I didn't realise it at the time, with the knowledge and insight which comes with experience and age, I can now see that Tapton House was a very good school. At the age of fourteen I couldn't wait to leave and I remember when I told Miss Lowe I wasn't staying on to take my school certificate examination she did her best to persuade me to change my mind. She told me I would regret leaving so early without any formal qualifications and she was proved right in this. At the time however, my life revolved around Stand Road swimming baths, The Lyceum cinema on Whittington Moor and the camaraderie of the streets around Newbold.

Some pupils of my year went on to be academics, most of them went into professional occupations and all of them, as far as I know, proved to be good citizens, contributing much to their community. I drifted into a job in engineering and it wasn't until much later in life that I got the chance to obtain a formal extension to a general education which had ceased for me at the age of fourteen. Through the Open University I graduated with a BA Honours degree in 1995 after five years' formal study. Although all my working life has been spent in engineering my interest in the arts must have been initiated at Tapton. When I think of Tapton House School it is with much regret in that I didn't see and use the opportunities which were available to me. Tapton didn't fail me - I failed it!

Personal Recollections 1943 - 1951

Brian Quartermain BSc, MSc, PhD, CEng; MIMechE, MIOA; FSS

I arrived at Tapton House School in September 1943 via the Whittington Special - the normal means of transport for those students living in New Whittington, Old Whittington, Whittington Moor and Stonegravels. The second world war was at its mid point and everything was in short supply including male teachers.

After assembly on the first day I was placed in form 1R, the R stood for remove, I think. My memories lead to morning assembly in the school hall, which was supposed to double as a gymnasium with wall bars, beams and climbing ropes. I cannot remember using the gymnasium equipment until year three when Mr Haddock took us for PE. However, the morning assemblies were of standard format with a hymn, the words written every day by the music teacher Mr (Nobby) Clarke on a blackboard on the stage - what dedication. The headmaster Mr Harry Mellor usually made the announcements along with various views and comments on life at large. I remember one which came annually when the daffodils came in the spring and were abundant in the parkland surrounding the school - *'Let no one say and say it to your shame that all was beauty before you came'*. This was a reference to those pupils who liked to pick the daffodils.

We move on to memories of facilities like books, paper and sports equipment. In fact due to the war we relied mainly on teachers notes written on wartime quality paper. I also remember that when it came to a double period of games we had one football, brought in by a pupil, for 40-60 boys to kick about what was called the bottom pitch. Playtimes and lunchtimes were taken up with playing on the playground with a small tennis ball. In the cold winter the playground became a huge slide for only the brave to embark on.

In my second year I went home to find no one there and it being Friday and homework having been set in English to write an essay I repaired to our outside toilet seat. I cannot remember the title but I know it was published in the *Rocket*.

Also in the second year I first cast my eyes on a new first-year girl - named Joan Lancaster - September 1944 - and as I write 1999 she is still my wife.

In 1946 I moved from the third year to the fifth and passed my school certificate in 1947. My memories of this year are a lot of homework and especially having to go to

Room 5 to copy down three blackboards of English homework set by the headmaster or Miss Wildin. Many times we missed the Whittington Special and had to run or walk to Whittington. It was also during 1947 that we suffered the heavy snow which made travel and attendance at school difficult.

During 1946-47 inter-school activities were getting back to normal and the Clayton Challenge Shield was recommenced. I have a photograph showing the football team which won every match including the final, which took place in April 1947 on the Recreation Ground.

Between 1947-1950 I remember being a member of successful athletic teams and indeed in winning the county 100 yards and 220 yards in 1948 and 1949 respectively. Perhaps all the Tapton House teams were naturally fit due to running up and down the park. It certainly was not due to the provision of first class equipment or facilities. Maybe the ethos of the school made up for the lack of sporting facility.

From 1947 a school sixth form was introduced and I progressed into this venture. Initially it was not well organised and I think initially the teachers at that time struggled with the new academic demands. I remember at first I was studying physics, mathematics, history and scripture - perhaps the basis for a future career as undertaker. The subjects were later reduced to physics, maths and geography.

During my sixth-form days I started walking out with the aforementioned Joan Lancaster. On one particular day at school we had a disagreement, so she caught the bus at the bottom of the park into Chesterfield, Stephenson Place. However, I decided to run and indeed was waiting for the bus when it arrived at Stephenson Place - Joan's face was one of surprise - mine was red through exhaustion - but Tenax Propositi saved the day.

Now I have started reminiscing I could carry on, but I am sure print is restricted and so I will close by saying like many other expatriates from Tapton House School - it was a good and worthwhile experience not least because of the standard set by Harry Mellor and his devoted staff.

Finally of the first intake of sixth form students I know at least three who obtained PhDs: Worrall, Hallowes and Quartermain.

Those Happy Uncomplicated Years

Rita Jackson 1944 - 1949

We hadn't heard of computers or clicky mice in those days. (I still lack the technology).

Soon after starting at the school the war was ending and the 'blackout' was lifted. It was such a novelty to go home in the dark with lights on all around.

Our music teacher during these years was Nobby Clarke. Who will forget the shape and smell of his trilby hat, as daily he stuffed it into his pocket with his pipe. I still remember every word of the hymns he played in assembly.

The Peace Gardens were built during our time to commemorate the end of the war. I enjoy having a visit when I'm in Chesterfield on holiday and feeling slightly wicked. The gardens were out of bounds to us at the time.

Harry Mellor was our headmaster. I can still hear him shouting 'Joyce, Joyce' up the well of the beautiful staircase. She was his secretary. We were all quite fearful of him in Latin class, as he thumped the desk with his fist and shouted at us, 'You will not fail my Latin'. No one ever wanted to sit on the front row in his class, we were fearful that the ever present dew drop on the end of his nose would splatter down on to us. One afternoon I remember Tubby visited each classroom in turn with a prize find. He and Joyce had been cleaning out an old cupboard and had discovered the old school cane. He grinned at us, gently tapping it against his hand. We never heard of it again - honestly. Where is it now, eh? Most of us, thank goodness, got through his school certificate Latin. Harry Mellor was an excellent teacher and we all had a great respect for him.

Some very personal memories of years at Tapton include the visit of the Australian cricket team to England for the 1948 Test series. Our crowd of friends (and they will know who they are), we were quite besotted with some of the younger members of the team; it's a wonder any schoolwork was accomplished at all. I'm sure Commemoration Days have been recorded by other contributors. I know there are photos somewhere. Also the deep snow and prolonged winter of 1947; wellington boots were in short supply; some children never had any. We sledged and plodded our way up and down the park for weeks. I'm remembering too, when the first ice creams (Walls) went on sale after the war at the now disappeared corner shop, opposite the park gates. We belted down the park to buy the simple, plain ice cream wrapped in flimsy white paper, hoping the limited supply wouldn't run out before we got to the counter.

Cookery classes were being resumed again after the war and one of the first things we made was something called coleslaw. None of us, at the time, had the slightest idea what it was - it just looked like a mess and not for eating. I discovered my friend tipping hers down the toilet. She said it made her sick and her mother wouldn't want such rubbish. I wonder if the old treadle sewing machine still stands in the old domestic science room as an ancient relic? I once made a pair of pyjamas on that machine.

I wonder - can you still walk from the school gates down the woodland path to the railway bridge and out on to Brimington Road? We would stand on the bridge and wave to the drivers and hope to get covered by the steam and smoke as they passed underneath. School dinners were supposed to be good for us, but in those days you ate them, like them or not, there was no choice. The sausages were indescribable, coated in an orangey brown crumby mixture, the inside, a spicy mash, all horribly dry and unappealing. They ended up in pockets and used as unidentified missiles on the way home! Some pupils were carpeted for this after being reported by an unsporting member of the public!

These were happy days - and - I'm grateful for them.

Lest We Forget

John Wilson - author of No Known Grave

After world war two ended in 1945, a dedication service was held in the entrance hall of Tapton House and a memorial plaque was unveiled to commemorate Old Taptonians who had sacrificed their lives.

At the top of the plaque are the words PRO PATRIA. Underneath are two columns of names commemorating the eighteen Old Taptonians who gave their lives, one of the names being that of my late brother Kenneth Wilson, a Taptonian during the 1930s. He failed to return from a mission over Germany on the night of 29 July 1943 and has no known grave.

PRO PATRIA

CHECKLEY FRANK	**WOTHERSPOON HUGH**
DODD COLIN	**DRURY DENNIS**
RICHARDS GEOFFREY	**DIXON ROY**

BOOTH MAX	WILSON KENNETH
TURTON HAROLD	MULVEY JOHN
HUGHES GEOFFREY	WAGSTAFFE JOHN W
WALE ALFRED	HENSHAW CYRIL J
SMITH ALFRED	KIRKLAND DAVID
THACKER CHASE	RODGERS GEORGE

When Tapton House closed for refurbishment, the memorial plaque was removed and I began to make enquiries as to its whereabouts. I placed the following letter in the Derbyshire Times: -

Will it Return?

Sir - As renovation work is in progress at Tapton House School the War Memorial to Old Boys who lost their lives during the war has been removed. As my late brother a Flying Officer V.R. (no known grave) was commemorated on the memorial, I would like to enquire whether it is to be returned when renovation work is completed.

J M Wilson

Chesterfield Borough Council then entered into correspondence with me regarding the memorial plaque and I placed the following letter in the Derbyshire Times: -

Thanks

Sir - May I thank Chesterfield Borough Council for entering into correspondence with me regarding the Memorial to Old Taptonians who lost their lives during the Second World War and for tracing the location of same. The Memorial is included in the Tapton Exhibition at Chesterfield Museum until 18 March.

J M Wilson

The memorial plaque was included in the Tapton House exhibition which was held in the Chesterfield Museum from January to March 1995 and I have since been given to understand that, after the exhibition closed, it went back into storage.

Everyone is entitled to their own views, but my personal opinion is that the memorial plaque should be fully restored and then returned to its original place and rededicated, regardless of whether the building is now referred to as Tapton House or Chesterfield College.

It Was A Very Good Time

Pamela Clark 1945 - 1950

I cannot remember my first day at Tapton - I do know that Joyce Bennett, an older girl who lived in our street, took me along and showed me around.

My first memory concerning Tapton House is of sitting in the gardens and being told by another pupil that the war with Japan was over.

The winter of 1947 - lots of snow. Games were not possible so we spent these lessons sliding down the park on bags or trays (supplied mostly by Mr Hicks, the caretaker). Time to go home and my friend, Beryl Morris, and I sat on our satchels and slid down the park. The snow got into Beryl's satchel and her books became very wet, mine remained dry.

Practical cookery lessons with Miss Carmichael and Miss Hoole - these lessons always ended with our scrubbing the long, very worn wooden tables, but on winter days the room was always warmed by a lovely coal fire.

Maths lesson with Mr Haddock - I wasn't paying attention and, suddenly, a piece of chalk came flying past my ear. Mr Davey, the English language teacher, was annoyed with our class and was giving us a real lecture. Suddenly, his top set of false teeth fell out - he caught it before it hit the floor but that was the end of the telling off as the whole class was laughing. Poor Mr Davey.

On occasional Fridays, Beryl Morris, sometimes Audrey Slack, and I would save money by walking to or from school and then buy chips from a shop in the Shambles. We stayed by the shop to eat them as we dared not risk being seen eating in the street by Miss Lowe or Miss Wildin.

I remember my first sight of Mr Pearson - very smart in his RAF uniform - when he came to look round the school prior to coming to teach.

Miss Pennington (French teacher) used to sit on a desk at the front of the class with her feet on the seat. Certain boys would speculate what colour undergarment she was wearing.

The boys collecting frogs in spring from the gulley and chasing the girls.

Playing snobs and ball games on the steps leading up to the hall during lunch time when the weather was too bad to go outside.

Playing rounders on the playground and having to chase down the park to retrieve the ball - no fence around the playground in those days.

If we just missed the bus when it left Stephenson Place, we would chase down Tapton Lane and be waiting for it when it arrived at Willett's shop. The bus had to go from Stephenson Place, along Cavendish Street, Holywell Street and then down Durrant Road to pass Willett's before going along Brimington Road, so we had plenty of time.

I remember that, at home time, we would run down the woodland path along to the railway bridge and stand on the bridge whilst the steam trains passed under.

Two memories of Mr Tubby Mellor.
He was walking outside, down from the hall, when he saw someone misbehaving - he bellowed the boy's name. I was always amazed that he seemed to know all the pupils by name. Christmas parties and having to sweep the floor and Mr Mellor showing us the correct way. Happy Days.

Beryl and I quite often would succeed in persuading Mr Ashton to change a mark of 91/2 for work done to 10 so that we could claim a house point.

Outside visits.
Going to the Odeon cinema to see Laurence Olivier in *Henry V*, and to the Civic Theatre (I think) to watch a performance of *Madam Butterfly*.

Commemoration Day - particularly the one celebrating George Stephenson's centenary (I was a spoke in one wheel of the Rocket). I remember the rehearsals after the casting of the various parts, all organised by Miss Wildin and, finally, the performance on the top lawn with the characters and the dancers entering from the trees. Very impressive.

P S. I cannot remember rain on Commemoration Day.

Tapton House Guides Revival

Sheila M Maycock 1945 - 1949

I was at Tapton from 1945 to 1949 and one of the bits that I think might be of interest to you was the girl guide company. Margaret Savage came to Tapton I think in about 1947 and she decided to restart the guide company and we were known as the Tapton House School Thirteenth Chesterfield Guides. Now I thoroughly enjoyed those guide meetings; we had some fantastic times. We played hide and seek around the school in the dark and only the very foolhardy dared to go into room five.

Another thing we found one night was that the door at the side of room twelve was unlocked and we opened the door and went up a little staircase and it brought us out on to the roof. This was an absolutely magical place; the views from the top between those chimneys were out of this world. I can't ever remember going up there more than the once. Of course it used to be the fire watchers station during the war, the ARP.

We used to take our torches and go down into the cellars; we would clamber over the mounds of coke looking for the secret passage reputed to lead to the parish church, and we never found it of course. We had such fun in the grounds. We'd set off tracking, tying knots in grass and leaving twigs as arrows, all simple things, but, oh, so happy.

The other thing I remember was when Sav decided to take us camping and the first camp we went on was in 1948 and we went to Thornbridge Hall. Oh dear, I can only remember being terribly cold, wet and so hungry. I'm sure it wasn't Sav's fault but really it was a dreadful week. The person who came as second in command was Dorothy Marriot, and Dot was such a lovely, jolly person. Years after that we went to Halls Farm, Danes Dyke, Flamborough. That was also a fantastic place to go camping; we walked into Danes Dyke to collect firewood and we walked into Bridlington and all the things kids got up to, eating chips and ice cream and really making ourselves sick because we were on holiday. It was such good fun. I remember we went to Flamborough at least three times with Sav. Then, of course, the time came when Sav left Tapton. By this time I had started going back as a helper because my mother would always let me off on a Friday afternoon so that I could go back up to Tapton to be with the guides. Then after Sav left, there was a Miss Thomas. She took over as captain of the company but then it became difficult because she also left and I think Janet Westbrook took over but things weren't very successful. Nobody seemed to have the company's interest at heart. The caretaker complained to the then headmaster Mr Jennings that the girls were running riot in the school before I could get there. I couldn't always guarantee to be there for four o'clock so consequently the girl guide company had to be disbanded. I think that must have been some time about 1957-58, I really can't remember, but I was terribly upset when I had to hand in our Tapton guide funds to go back to Miss Hasland, the Guide Commissioner.

Now, the other thing I remember so vividly was the winter of 1947. It snowed and snowed that year. My sister and I used to take the Brampton bus into town. Then we always walked from town up to school along Brimington Road, over the bridge and up the woodland path. We'd be snowballing all the way; you would jump up and pull a branch down so that the snow fell off the branch on to the people who were walking behind. So many of us walked on that woodland path in those days and I went back there recently and it was so overgrown. I know the school's been closed a few years now but it seems like no one's used that path for donkey's years. I just can't imagine how times have changed.

During the winter of 1947, the boiler broke down. We young ones were allowed to stay off school but the seniors who had exams to sit had to carry on with school. The caretaker had to make fires in the classroom and I think rooms 7 and 8 had two fireplaces in each of them. Most of the rooms had fireplaces and there were these big roaring fires. As far as I can remember the coke lorries couldn't get up the drive, because of the snow and ice. When we returned to school a lot of us took our sledges to school. Every lunchtime we would go sledging down the park. If you got a flier, it would go down the park, over the drive, up the bank on the other side, through the hedge and deposit you in the field at the bottom. There were a lot of us with wet knickers. It got so bad that we even got fed up of sledging. There were all of the sledges leaning up against the cloakroom and you just used to get hold of one and went and have a session on it. If the owner wanted his sledge, he or she knew exactly where to find it.

The shop at the bottom; in those days it used to be the Co-op. They used to have a delivery of ice cream on a Thursday. Every Thursday we would be hovering about at the bottom waiting for the delivery to come. Sometimes it didn't arrive before half past one, and so obviously you couldn't have your ice cream. If we were on one and half break, we would dash down the park, collect our ice cream and be eating them on our way up the park. I remember this one day when we got to the top we looked up and, lo and behold, there was Tubby Mellor, the old headmaster, waiting for us on the drive. He didn't say anything to us apart from, 'Come along there, hurry up, get into your classes.' The old devil. He followed us into our classroom and he knew we had got ice creams and there we were sitting down with ice cream melting away in our pockets, because none of us dare eat them.

You must realise that in those days ice cream was a luxury to us. Tubby was a fantastic headmaster. Love him or hate him, you had to respect him. He may have ruled with a rod of iron, but even so he was quite approachable. You never felt uncomfortable going to ask him anything; well, we as girls didn't. He always treat us very kindly, as did most of the staff. We used to have most enjoyable lessons. If they weren't, I don't remember them.

About ten years ago I was walking along the back of M&S and I saw this couple coming towards me. I realised that it was Mr Routledge and his wife, the former Miss Hoole, and they had recognised me too. It was such an embrace and Mr Routledge said, 'Oh, it is Sheila Mycock' I was absolutely amazed and annoyed at the same time, as my name was Maycock and not Mycock. Nevertheless, to think that he had remembered me after forty years since I had left school. He had remembered me as a person and my name. I still can't understand why he should recall me since I'm sure I didn't do anything too bad at school. That was the calibre of the teacher at Tapton. They knew you as pupils and were as friendly as possible.

Memories from Eastbourne

Tony Cable 1946 - 1951

Miss Pennington - French
Tall, very thin, spindly woman, almost skeletal, and would have played Helena in the *Dream* and would have the description Hermia gives her, 'low and little, nothing but low and little. How low I am thou painted maypole'. She didn't wear make-up, which accompanied the rest of her appearance, frizzy light auburn hair and clothes almost matching. If we were slow on the uptake she would adjust her spindly glasses by the hinges with her thumb and little finger, accusingly widen her already thin lip to wafer thin proportions and, looking over the top of her glasses, would say in equally thin, thin tones, 'Really 3B'.

Routledge - Geography
Threw blackboard dusters and other lethal warfare catching his target for not knowing or misbehaving. I think he suffered asthma.

Haddock - Maths and Sport
Could have stepped out of a Damon Runyon novel, gangsters and all. Harry the Horse, or Nicely Nicely Maybe. He was tall, slim uneven discoloured teeth, very boringly dressed and made no sense to me with his maths at all, if only he could apply the theories to a practical usage, well maybe yes. He had a bad temper and he hit Joan Clarke across the face, made her cry, which resulted in her father going to school to see Tubby about it.

Mr Bates - Chemistry
Again, what was he trying to tell us in his lab? Maybe it was me not adjusting properly, but all those burning things in test tubes and holding hands to acquire electric shocks from a generator. Was he trying to electrocute us in this torture chamber?

Miss Dorothy Woodall - History
Worldly sort of woman, nice honey coloured hair. But where was all the romantic background to Mary Queen of Scots and Elizabeth I which would have helped no end in putting her message across? But no, we had to take her dictation down all about dates of wars, reigns and parliaments. When finished, out she would flounce, happily with books, clasped to bosom, already fit to flounce out of school on the stroke of four. No extra-mural activities woman she.

Mrs Lloyd R I - Vicar's Wife at Bolsover
Very nice she was and talked a bit far back, certainly for Bolsover or 'Bowzer' as the

locals call it. She timed things very well. We were reading a passage from the Old Testament in the Bible when those of us reading a little further came to the word 'shit'. Just as we neared the said four-letter word, the bell rang for end of lesson, much to our dismay. When we picked up next time, the reading continued from the following verse, so we missed the treat.

Nobby Clarke - Music
Now here was someone in my league, as music is my hobby and I just loved his lessons and being in the choir, singing at Bradbury Hall school choir festivals and solos in the carol services at Trinity Church at Christmas time.

Mr Ashford - Art
He was rather a nondescript man who seemed to wear the same grey herringbone pattern jacket and had a speech defect, pale face, black hair and glasses. He seemed to content himself with letting us paint or draw still-life things in bowls and slippers - just that.

Wilf Pearson - Physics
Oh dear! Terribly ex-RAF. Again I wasn't at all interested in what he was talking about (prisms, fulcrum, effort and load). He was very daunting with added temper on being given the wrong answer. This particular day I woke up with the strong premonition that he was going to ask me a question, which I couldn't answer and into trouble I would get. So strongly was I convinced that a continuous wave of panic struck me on the way to lesson. Further so scared was I that on the way to school my corner sharp tooth on the upper gum bored a hole through my tongue to meet its lower gum partner. I jest not - so it came to pass I was asked a question, I didn't know the answer and the wrath of Pearson descended upon me!

Mrs Bamford - Girls' PE - I Think
She held lunchtime optional ballroom classes in the gym, which were very popular. This particular session she was teaching the waltz. Her bosom was of more than generous proportion; she began by doing a solo demonstration of the steps. She would clasp our hands to her chest and call out. Two things then would happen; she would call out the rhythm of step one, two, three but the word 'one' was pronounced as 'wan' with a short 'a' sound, 'wan, two three, wan two three' with great accent on the 'w'. As the performance proceeded the ample bosom automatically brought forward the crooked arm and elbow with such gusto, our attention was drawn to that event, rather than what was taking place at feet level!

Other Thoughts
Winter time, sitting in a top floor classroom looking down on the swirling mists and fog through the trees in the fading light and feeling the thrill of walking home in it.
A Trip To Stratford
A Branson bus from Brimington. Day trip early departure.

First stop Lichfield for coffee in the home made chocolate shop- very old worldly.
Warwick - look inside the castle.
Stratford - picnic lunch round the memorial statues by the theatre. Bus tour of the town.
Run down to Broadway and Chipping Camden for tea.
Return to Stratford for dinner at the theatre in the riverside terrace restaurant. We had grouse and I remember the first coffee-pot I had used with the spout on the side of the pot. All this overlooking the river and the swans of Avon.

Evening performance of *Henry V* with an old theatre trouper of the day - Gwen Ffrancon Davies.
Return to Chesterfield at 2.00 am.
Cost to my parents 12s 6d - sixty-two and a half new pence - don't forget the halfpence!

Sam Dunkerley
Woodwork master - smoked cigarettes among the shavings and sawdust so he did - smashing teacher, lovely man. 'Today you are going to put this piece of unlevel wood in the vice at your bench and plane it down so that it is nice and smoothly level on all sides.' Little did he know what he was asking from me. By the time I had finished there was not a sign of any block of wood in my vice. It was all in a state of shavings and sawdust on the floor. His end-of-term comment on my school report was, 'Definitely not his subject'

Bellows Through The House
Tubby Mellor shouting for Joyce his secretary, who would be on the top floor above that lovely wooden staircase - the holy of holies - except to staff and prefects and for open Commemoration Day, when we were all allowed up and down as well as parents. In the ceiling high up was the glass dome. He would stand at the foot of the stairs in his dark grey suit, pot belly protruding forward, arms thrown back as far as they would go, likewise his head bespectacled in tiny gold wired frames and he would bellow forth 'Joyce' which would resound in echoing fury as Joyce came bounding down the staircase to meet his secretarial requests.

Detention At 4.00
What for? Who knows now, who but the headmaster himself no less. Room 6 it was; I was sitting at the front-row desk. He was really letting rip about something and as his anger grew his hot round face increased in colour. Now whether it was that situation, or whether it was a sneeze that seemed to develop, who knows? A combination of the two maybe but the resulting next thing was that his false teeth had relieved themselves of their normal position and descended from his mouth, landing on my desk.

Sibelius and a Book
Phil Wildin, whom I would follow to the ends of the earth for giving me my love of Shakespeare. She was giving us the idea of mixing reading with listening. That we

didn't have to keep the two separate; that we could read and have some music playing in the background. As an example, we all took out our novels we were studying for exams and she played a record on the gramophone, as it was in those days (1951). Now the influence of people's enthusiasm for music affects me greatly and I have a lot of people to thank for introducing me to great works in this way. Phil's choice, this day, was the tone poem *Swan of Tuonela* by Jean Sibelius. It is very gentle music, picture music depicting a swan gracefully gliding along its watery path. That memory and the music have been locked in my memory box all these years.

Snacks in the Afternoon

Food has always been my hobby and interest and work later in life. It and I have lived in a close magnetic field together. So it was that when home-made sausage pie came round for school lunch, I would be first in the queue. Now the cook, Mrs Beresford, a lovely homely buxom motherly lady, who understood young people's needs in the eating department, recognised my recognition of her domestic acumen and both rejoiced when I arrived at the kitchen back door for another slice of the celebrated sausage pie during afternoon break.

Chain Gang

As the school was at the top of a public park, added problems were forced upon us by people coming for their walks and distributing their litter all over the vast wide area of parkland, so it fell to our lot to clean it up periodically. I can't recall what we used for containers. Did we have plastic sacks in those days? However and whatever. The whole school would move downhill to the drive curving its way to the top of the hill and we would form a chain line like the black slaves in the deep south, and we would proceed slowly uphill, backs bent, picking up all the debris we could find. Of course, in those days sex and anything to do with it was never discussed with youngsters as it is today, so that when any sexual deterrent, used of course, was found, there would be an outburst of adolescent glee and delight. Tubby had a great thing about litter and made us all feel very guilty. Even now I would never dream of leaving anything dropped in the streets or open spaces and deplore those who do. Why? Because his motto was this - *'Let no one say it and say it to your shame, that all was beauty here before you came'* and I'm forever quoting that today, forty-seven years later.

Drama on the Lawn

Oh! My goodness, what a feast of pleasure Tubby gave us with his own written plays for open commemoration days. *Chessmania* was one on the large open lawn backed by tall trees and bushes. The ground was laid with large black and white squares, chessboard fashion, and the theme was rival warfare between black and white chessmen. Again, for me, the music he used played a long and happy collection piece in my musical store. It was the march from *The Love of Three Oranges* by Prokofiev. Still hear it lots today on Classic FM and Radio Three.

More Drama on the Lawn

After Tubby retired, Mr Hall from Sheffield was our new head and he was happy for Phil Wildin to take on the drama life of the school. Our Shakespeare for O levels was *A Midsummer Night's Dream*. She decided to direct it for the annual school play, all and everyone invited. Who did she cast as Lysander, one of the four lovers, but me? I was in my element - forget the woodwork bench, the physics lab and any other lab, let's get on the stage. We only did two performances, both on the same day and did what you might call a 'tour'. The afternoon performance was outside again on the lovely natural setting lawn with the trees and bushes through which we made our entrances, and the second showing was the same evening in Bradbury Hall, Chatsworth Road, hence the phrase 'we toured'. I remember the afternoon was rather windy which caused noise disturbance in the trees and so, with no amplification and a certain lack of professional projection of our voices, a lot of the dialogue must have been lost. But the evening performance was quite different on stage with lights and effects. I remember I wore a silk doublet with an elasticated bottom. In one scene my arm had to extend heavenwards as I crescendoed into one of my speeches. As I did so I could feel the blouse rising from base up to bare midriff proportions. No make-up - all white.

My last one - the Lowe Car

This is my own memory and doesn't involve school or any pupils. I lived across town with level viewing of school from our house. I would say the distance would be about two and a half miles to walk down Sheffield Road, down Wharf Lane, across the canal, on to Brimington Road and henceforth up to the Skull and Crossbones and on to school. It always seemed to coincide at a certain stretch of the road between the canal exit and the Skull and Crossbones corner an old Austin Seven car would trundle its way along heading for the same destination as myself. The driver was Dorothy Lowe, the geography mistress and her friend, Phil Wildin. They travelled and worked together. The car looked hardly secure, not through any fault of the driver, but merely its style and make. I remember the paintwork was dark blue with the haunch-like black mudguards and (did they call them running boards?), the platform step running alongside the door, and I still vividly remember to this day the registration number DRB169. The letters RB determined the county of Derbyshire and still do to this day. I now live in Eastbourne in the deep south and we see a lot of cars here with holidaymakers. Which all serve to remind me of my roots and school days.

As an added bonus to living in Eastbourne, much of the property and land belongs to the Chatsworth Estate and, as such, many of the roads and buildings take their names from the towns and villages in Derbyshire as well as from the Devonshire family. We have Chesterfield Road, Bolsover Road, Chatsworth Hotel, the Burlington - the list is endless.

Happy days!

* Tony died on 5 January 1999

All Was Beauty Part 1

Peter Wagstaffe 1947 - 1954

A chilly September morning in 1947: boys and girls segregated, the whole school assembled for the ritual registration on the sloping playground, its lower edge bordered with remnants of nets. After most had crocodiled off to classes we were left, the new intake, awkward in uncustomary uniforms (caps compulsory) and shouldering new satchels. Names were called; we reassembled, separated into lines of sheep and goats. I was a C streamer. Was I really that much of a dolt? Hopeless at maths - that probably did for me. Little did they know they had a future head boy in their ranks!

Form 1C waited silently in a top-floor classroom as a grey-suited lady of ample proportions bustled in and introduced herself as Miss Lowe, adding with a wry smirk, 'Lowe by name and Lowe by nature.' We were too afraid to smile... or perhaps simply ignorant or irony - but dutifully copied down our first timetable, containing subject abbreviations like Dom.Sci., Phy/Chem., WW, and PT - alien invaders of our junior school minds.

Dorothy Lowe and her lifelong friend, Phil Wildin, must have had a lasting influence on countless Taptonians - and certainly on me. Dorothy tore strips off bumptious 'little Hottentots' who crossed her path; Phil had a no less daunting reputation. My first 'contact' with her was when she hauled up by his collar this stupid second year lad who was adding to the mayhem in a packed corridor: she gave him a dressing down, face close, eyes blazing in anger. And she wasn't acting! Three years later, when we were on speaking terms, she introduced me to Chloe Gibson, resident producer at the Civic Theatre (now the Pomegranate), and I took walk-on parts in some of the shows: an invaluable by-product of the Tapton Experience.

Dorothy was often on duty as we entered the canteen (newly opened in 1947). She scrutinized both sides of our hands to see whether the Great Unwashed had dared live up to their name, and was one of the few to perform this unappetizing duty with exemplary zeal. Today's teachers would never see such tasks in their terms of contract (but soon they'll be trained to sniff our cocaine.)

After school dinner (never called lunch) we had a blissfully long hour or so to run wild in the tree-graced spaces of the hill or scramble on the precipitous railway cutting: we did this for kicks, as they'd say nowadays, and from time to time the caretaker, short and bald Mr Higgs, went on patrol but rarely were culprits caught. Today, they would doubtless be prosecuted for trespassing; local authorities are alert for anyone at risk, but I wonder if pupils are any happier. None of us in those drab postwar days came to grief, but neither its setting nor ethos made Tapton a 'normal' school, luckily!

The shrubberies were another venue for shenanigans, their spreading rhododendrons and overgrown wildernesses covering a multitude of youthful sins (or boasted ones!) Two friends and I were hauled up before Tubby Mellor for charging along and allegedly crushing daffodils; we received a sharp stroke of the cane and thus learnt the hard way to respect the head's oft-repeated adjuration: '*Let no one say it, and say it to your shame, all was beauty here before you came.*'

The fine green level of lawn fronting the tempting bushy shades was the setting for memorable drama activities on Commemoration Day in June. Mr Mellor would write and produce pageant-like plays based on Classical myth. To us they were incomprehensible but offered exciting opportunities to dress up as Nubian slaves, Greek dancers or bearers of the flags of all nations. Phil Wildin later took over and I made my first appearance in tights, as Philostrate in *A Midsummer Night's Dream*. Tapton's gardens had become a wood near Athens, but not for long: the dark clouds burst and we were duly rained off. Flimsy gauzes worn by a host of fairy nymphets were soon soaked and see-through, producing an erotic charge to galvanize the ogling boys! After a long delay we presented the Bard (twice) in the confines of the wall-barred school hall, and later at the Bradbury Hall in town. For many of us, that first taste of Shakespeare would linger for years.

Assisted by Spot Stanley on lighting, Dorothy on make-up and Mr Dunkerley as master carpenter, Phil's reputation as a producer gathered apace. My happiest memories are of appearances in Henri Gheon's nativity play, *Christmas in the Market Place*, Shaw's *Saint Joan* (with the inspired Sylvia Swallow), *Beauty and the Beast* (again with Sylvia), and the stylised fantasy of Housman's *Prunella* (Sylvia triumphant). After my first-year at university I made one positively last appearance on the old stage in 1955, when I stood in for an absent student, playing a small part in *As You Like It*, with Des Baker as romantic Orlando and, need I say, Sylvia as Rosalind. I recall looking down at the front row while spouting Le Beau's lines and seeing the then head, Arnold Jennings, grinning broadly in his usual fashion.

I often visited Phil and Dorothy at their book-lined home in Whitecotes Lane, but the years and declining health took their toll on those dear friends. With deep sadness I learnt that Phil had taken her final curtain last year; Dorothy had preceded her. All schools produce characters among staff, of course, but I think hundreds of students have gained immeasurably from contact with these two remarkable teachers, whether on social or academic terms. Schooldays have their agonies and anguish but most Taptonians will surely look back on them and say, with Wordsworth:

'Bliss was it in that dawn to be alive,
But to be young was very Heaven!'

A Super Sojourn

Sam Dunkerley - Woodwork (THS 1947 - 1955)

In 43 years of experience in teaching, my time at Tapton House was the happiest of all. This was due to a large extent to the aura in the staffroom. When I arrived, I knew at once that I was embarking on a pleasant and elevating experience. This was mainly due to the then deputy head, Frank Silcock, who had time to spend on any colleague and acted so successfully as the bridge between staff and headmaster.

Mr Mellor was the head at that time - a man who put faith in his staff to do their work well - his reward was that by and large he had the right response. I well remember him saying in assembly, on one occasion, 'I know you refer to me as Tubby - that's all right but don't let me catch you'. However he it was who established the standard (and what a standard) of general ambience in the place.

Male personnel on the staff were Wilfred Pearson - a role model for organisation, neatness and industry, Doug Gillam, who met so much adversity with equanimity and Christian spirit, Norman Clarke, a good amateur pianist with a flair for training school choirs. He was also responsible for a certain amount of religious instruction - I believe he was assured of complete good behaviour by holding up a cane while saying 'Whom the Lord loveth, he chastiseth'. There was Stewart Haddock, a teacher of maths - known generally and not surprisingly as 'Finn' - who always forecast that he would score 50 runs in the Staff v School cricket match - strangely enough he never failed. Doug Cox was a language specialist (I have been pleased to call him a friend for many years, but he has not been well recently). Frank Booth, who, like Doug and Jim Lennon left to become headmasters, was a good mathematician. The geography specialist was Harry Routledge, who of all the staff came closest to the term 'gentleman' - impeccable. We had good artists in Bob Furber and Aubrey Jensen.

The ladies were less well-known to me, but there is no doubt that our school plays were under the best of care with Phil Wildin. She could make a triumph from a simple play no matter what it was. I recall with great pleasure *Christmas in the Market Place*, a very simple play, which she turned into a spectacular. I remember Johnny Wheatcroft miming the herding of a flock of sheep across the market place - one could almost see them and the 12-year-olds Pat Ramsdale and Barbara Hogg singing the carol *Rocking* in perfect (not a word I use willy-nilly) harmony. Saint Joan, too, was a great success (Doug Gillam played a convincing part), as was *Sleeping Beauty*, with terrific scenery devised by Aubrey Jensen. Dorothy Lowe taught geography, Mrs Lloyd religious instruction, Mary Inger and Lorna Hale taught art in succession, Hazel Hoole (later

Mrs Routledge) was in charge of domestic science. Spot Stanley was a well-respected teacher of biology, Dorothy Woodall was a history specialist and Miss Pennington taught French and history .

Mr Mellor, on his retirement, was succeeded by Mr Charles Hall. I remember Mr Mellor saying that he was the only candidate with a sense of humour. Mr Hall did not stay long - he transferred to a larger place in the North, whilst his place was taken by Mr Jennings - an ardent politician.

When Mr Mellor walked into assembly at the start of a new schoolday, he would react strongly to the amount of buzz in the hall. If there was too much for him to tolerate, he would turn the whole lot out on to the nearby square and then have them marched back in silence. If he was still in a bit of a tizzy, he would give a short sharp lecture and carry on with the service. Naturally everyone would feel subdued. I well recall one occasion when the head had been particularly sore and the chosen hymn was *Onward Christian Soldiers*. When we arrived at the phrase 'Join our happy throng' Dorothy Lowe cracked in amusement and had to turn to the wall until she had composed herself.

Also in one of our assemblies, Norman Clarke was thumping away with great enthusiasm on *All Things Bright and Beautiful*, when the front of the keyboard fell away with considerable clatter - no one dared smile let alone laugh!

As craft teacher, I was responsible for the construction of scenery for school plays. When preparing for *Christmas In The Market Place*, a cross was required as the focal point of the square. Phil Wildin as producer wanted it to stand six feet high above the base. This we did, but Miss Inger said it was too big, dwarfing scenery of her design, and she thought that six inches taken off the height could well be spared. We complied and shortly afterwards she said that it was still too large and she would like a further six inches removing. The following day, however, Phil Wildin came to see me and greeted me with, 'Oh! Sehm (Sam) what have you done to my cross?' It was rather more difficult to build it up again but of course we coped.

After Spot Stanley left we had a young lady arrive who, in teaching her class how to dilute sulphuric acid, unfortunately added water to a Winchester full of the stuff. Alas poor Winchester!

One of our ladies of rather generous proportions came to school wearing a loud check coat reminiscent of a horse blanket. One of my colleagues said, 'I hope she doesn't go to Kempton Park today else they'll whip it off her, give her a quick rub down, smack her on the backside and put her in the two-thirty.'

There were narrow staircases at Tapton House and Stuart Haddock (Mistaddick to the less erudite) told of the time when Mr Mellor was pushing a class upwards while he (Stuart) was kicking a class downwards, resulting in stalemate and pandemonium in the middle. I think if Stuart had used the word 'urging' instead of 'pushing' and 'kicking' it would have been nearer the mark.

One day in my craft room, I urged some of my more senior lads to be less rough with each other and try using good manners for a change. The following week Ben Broadhead and Ralph Brailsford were the first two in the queue to enter the room. They made great play of 'After you, Ralph', 'Oh no! after you, Ben', 'Thanks old boy'. I gave up. There are times in a teacher's life when he has to see the joke.

When Tapton House was started as a second-stream grammar school, there was much discussion in other schools as to who ought to be staffing it. I know that a member at William Rhodes School turned up in a new suit and was said to be wearing his 'Tapton suit'.

Commemoration Days were generally enjoyable with plays in the natural amphitheatre and local officials there to enjoy the food. There was the occasion when the speaker for the day was Rear Admiral Breaks. Pat Morrison gave the vote of thanks - so confidently, so freely that the Rear Admiral sat at her feet. (The ground was dry). In response he pointed out that he paid hundreds of pounds per annum to have his children so well educated and confident - 'And you get it free'.

I once heard a clergyman say from his pulpit that the big difference between Tapton House School and Chesterfield Grammar School was that there was no discipline at Tapton. What he should have said was that there was less repression at Tapton but much greater happiness. It was a special type of school that adapted to the needs of the students whereas the grammar school expected their children to adapt wholly to itself.

One of the Privileged of '48

Barbara Johnson 1947 - 1954

It was a sunny afternoon in July 1948. I sat listening to a history lesson when the door opened and Phil Wildin came in. This was usually an interesting event in itself. We were told that we were highly privileged because we had been chosen to watch this very special dancer perform. No one told children in 1948 that we were privileged - thick, dim, daft maybe, noisy and inattentive certainly, but privileged never. A dancer - intriguing. Of course I had seen chorus-line dancing, ballet dancing, and tap dancing in the pantomimes or on films. But a single dancer on a lawn? I pictured her in a tutu and crown.

We were led out to the bowling green where we sat cross-legged on the grass. At one corner of the green stood a small wigwam. Now all was explained. She was an apache dancer. Until then I hadn't noticed the wind-up gramophone; it did not usually figure largely in apache dances. By this time there was a subdued hum amongst the audience who were speculating on the possibilities of this performer.

Then the music began; some classical piece that I cannot remember. She was no ballet dancer and there were no feathers. A plump lady ran round the lawn trailing several chiffon scarves. Her hair was bound with yet another; at one time she seemed like a minor, impish wind, then a whirling dervish; she came to a full stop and her face looked thunderous.

Murmurs on the quality of her chest ran rife. The record was changed and now she was vigorous and full of humour, all of her smiled. In her sheer joie de vivre she cast several scarves, she did not miss them; she had many more. For her last dance she was in the doldrums, languid, listless, the music altered and became faster and so did she. Round and round she sped until she seemed to disappear in a whirlwind of scarves. The music paused and crashed, she dropped like a shot bird to the ground and lay abandoned, her wings spread, her chest heaving, her heart still beating. We knew she was not dead, but the music had stopped. What were we supposed to do? A member of staff began to clap and we all followed suit.

I chose this memory because it was quintessentially Taptonian. Many schools stopped lessons for a special event, some schools may have had entertainers, but only Tapton took unprepared children to watch a solitary dancer emerge from a wigwam and perform a series of expressive dances accompanied by a wind-up gramophone and expect them to behave with all the sang-froid of a seasoned bon viveur.

I have deduced now that the dancer was probably trained at one of the Isadora Duncan schools. We were, indeed, privileged to see her but we were far more privileged to be at Tapton, where the staff succeeded in providing opportunities to enlarge and enhance our lives.

Beyond The Walls of The Classroom

Douglas Cox - Latin (THS 1948 - 1956)

Jim Lennon and I used to work with the school soccer elevens on Saturday mornings and ourselves play soccer in the afternoon for a local club, probably now defunct, the Chesterfield Ramblers. I'm sure you will remember that one of the school elevens included young Bobby Wilson in goals. I don't remember an opposing team actually getting a goal past him. I recall one soccer match when someone called out to a stocky chap call Quartermain, in a broad Derbyshire accent, 'Th'art thwarted, Quart.'

Oddly enough my memories of my Derbyshire days are mainly of the extra-curricular variety, little mental snapshots. I recall going with a group climbing and fell walking to Jack Longland's newly opened Open Country Pursuits Centre at Buxton. Wilf Pearson and I took a group for about a week to London. I remember finding one boy after about only twenty minutes sitting on the steps of the British Museum. When asked if he had seen the Elgin Marbles and all the delights of the museum, he said, 'I've done it, sir.' On a very enjoyable tour to Rome with mainly older pupils, I remember traipsing around Rome at dead of night looking for first aid for a boy who had gashed his hand. A mixture of Italian, French and Latin produced a result.

No doubt others will have mentioned the Christmas parties with goodies, games, *Dashing White Sergeant* and lusty singing of *The Twelve Days of Christmas* in the school canteen at lunchtime.

I look back on my Chesterfield days with great warmth. Good luck. Tenax Propositi!

Chalk Dust or Greasepaint

Douglas J Gillam - Chemistry (THS 1948 - 1953)

I first became aware of the existence of Tapton House School soon after it opened as a school in the 1930s. At that time I was a teenage pupil at the old Chesterfield Grammar School in Sheffield Road. Most of the pupils, my contemporaries at CGS, were sufficiently snobbish as to pretend that Tapton didn't exist. Although I played a lot of rugger at the grammar school, I never recall ever playing against Tapton, or even visiting the school. One of the reasons for this was that it was a mixed school. We had been trained to believe that girls should be kept in a separate institution, from which we were permanently excluded.

Before the outbreak of the Second World War, I left Chesterfield to go to university in Manchester, and from there I joined the RAF. I had not completed my teacher training, but in 1940 I felt that I should be doing something more useful than remaining a student, so I began flying against the enemy in Europe. In 1943 I was shot down, parachuted into enemy territory, and spent the rest of the war in a prisoner-of-war camp in Saxony. For two years I had to occupy my time as usefully as I could. I began my teaching career, teaching mathematics to fellow prisoners, and I was also the secretary to the church in Stalag IV B. During the last year, I worked full time as an actor in the theatre we had built.

After the war I returned to university to complete my graduation and got my first appointment as a teacher of mathematics in the grammar school in Penistone, in the West Riding of Yorkshire, in 1947.

Although I was happy in Yorkshire, I soon had to look for a job nearer home. This was because it proved to be quite impossible to get a house in Penistone, and I quickly got fed up with the travelling. Throughout the summer term of 1948, I went by train daily from Chesterfield central station, changed at Sheffield, and proceeded by a slow, stopping train to Penistone. The reverse journey had to be performed every day after the end of afternoon school. As I look back on it now, I wonder how I stood it for so long.

This, therefore, was how I came to be on the teaching staff at Tapton. A vacancy arose which enabled me to leave Yorkshire, and I was appointed to work in both the mathematics and science sections of Tapton House School, and I was fortunate that my immediate superior was also an old boy of the grammar school, although I couldn't remember him as a pupil. He was considerably older than me. I soon discovered that there were several Old Cestrefeldians on the staff. Names that come into that category that I can still recall include Mr Pearson, Mr Haddock and Mr Ashton. There were probably others, but I don't remember any more names.

I served at Tapton from September 1948 until December 1953. Although I was the only graduate mathematician on the staff, I was only a junior member, and I therefore had to teach many other subjects besides my own. My headquarters was in the physics laboratory, which I recall was next to the woodwork department, and I quickly became quite friendly with the woodwork master, whose name, I believe, was Dunkerley. I never got much of a chance to teach senior boys and girls, but I had a very happy time at Tapton, teaching physics and chemistry, as well as maths, to youngsters in years one, two and three.

The headmaster of the school at that time, Mr Harry Mellor, was a man who was very well known in the town. Part of his reputation was built on his skills and success in fields other than his prowess as a schoolmaster. I knew him as a keen supporter of amateur dramatics, long before he became my boss. He worked as producer for the Chesterfield Playgoers' Society, and also for the Chesterfield Teachers' Dramatic Society. I had not long been on the staff of the school when I was enrolled by him to work on the school plays. To begin with, I was asked to help with the lighting and sound system, and later I worked on the make up for the pupils. I remember designing and executing the make-up of the fairies in a production of *A Midsummer Night's*

Dream which, I believe, was performed at the Bradbury Hall in Brampton.

It wasn't long before the inevitable happened; I was asked to take an acting role in one of the school plays. My first part was in a production of Shaw's *Saint Joan*. I played the part of Stogumber, the monk who attended Joan of Arc at her trial. Another part I recall playing was in a most peculiar play by Laurence Houseman and Granville Barker. The play was *Prunella*, and my part was Scaramel. It was such an odd piece that I can remember hardly anything about it. The only memorable fact was that the scenery required a statue to be on the stage. In the last act the statue came to life. The statue was played by a sixth former named Neil Watson, and his whole body was covered in stone-coloured greasepaint. He spent most of the play motionless on the stage until he eventually slowly began to move as Love came to life. I imagine he must have been very relieved.

Both these plays were staged in the school hall, *Saint Joan* in July 1952 and *Prunella* in July 1953. Mr Mellor didn't produce the plays himself. They were both directed by Miss Phil Wildin. Other teachers associated with the productions were Miss Dorothy Lowe, Mrs Lewis Lloyd and Sam Dunkerley. Miss Wildin was an accomplished actress. I remember seeing her on the stage of the Chesterfield Civic Theatre, and I recall her performance as Lady Macbeth at the Great Hucklow village theatre. Acting has always been a hobby of mine and I enjoyed the Tapton school plays, but it was a difficult task performing as a member of the company, where I was the only teacher among a complete cast of my pupils.

In the early part of my teaching spell at Tapton, I taught mathematics, physics and. some chemistry. It was all very strange. Because I was a 'Junior' master, Mr Mellor would only let me teach in the lower part of the school. This meant that I had to swot up some chemistry in the evenings, so that I could teach it next morning. In return, I used to coach the senior chemistry master in mathematics. This was so that he could take maths lessons in the sixth form. It wasn't until Mr Mellor retired and was replaced as head by Mr Hall, that I got the chance of teaching sixth formers.

Mr Mellor firmly believed that a fully qualified teacher could teach every subject on the curriculum. He was a classicist, but I have seen him teach science, maths and even music. He was so good at his job that pupils usually managed to learn whatever he taught them, even if it was really a load of rubbish. I remember he once took over a chemistry class of mine and I listened to him talking a lot of nonsense. Weeks later, the class remembered all he had told them, but I am sure they hadn't learned much from me.

Occasional incidents at Tapton indicate what sort of man our head was. I recall an incident when he was reprimanding the whole school about some rule that had been broken. He suddenly declared, 'I explained the rules in simple language: in words that even your parents could understand'. More amusing was the occasion when he was taking morning assembly. Using a prayer from the prayer book, he thanked God for the healthful wind and quickening rain. At that moment a sudden gust of wind blew open the outside door and rain showered on him and all the teaching staff. He never paused and continued as if nothing had happened.

I found that teaching at Tapton was a rewarding experience, despite the fact that there were times when we felt we were in a public park. Before the school was opened, the house was empty, but the grounds were part of a municipal park. As a small child I was often taken by my parents to picnic in the park, and I recall looking through the windows of the empty building, and wondering what it was for. In 1928 I took part in a huge Scout and Wolf Cub jamboree in the grounds. The grounds were still open to the public even after the school was founded. It was not unusual to find a family with young children having a picnic in the park, just outside a classroom window, while I was trying to complete a lesson inside.

The buildings were very mixed. Some were parts of the original house, while other sections had been built when the school was first opened. There was some difficulty getting accustomed to the different levels - corridors seemed to have steps at all sorts of odd places. I remember taking a small sixth form maths group in the room in which George Stephenson is reputed to have died. The door was ill fitting and occasionally it would open of its own accord. The class accepted this as normal, and without any disruption to the lesson, they made room for George's ghost to come in and join the class.

Unfortunately, Mr Mellor never considered mathematics very important. As the only graduate mathematics master in the staff, I was asked to rewrite the whole of the mathematics syllabus for the school. This exercise took a considerable time and I was devastated when it was published bearing the name of the head of the physics department. My name appeared nowhere. I soon realised that this is how things work, but at the time, it hurt. I had to learn what it meant to be a junior master. It wasn't long before it happened again. In preparation for a forthcoming open evening, I spent many evenings designing a set of exhibits and experiments as a contribution to the occasion from the physics department. I had a whole crowd of youngsters doing demonstrations in electricity, magnetism and optics. In his speech to parents, the headmaster congratulated the head of the physics department on his display. I was somewhat dismayed that my name was never mentioned.

It was during the summer of 1953 that I began to look at the possibility of getting some promotion in my profession. There wasn't a separate department of mathematics, so I realised that I would probably have to look for another job elsewhere. At that same time, another of the teachers at Tapton went for an interview for another job. When he came back to school, he handed me all my syllabus and lesson notes, and thanked me for assisting him in getting the job he wanted. I immediately decided that if they were good enough to get him a job, then they would probably get me one too. I therefore applied for a position as head of mathematics department at a technical school in the Midlands. My application was successful, and I left Tapton in December 1953.

Baby Brownie Box Camera Days

Gill Ashley 1949 - 1956

A few thoughts about Tapton House. My thoughts about that time are usually triggered off by something. I can be clearing out under the stairs, when in the dusty corner I see a hockey stick. I am then taken back to Saturday afternoons when the Tapton School team played Robinsons. That was always a tough game; Kath Forrester in the goal, she would scare the opposition by lying on the ball at the entrance to the goal, and with loud shrieks dare anyone to approach her to place it in the net. Other matches at neighbouring schools were more sedate and always followed by a feast afterwards in the school canteen

If I see some large polished Cox's apples, I'm taken back to a Tapton Christmas when Phil Wildin and Miss Lowe once made an elaborate kissing ring. They walked down the staircase holding the structure of greenery, apples, baubles and all; then there was a constant banter of how to hang and where to hang. The excitement was palpable.

Whenever I see a trip to Paris in April advertised, I am again transported to a trip we made with a group from Tapton with Mr Hall, the headteacher, Miss Pennington and Miss Woodhead (1952). We stayed at a lycee for bed and breakfast and visited the sites during the day. The nights were our own. We were allowed to walk the boulevards at night. They were packed with promenaders of all nationalities. Some would come to our group and begin to chat in voluble French. I was quite happy to be sold into slavery in my innocence, but I am eternally grateful to Edith Wynn (Edith where are you?) who stealthily guided me to safety. Kathleen Forrester and I were so tired we missed the trip to Versailles, which I still regret. I have quite a few photographs taken with a Baby Brownie of a group of us sitting about the Notre Dame, all of us wearing those hopeful smiles for the future.

I was lucky to go on another trip to Amsterdam where we saw the graves at Arnhem which still haunt me; again I can stare into black and white photographs and see faces from the past, and I always place them back in the drawer with such pleasure.

During Easter about 1954 another trip was arranged in Scotland. A group of us went with the biology teacher to stay in a youth hostel near Ben Nevis. Strong shoes were recommended. I remember taking a pair of small size pit boots, to run in. When we arrived at the train station we had a long walk in the dark to the hostel. The pack on my back was enormous for my size, extra blankets were put on board by a worrying mother, and by the time we reached the hostel both my heels were rubbed raw. I had to visit a doctor in the end at Fort William before I could get any relief. We walked up Ben Nevis. I'm sure I was only wearing Clark's sandals at the time. What I am really saying is that none of us wore the sort of gear that is worn today. As we walked up the path, a blizzard blew up. We just turned around and headed for the hostel. The idea of the trip was to camp out in tents - Easter, remember in Scotland. We headed up the boreen for a few miles, found a likely stream, pitched our tents, huddled in, and then down came the rain in torrents, literally rushing through the tent. We found the boys' tent, which was less wet and brewed up a hot Oxo drink. That was our last night under canvas. We headed back to the youth hostel for a luxury holiday in the highlands. The Baby Brownie did not join me on this trip but I have amazing pictures in my head.

That's really all, but there's so much more I know I was always sad at the end of term and I couldn't wait for the school holidays to be over.

Reminiscences from Cutthorpe Days

Roger Webb 1949 - 1955

We had to wait for the school bus down Durrant Road, at the side of the Royal Hospital. If a schoolmaster appeared, one instinctively sprang to attention and doffed the cap. If one failed to do this, it was a telling off on the spot. Silcock often waited at this bus stop. He was strangely impressed by Cutthorpe and when I transgressed he would rebuke me, saying 'You live in Cutthorpe - you should know better', as if, in some strange way, Cutthorpe-bred pupils were expected to be above the norm where manners, behaviour and academic ability were concerned. If you weren't interested in sport or drama (as I wasn't), or was only mediocre academically (as I was), then you were shunted into the sidings of obscurity until you showed some promise (as I did eventually)

A group of us always ran down to the railway lines after dinner (for some reason, never called lunch). We would collect the details of the locomotive hauling the Thames-Clyde Express. While waiting for this event we would sometimes place halfpennies on the slow freight line and watch the Beyer-Garratts squash them to the size of half-crowns. Cox once rebuked me for running on the corridor. 'You'll soon be serving your king and country, Webb. Isn't it time you grew up?'

The school was run on public school lines. Gowns and all that. Nobby Clarke was often late for playing the piano in assembly. His gown was covered in chalk dust and he made a habit of walking around with his flies undone. In a singing lesson, on one occasion we lads were behind the piano pulling the cover on the back of the piano in time with the music. Suddenly the curtain cord at the top snapped and flew up in the air and Nobby went ballistic, smacking each boy on the back of the head in his fury. As the girls were laughing he turned his attention to them, only to discover not only that his flies were undone, as usual, but his underpants were sticking out. To hide his embarrassment he dismissed us all, and the girls escaped.

Mr Jennings became the headmaster after Hall, I think. He resembled Mr Punch where his features and meaty grin were concerned. Discussing my retake failure at O level scripture, he said, 'You and Christianity seem destined to go in different directions. If I were you I would forget it and try something else'.

Patrick Yates lived in Holymoorside and was a bit of a rogue. On one occasion someone dropped an expensive fountain pen from the top landing which fell down the well where the teachers' stairs were. Patrick Yates had, to use current terminology 'eyes like a shithouse rat', and grabbed the pen before it hit the ground, out of midair. It was never seen again. I think Yatesy was a member of the smoking group who met at every opportunity in the laurel bushes near the back of the cultivated garden which we were only permitted to enter on Commemoration Day. Jack Lambert and Alan Cresswell were prominent members, as I recall.

Mr Higgs was the caretaker with several assistants. He was small, with a totally bald head. His room was out of bounds, but always seemed to contain a medley of old women who would take great pleasure in shouting at you if you stepped over the threshold.

I remember the dead rat beneath the floorboards of the room occupied by either Pennington or Woodall. The smell was unbelievable.

Room 5 was reputed to be haunted by the spectre of George Stephenson.

My first geography report from Routledge in December 1949 stated, 'Seems to be in a complete daze so far'. How right he was. Coming from a school of 41 to a school of 450 was such a shock that it took me six months to come to terms with it.

Occasionally Mesdames Wildin and Lowe would sweep down Durrant Road, shriek to a stop and Wildin would shout 'The first four of you - IN' The car was a Standard 12 saloon and getting into it was like entering the jaws of hell. You couldn't breath as they both smoked furiously. They would bicker all the way there and on arriving at school would ease themselves out of the car, still arguing and walk in that peculiar way - knock kneed, handbags rammed under one arm, fags and Daily Telegraph under the other. In spite of their peculiarities, they were well liked. Other teachers were despised. Haslam was moody and could be brutal. Savage could be - well, Savage, particularly if her tie was too tight. Miss Hoole seemed spoilt and petulant; Davey, Haddock, Silcock, Routledge, Ashton (always called Daddy), Claxton, were revered for their ability. They were a bit remote. Some of the younger teachers were fancied. The art teacher with the beard and the young chemistry teacher (female) were two I recall.

I had a brief liaison with Anne Sinclair. I think she was embarrassed by my lack of a cultured accent. We would meet in 6a (remember 6a?) She resented me watching her play hockey in her knickers and tried to make me promise to look away when play was in progress. Her ample charms prevented me from making any such promise and the relationship faded away. I then went out with Barbara Peck, who was, I think, adopted and lived in Newbold.

I reckon those days at Tapton were some of the best we ever had.

Roger Webb 1R-1B-2B-2C-3alpha - 4 arts - 5 arts - Lower sixth (2 months)

Further memories of Tapton House School

My first and perhaps most vivid memory of Tapton was experienced on my first day there when we all witnessed the sight of Harry Mellor overcome with emotion at the prospect of having to leave his beloved school. As I had come from a village school where nobody showed any emotion whatsoever and the education we received was basic and somewhat agricultural, I was overwhelmed by this spectacle. I had gained a sort of notoriety at Cutthorpe Primary school by my willingness to become a member of the village gang and terrorised the girls by my splendid wheeze of chasing them holding a bunch of stinging nettles wrapped in a dock leaf and shoving them up their skirts. At Tapton, however, there was clearly no chance of carrying on in the same primitive way, and I was now faced with an army of formidable females clad in bright blue skirts and Clark's sandals who were clearly not going to take any nonsense from a hick from the outback. I was introduced to places I had never heard of - The Brushes, Boythorpe, Langer Lane and Stonegravels. It took me a long time to get used to having books, which one had to carry from schoolroom to schoolroom at the ringing of a bell. I had heard vaguely of periods but I thought they were something to do with girls. Then there was the business of having to scrub hands before dinner and eat the disgusting gristly meat and grey potatoes. At the end of the day there was the frantic chase down the park to catch the bus to Chesterfield. It was all too much for me and, as Mr Routledge indicated - I was really on Fuller's Earth for the first six months. I eventually became aware that there were older fellow students who were in a very privileged position - they were allowed to wear sports coats and use the teachers' stairs. At some stage they were given their own quarters which seemed to be a converted storeroom in the little paved area adjacent to the caretaker's room. They had a rapport with some of the teachers, and I seem to remember Christian names being used on occasion. The ones with a military bent were persuaded to become prefects and abused their positions by standing at the bottom of the stone stairs after dinner and taking names of miscreants and shouting insults at everyone in general. How we despised them. I was only in the lower sixth for a brief period, but I experienced the thrill of also using the teachers' stairs and wearing a sports coat, but I clearly wasn't one of the elite; I wasn't going to do A levels, so I was of no interest - socially or academically. Robert (Primrose) Wilson was with us briefly but was suddenly transferred to what we called the grammar school. He was tall, rather gauche and we would torture him occasionally in the boys' lavatories by grabbing him and holding his hand on the hot water radiators until he begged for mercy. Perhaps we were too rough for him? My best friends were David Buckley and David Sims. Dave Buckley lived at 1 Queen Street, and David Sims lived on Princess Street in Brimington. Dave Buckley was absent for some time following heart surgery. He was very clever; with far more ability then I had, and coped with foreign languages easily and naturally. Daddy Ashton considered him to be his star pupil. David Sims was destined to go to teachers training college. He liked girls. So did I but he had more success than I did (He also had more hair). I later discovered I had a flair for English (both language and literature) so perhaps my time at Tapton wasn't a complete waste of time after all. The two Davids and I would go on hikes and walks and we persuaded Rusty Barnes and Stella Moulson to accompany us. I even have a photograph of Joan Smith looking very demure and alert outside the Robin Hood pub at Baslow. I seem to recall that Joan ran with the sheep and the goats in that she was rather athletic but at the same time acceptable with the dramatic art enthusiasts. She was, in modern parlance a good all-rounder. Norman Bircumshaw was one of our contemporaries and after he eloped with (Miss) Celia Timmins we lost touch with him. I remember being introduced to Celia Timmins at a semi-formal social event somewhere in Chesterfield and how strange it felt talking to her (rather stiffly) as an equal rather than a teacher. Somewhere in the house is a copy of The Daily Mirror showing Norman and Celia on the front page smiling broadly for the camera.

Schooldays for the first three years at Tapton for me were characterised by a series of failures to understand virtually anything I was taught. PT was always a disaster and I don't recall ever mastering the forward roll over the box or the leapfrog over the horse. Jock Lennon despaired early on, I am quite sure. Incidentally, why were those huge soft (but heavy) balls that we had to throw at each other called medicine balls? I wonder if my memory is playing tricks, but were there brass protuberances fixed to the banister adjacent to the back stairs? Hardy souls were prepared to slide down the banister in spite of the threat to the genitalia. By skilful braking and a slight elevation on approaching the spikes, a successful descent could be made I seem to recall. One had to have a very good excuse to enter the staffroom, the reason generally being to purvey messages from one member of staff to the other. There was always a smell of animal heat and cigarette smoke coupled with an atmosphere of slight tension, it seemed to me. Next door to the staffroom was the sickroom, I think. There was a couch in here on which one could rest following some trauma or other. Did we have a matron or am I imagining it?

People I recall are Ann Bebbington who lived in Brimington and was slender with blonde hair; Eric Smith who had what is now fashionably short hair even in those days. He would run about clutching a top pocket of pens and pencils, seemingly always in a desperate rush. Terry Genders had very red hair (like Rusty's); Jack Lambert - a big lad who lived at Whittington; Mick Wells, another big lad from Calow; Kath Rhodes and Hazel Deakin who both lived in Stonegravels, I think. Commemoration Day was a big event as it signified the start of the school holidays, an opportunity for family and friends to visit the school and a big chance for the budding thespians to demonstrate their ability by performing one of William Shakespeare's masterpieces on the top lawn. This was also the occasion when the creme de la creme received their books and other prizes for being clever. I never received one. I recall one occasion when three of us (myself, Dave Buckley and ANO) conjured up this wheeze to go on to the Tapton golf course and paddle for golf balls in the pond which was in a depression some distance from the school. We gobbled up our dinner and had great success on the first occasion, collecting some 25 golf balls and also a good selection of leeches, which we pulled off our legs as we dashed back up to school. We couldn't wait to repeat our lucrative stunt. On the following day when we were all at it, paddling away and throwing the balls back on to the bank, we were apprehended by a chap who turned out to be the chief greenkeeper or master of the balls or something. Anyway, we had to give the golf balls to him along with our names and sure enough, during the afternoon we were all called to the headmaster's study to be confronted by Jennings and the man who had confiscated our balls (fair makes your eyes water). We were rebuked for trespass and had to apologise to 'Mr Balls' and that was the end of our little escapade, but it was fun while it lasted, in spite of the leeches.

Although I was the only lad to attend Tapton from Cutthorpe, it never occurred to me that I was in any way different from the rest of the lads in the village. They all went to William Rhodes or the Manor or Violet Markham or Peter Webster's and they never carried satchels or had to do homework as I did, which seemed unfair, but on the bus on the way home there was the usual horseplay involving fights, snatching of caps and fountain pens and in retrospect; it seems a miracle to me that we weren't all sent to Borstal. The bus left Rose Hill at 4.20; no adults dared to travel on the upper deck and the fracas that we indulged in was the highlight of the schoolday for many of us. On one memorable occasion I delivered an uppercut to a girl called Joyce Taylor who had snatched my fountain pen (the sexes were equal in Cutthorpe where violence was concerned) and as Chesterfield buses had a single seat upstairs with the aisle on the right, not in the middle, she went sailing along the shiny leather green seat and her rear end disappeared through the window. This happened at Chain Bar on the Newbold Road, and the driver, clearly at the end of his tether ordered us off to walk the last mile or so. As we alighted all the adults on the lower deck were shouting, 'Bring back the birch', 'Hanging is too good for them', 'Animals - they should have to walk in the gutter', and similar light-hearted observations. I got my pen back, Joyce picked pieces of glass from her buttocks and we plodded home, somewhat chastened and subdued.

Tapton House School was a wonderful experience for most of us, although naturally, we never thought so at the time. When we meet up as sixty-year-old Taptonians, I am always struck by what I can only explain as a sense of belonging, as if we had all been sat in a classroom just a short time before. Another strange thing is that we are all good at spelling and the use of the F written word. Of the ones who make the effort to come to the Gate Inn at Pratt Hall, there is a fair percentage of graduates and quite a few academics as well but the emphasis is on the pleasure of eating and drinking, along with the summer picnic, in good company and with lots of interesting, and often outrageous conversation. To end on yet another amusing anecdote - when we gather at the Gate we have to undergo the ritual of trying to identify a strange face, probably not seen since 1954 or 1955. Dredging names up from those days is difficult to say the least. We had a visit from one old scholar, now living in Nottinghamshire, accompanied by a woman of similar age. 'Who am I, then?' she asked me. I spent about half an hour going through every name I could remember, and lots suggested by other Old Taptonians there. In the end I had to admit defeat. 'Well, go on then', I said, 'put me out of my misery'. She did - she was the other woman's next door neighbour who had driven her there in her car so she could have a drink. Inebriation and mortification all in one evening!

Other names to jog the memory:- Mrs Brailsford, gauleiter of the canteen and the pieces (squares) of sponge pudding she made available to those of us who were prepared to hang round the back door of the canteen like prairie dogs. Killer Kay and his band of neo-fascists who wore swastika arm bands and roamed the gardens intimidating innocent strollers and cigarette smokers. The tuck shop provided by the friends of Stephenson House. Marbles (mabs) played in hollows made in the roots of the beech trees at the top of the park (Patrick Yates was the undisputed champion). The frenzied enquiry into the introduction of copies of the KamaSutra by persons unknown, and the investigation by concerned parents and teachers that sex might be rearing its ugly head (As if..............).

Form 4Scii Summer 1946

Back row: J Oxley, R Robertshaw, J Whiteley.
Middle row: E Prince, B Annetts, G Booth, D Moore, T Connaughton, R Mathews, M Brocklehurst, Roberts, J Chamberlain, G Shaw, G Briggs, E Noble, D Smith
Front row: J Beardall, C Keller, M Bird, ?, ?, Mrs Lloyd, J Charlesworth, L Walker, M Ford, M Smith, J Cropper.

Group of senior pupils 1946

Back row, left to right: F Kerry, G Beresford, ?. Centre row: H Mellor (head), J Mitchell, ?, A Jones, K Stockton, P Morrison, M Hobson, P Wildin (snr mistress). Front seated: J Welton, J Croft, S Renton, M Pollard, J Hall, Miss Stanley, J Orton, B Nuttall, ?, J Fox, B Cater.

Netball team 1947-48

Back row, left to right: Miss Savage, B Rhodes, L Paulson, D Walker, Mr H Mellor (head). Front: P Smith, M Davis, J Bennett, M Poll, B Lord.

Clayton Challenge Football Shield winners 1947

Back row, left to right: Mr Lennon, Lethbridge, Cropper, Eyre, Woodhouse, Woolgar, Mr Silcock. Seated: Mr Mellor (head), Jones, Quartermain, Sims, White, Bradshaw, Mr Haddock. Front row: Welton, Winnard.

Boys athletics team 1948

Back row, left to right: Mr S Haddock, Mr J Lennon, Barratt, Bramley, Worral, Twelves, Callaghan, Woodhouse, Smith, Marsden, Mr F Silcock, Mr H Mellor (head). Centre row: Orwin, Walkley, Lethbridge, Barlow, Bradshaw, Quartermain, Pidcock, Broadhead, Mundy, Bradshaw. Front: Roper, Elliott, Bramley, Walton, Astell, Fane, Key, Hanshaw.

Boys athletics team 1949

Back row, left to right: Ralph Brailsford, ?, ? 2nd row:Mr Sam Haddock, Mr Douglas Cox, ?, ?, ?, ?, ? 3rd row:?, Archie Walters, ?, ?, ?, Key, ?, Jack Lambert, Ron Padgett, ?, Mr Jock Lennon, Mr Harry Mellor (head). Front row: ?, Snowy Walker,?, ?, Ben Broadhead, ?, Gus Holloway, ?, Key.

George Stephenson Commemoration Day 1948

Netball 1949

Back row, left to right: Mr Mellor, Doreen Fisher, Pamela Clark, Miss Savage.
Front row, left to right: Brenda Rhodes, Margaret Davies, Viola, Vera Cutts.

Girls hockey 1949

Back row, left to right: Mr Mellor, Jill Booth, Pamela Clark, Pam Purdy, Jeannette Miller, Brenda Goodwin, Hilary Norman, Miss Savage. Front row, left to right: Joan Gales, Ethel Reno, Edna Barson, Barbara Greaves, Dorothy Wilson.

Commemoration Day scene

Back row, left to right: Brenda Rhodes, ?, Sybil Hopkins, Pam Smith, Kitty Bellamy, ?, Dorothy Marriott, Peter Roberts. Front row: ?, ?, ?, Viola Granfield, Carol Harrison, ?, Audrey Shaw.

School play 1949 at Diana's shrine

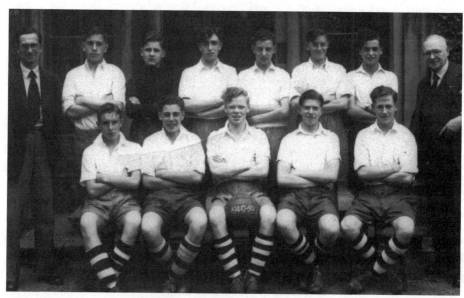

Tapton House 1st XI 1949-50

Mr Frank Silcock, Orwin, ?, Brian Quartermain, Bradshaw, ?, Bradshaw, Mr Harry Mellor (head). Front row: ?, White, Eric Twelves, Potter, Parsons.

Presentation to Mr H Mellor

The Derbyshire Times - Friday, 21 July, 1950

Mr Harry Mellor, headmaster at Tapton House since the school was opened in 1931 is retiring. On him fell the responsibility and honour of creating a school of a new type in Chesterfield. Pupils came from all classes of homes, their only qualification was success in the entrance examination. From this cross-section of school life, Mr Mellor had to mould spirit and tradition.

Now this young school has a great tradition and one of the finest spirits in the country. If proof were needed, it was given on Wednesday.

Old students assembled in the hall to pay tribute to their headmaster and see John Godfrey, the first head boy present him with a television set and a cheque raised by voluntary contribution.

A Grand Chap

I don't think that the link between Mr Mellor, old scholars and Tapton House can ever be severed, said Mr Godfrey. I think the foundation he has built will be carried on with great care by those who follow - his spirit will always be at Tapton. He has been a grand chap - I don't think we could have had better.

'If any of us were asked to give an example of a good headmaster, we would all point to Mr Mellor', he said. He is not one of those people who have let their brains go to their head. (Laughter). He has always had two feet on the ground and a true respect for all sources of knowledge'.

Stressing that Mr Mellor had been a great influence on the lives of all students, Mr Godfrey added, 'We know that when you leave Tapton it won't be the end of all your activities. We know that you are not the kind of person who can be idle.'

Commenting that Mrs Mellor too, had always been a part of Tapton House, he concluded, 'We hope that when you both look in (at the television) sometimes a vision of us will come before you and you will remember the affection in which we hold you'.

A bouquet was presented to Mrs Mellor by Dorothy Marriott, the newest of the 'old scholars'.

Mrs Mellor expressed her thanks and Mr Mellor thanked all the old pupils 'from the bottom of his heart' for their kindness. 'That has been the remarkable thing about Tapton House - kindness', he said. 'We have tried to make a spirit and I hope that spirit is going to live'.

A Happy School

'Visitors always say, 'what a happy school'. That is three-sided, it comes from the children, the staff, and a little bit from myself'.

'Brains don't matter so much so long as you get a happy spirit. It will take you through all the hardships in the world'.

He said that he liked to look upon his pupils as friends; his home was well known by most and if anyone needed help they knew where to come. Turning to the staff, he remarked, 'We have had a wonderful staff here. No man has ever had a more trustworthy staff. But it is not I, it is not the staff, it is you who have made Tapton House....You have the right spirit'.

Ald. Mrs D M Sutton, (Chairman of the Governors), who presided presented Mr Mellor with a brief case on behalf of the Governors and Harry Draycott (the first student admitted) led the pupils in singing 'For he's a jolly good fellow'.

The Mayoress, (Mrs R Brightmore), joined in the informal get-together which we held in the canteen after the presentation.

Today, (Friday), Mr Mellor will receive a raw hide travelling trunk from the school and the staff are to present an album of photographs of the school bound in blue Morocco and a set of Dunhill pipes. The staff is also entertaining Mr and Mrs Mellor at dinner.

School Day Thoughts

Malcolm Nicholas 1950 - 1955

Summer, 1950 and my 11-plus examination efforts had earned me a place at Tapton House School. My earlier days had been spent at a small village school 200 yards from home. Now I was to travel to some unknown location over 12 miles away, on the other side of Chesterfield. The first day arrived with some apprehension. This was a large school but I had liked Mr Mellor, the retiring headmaster at the initial interview.

We were ushered into the assembly hall where the new headmaster, Mr Hall, and many of the teachers were dressed in gowns. How important they must be to wear such clothing. There were around 100 new children and we were divided into three classes. Our names were read out and we were to congregate in the yard area outside the physics and woodwork rooms. I was allocated to form 1R and we were introduced to our form teacher, Miss Savage. Was this really her name or some pseudonym? We did learn that Miss Savage did not live up to her name and was really a kind lady. I remember others who had earned frightening reputations - Miss Lowe, Mr Haslam and Mr Pearson should always be treated with great respect.

With larger numbers than I had previously encountered, competition was more intense. This was probably good training for later in life. There were good cross-country runners in our year but this was not for me and I, and others, would wait behind the hedge in the top field and follow the genuine athletes back.

The school made headlines in the national press when the PE mistress and a sixth form student eloped. An additional holiday was granted when the first student from the school gained a place, at, I believe, either Oxford or Cambridge University. Another high note was when a pupil (B Holloway) was selected to play football for England schoolboys.

Probably the highlight of my school life was the Christmas when Miss Wildin asked for volunteers to join the chorus of the Civic Theatre pantomime. The cast included Wilfred Brambell (*Steptoe*), David McCallum (film star and *Man from Uncle*) and Nigel Davenport (Film and TV Star). I can claim to have been a professional actor (£1 per week) but I was not offered another contract. My colleague that Christmas was Michael Hopkinson, who remained a friend until he tragically died in December 1997, following a motor accident in Russia. Michael had qualified as an architect and became an internationally known authority on the design and construction of hospitals in the third world.

I never appreciated how privileged we were to have such a beautiful building and park for our school. My memory recalls regular walks in the woods and later in the Peace Garden. I do not remember rain, fog or frost. Is this selective memory or were summers better in the 1950s?

The area now includes large modern buildings, not really in keeping with the house of George Stephenson. I suppose some sacrifices must be made in the name of progress but perhaps I am fortunate to remember this particular establishment as it was.

School Events 1951

David Ashton - The Taptonian 1951

The morning of Commemoration Day is always one on which members of Tapton House, especially those who have been present at previous Commemoration Days, listen with great keenness to the weather forecast. Tapton's setting of park and garden, above all in early summer, is so perfect that it seems particularly galling that so often what our headmaster calls cyclonic conditions' should drive us out of the spaciousness of the gardens into the cramped accommodation of the Hall.

In preparation for the worst, arrangements were made that the 1951 service on 11 July should be relayed to those members of the school who had to be excluded from the hall and so everyone took part in the ceremony which, this year, seemed even more than usually a 'family affair'.

The reading and entrusting of the school charter were performed by Alderman Cropper whose signature the charter bears and who is, in a very real sense, one of our founders. Mr Mellor, our former headmaster, read the lesson most movingly and the address was given by Canon Lewis Lloyd whom we regard as an old friend.

A special feature was the ceremony in which one of the first old boys, Mr H H Draycott, the chairman of the Old Taptonians' Association, handed to a first-year pupil a Bible which now stands in the entrance hall as a memorial to those members of the school who gave their lives in the war.

After the service and the presentation of awards to the prefects, it was decided that the school play, *A Midsummer Night's Dream*, should take place on the lawn, but, hard upon Titania's speech about the unseasonableness of the weather, came the worst downpour that Commemoration Day has ever seen. Everyone felt great disappointment that the play could not take place in a perfect setting, but the situation appeared to be even more serious: the performers were drenched, many of the costumes seemed ruined and the play was to be put on in Bradbury Hall on 16 July.

A full-length school play always involves a tremendous amount of hard work but this time the haste to repair costumes damaged in the storm was almost frantic. By Monday, all was restored and the two full audiences saw an admirably acted play, beautifully dressed on a charming set. Those of us who had glimpses of the play in its early, raw stages know how hard the producer Miss Wildin worked, but it was, above all, her skill and knowledge and her insistence in rehearsal on nothing less than the best from each performer that produced a play of remarkably high standard.

In previous years the distribution of prizes has taken place on Commemoration Day. In 1951 it was decided to make commemoration primarily a service of dedication and on 21 November the school was 'taken to town', as our visiting speaker phrased it, for its first Prize Distribution and Speech Day in the Civic Theatre. Owing to the inadequacy of the hall at Tapton there have been few opportunities in the past for the school to be seen as a whole by parents and visitors. In his report, our headmaster, while giving due attention to the academic side of school life mentioning that in several subjects in the General Certificate of Education the number of successes exceeded the average for the country - stressed that our school is much more than a disseminator of knowledge. His report showed what variety there is in the social life of the school.

The chairman of the governors, Councillor E C Hancock, presided and the Director of Education for Derbyshire Mr Jack Longland MA, distributed the prizes. Perhaps the most amusing incident on Speech Day to an onlooker was our head girl's firm reminder to Mr Longland that he had forgotten that most important duty of a Speech Day visitor - the request for a day's holiday for the school - but the thanks she conveyed for a witty, entertaining and thoughtful speech expressed everyone's feeling. She was followed by our head boy, who presented Mr Longland with a cigarette box made in the school workshop.

Christmas is the time of the year when the social life at Tapton becomes almost exhausting. The school dance at the Cooperative Hall began our celebrations and provided, particularly in the customary *Dashing White Sergeant* and conga, a preliminary training for the strenuous activities which followed in the five 'year' parties at school. The school dance is, too, an opportunity for both past and present members of the school to get together and we must mention the pleasure that Mr Mellor's presence gave to us.

The school parties involve a good deal of hard work for many people, especially for Mrs Brailsford and her staff. We all realise that what for the school is a time of enjoyment is for them a tie when their work is increased and we all thank them for what they do.

The term and the year ended fittingly with the carol service at Trinity Church. This is the second year in succession that our school, which occupies Stephenson's house, has held its service in the Church in which Stephenson is buried. This service seems to the writer to have a double significance. It is yet another opportunity to unite present scholars, old scholars and parents to remind us that school life is part of the greater life of the community and, most important, we break up realising the true meaning of Christmas.

In April, 1931, the School was opened for the first time and on the second of April this year the coming of age of Tapton House was celebrated by a dinner and dance at the Victoria. The gathering included past and present members of the School, both pupils and staff. Miss Violet Markham, who was the guest of honour, claimed to be the oldest Old Taptonian, since she came to Tapton, long before it became a school, in a pram. There were many reminiscences of the early days of the School. Mr Mellor, who proposed the toast of 'The School and Association', traced the development of Tapton House into a Grammar school preparing pupils for the General Certificate and for Training Colleges and University. Our headmaster, Mr Hall, replied. Mr Dennison, in proposing the toast of 'The Borough and Education of Chesterfield', to which Alderman Cropper replied, spoke of Chesterfield's distinction in the field of education. In replying to Mr Draycott's toast of 'Our Guests', Dr L du Garde Peach, in an amusing speech, told us that our school days were far from being the happiest days of our life and that when he came out into the world after attending two universities, he was over-instructed and under-educated. No birthday party is complete without a cake bearing the requisite number of candles, and Miss Markham showed her vigour both in blowing out the candles and in cutting the cake. She spoke briefly, and forcibly reminded us that we must be forward looking and optimistic. After the dinner, the guests joined those who were already dancing, sometimes audibly, in the ballroom overhead. We must thank all those Old Students who worked so hard to bring about such a successful and worthy celebration.

I Remember, I Remember

Marion Yeldham 1951-1956

In the winter, when it snowed, I used to take my home-made sledge to school. As we lived at Boythorpe this entailed taking the sledge on two buses. However it was worth it for, at lunchtime, I was able to enjoy the exhilaration of sledging down the park.

The sixth form played an April Fools' Day joke on the teachers. As far as I remember, they closed the school gates and smeared the latch with treacle so that, when Phil Wildin and Dorothy Lowe arrived in their car, they had to get out to open the gates. They also locked the teachers in the staffroom. As a punishment, all the boys involved were caned.

Celia Timmins was the games mistress, age 23, and Norman Bircumshaw was one of the pupils, age 17. They ran away together and, as far as I know, were married at Ashby de la Zouch.

Tapton House had historic links with Trinity Church as George Stephenson was buried there. Every Christmas, a carol concert was held at the Church, which all the school attended. There were the usual carols, my favourites being *The Holly and the Ivy* and *God Rest Ye Merry Gentlemen*.

I can still remember the smell of stale cooked potatoes that seemed to permeate the canteen. Mrs Brailsford was the cook. I recall the liver casserole when the liver was like boot leather. The puddings only varied in colour or flavour (eg. jam, treacle, chocolate) and always with lumpy custard. The days when we had biology always seemed to coincide with the day sago (or frogspawn, as we called it) was served. The teachers, needless to say, had different food from the pupils. At Christmas time, the canteen was decorated with large pictures (done by the art class) of each of the 12 days of Christmas. These acted as reminders so that we could sing the song with great gusto.

It was a tradition, at Christmas time, for a kissing bough to hang in the main hall by the staircase. This consisted of colourful intertwined garlands with a sprig of mistletoe at the base.

In my first-year at school (age 11), we used to lay wild flowers on two dogs' graves. I forget their names. These were situated next to the wall in the wood adjacent to the top pitch. The dogs were said to have belonged to George Stephenson. I have recently tried to find the graves but cannot locate them.

Springtime was my favourite and strongest recollection of the park. The driveway going up to the school was flanked on each side by hundreds of daffodils, and the horse chestnut trees were laden with white and pink candles. At the approach to the sunken lawn there were beautiful Japanese blossom trees with short shiny trunks and pink blossom. (I regret to report that these trees were removed in 1999)

Without doubt for me, the best and most influential teacher in the school was Miss Wildin (sadly Phil died in 1998 aged 92). I can remember quite clearly how she read *Pygmalion* to us. She made the play come alive by speaking each part in the accent of the character.

Reminiscences

Evelyn Henighan 1946 -1950 The Taptonian 1952

As an old pupil (well, 'past' would be a better description), I was very flattered when asked to contribute to the school magazine, both flattered and pleased that is, until I realised that I was quite devoid of ideas of a subject. In sheer desperation, therefore, I pulled out my old school satchel the other night and started to look through my old essay books in the hope of finding some inspiration there. Well, you know how it is when, in the throes of clearing out odds and ends; one has to keep stopping to examine various articles unearthed for the first time for ages! So it was in my case. I should like to take you, therefore, with me on a journey down Memory Lane as I look once again through these dear old exercise books.

Here, on the 16 September 1946, did I write my first essay - or here is what remains to be seen of the masterpiece under the welter of rings and crosses and cryptic comments inserted in the margins - comments which I prefer not to quote. It is noticeable that while the essay itself takes up only one page, showing that I hadn't much to say, the corrections which inevitably follow it take up three pages. Evidently the marker, whose name I will not mention, had much more to say on the subject than I.

We must move on, however, and we arrive at my domestic science book. Why, what have we here? Something resembling a prehistoric monster, but, to judge from the description beneath, it is a sheep depicting the various cuts of mutton. Here, too, is the most deceitful-looking cow I have ever seen, with eyelashes fully half an inch in length (obviously added after I was awarded nine marks out of ten!). A recipe for Welsh Rarebit now catches my eye, bringing back memories of a decidedly pungent smell of burnt cheese-on-toast, which, when it wafted through the school and joined forces with one of those brimstone and treacle odours which issued at regular intervals from the chemistry laboratory, almost resulted in putting off all the pupils from the school dinner (and in view of the excellence of these dinners this was quite a feat).

Let us pass hastily over my French Grammar book, and my mathematics books (always too numerous for my peace of mind), one look at Theorem One in my Geometry book being enough to warn me that here lie many painful memories which I do not wish to recall. My English Grammar book is likewise spurned (Oh, those clauses!) and we come to my biology book where a further weird drawing declares itself to be a tadpole. If this is really meant to be a tadpole I must either have had a warped view of things then or have been suffering from defective vision.

Throughout this journey into the past, one thing which is striking me is the nature of the handwriting in these books. I have looked repeatedly at the covers but it is my name which is written on them. I must say that the caustic remarks, which are as plentiful as daisies on a lawn, are quite justified. Yet - of course, some of the more weird-looking script could have been the forgery of some of the dear little thugs with whom I roamed the school.

Now, I think we have exhausted my stock of brown-paper covered exercise books, but what is this folder with the broad, black, funereal border? On, no! Put it away. Do not let it see the light of day. Do not delve into its horrid depths. Yes, it is my School Report! What black secrets and turbulent mysteries lie between those mildewed pages! What stinging phrases are written there - phrases which hard-boiled theatre critics attending a first night would give their opera glasses to be able to use! The mere sight of that cover is enough: no need to open it to stir up muddy waters.

So I bid you adieu and return the relics to the confines of the dear old satchel - and maybe some day I shall take them out again to chuckle and shudder alternately at the memories they evoke.

Impressions of a Visitor to Tapton House School

Elizabeth Jennings, wife of Headmaster1953 - 1959

To pupil and visitor alike Tapton House, set on a hill looking across at the city of Chesterfield , surrounded as it is by a beautiful park presents a very pleasing sight for a secondary school.

I remember especially Commemoration Day, when the sun always shone, and in particular that one when Deborah, the Duchess of Devonshire, presented the prizes, and gave a remarkable address in which she pointed out how lucky they were to be at a school, as she and her sisters had never experienced such a pleasure.

Other memories include the wonderful plays put on by Miss Wildin and her band of helpers. In particular there was a youthful and jolly *As You Like It*. In contrast another year was given Thornton Wilder's *The Long Christmas Dinner*, something completely different, and finally Berthold Brecht's *Caucasian Chalk Circle*, a complete contrast and experience.

During the time my husband was headmaster three visitors appeared there, all of whom had connections with Tapton House before it became a school. The first was the owner of the original house - Stephenson himself. When my husband worked there of an evening alone he was astonished by the noises, creaks and thumps which grew familiar to him, but put it down to old floorboards and mice. However, one morning one of the cleaning ladies after her early morning shift reported that a strange man was seen wondering in one of the labs, wearing odd clothes. When questioned she was shown a photograph of George and remarked that he was wearing a stock round his neck just like the photograph. No further sightings were reported. Maybe just a chance hallucination:

Two other visitors came to see him. Violet Markham - whenever she was in Chesterfield she would visit and instruct my husband about the layout and use of various rooms when it was the Markhams' home. His study had been the morning room where her father and mother had an office and directed the running of the house. She was concerned that the fireplaces in the main rooms should be cared for and not misused or removed. She was a very considerable force to be reckoned with in those days.

Then one morning the secretary brought in a remarkable late middle-aged tall gentleman speaking English with a distinctive Polish accent - Count Edward Raczinski. He was holding a large bouquet of white flowers and came to ask if he might be permitted to leave them on his wife's grave. She was one of the Markham daughters. Apparently down in the park is a small walled area of consecrated ground, which has the Markham burial plot.

So Mr Jennings accompanied Count Raczinski to the spot, and waited while due respects were made. So in many ways Tapton was always full of surprises and new experiences.

Miss Wildin Remembered

Bob Doughty 1954 - 1961

I do have one major specific memory, which could be useful. It was when I was in either the second or third year and Miss Wildin was taking us for English literature. I forget what we were actually doing but she stopped in mid-lesson and told us about the time (not a clue when) she was camping in Wales with her BBC friend Chloe Gibson. The people where they were staying told them, when they learnt about their literature connections, to go down to the pub that night as they would meet someone interesting there. Unfortunately it rained heavily and they did not go and as it continued the next day they packed up and went home. She then said, 'I realised later I had missed the chance of meeting Dylan Thomas. The point is, boys and girls, if ever you have the chance of doing anything, do it - otherwise you will live to regret it.' I have not always followed her advice but I still remember the lesson as it has always stayed in my mind.

I also remember her telling us that she thought teddy boys in drainpipe trousers etc were far smarter than us in our grey flannel bags. As teddy boys were definitely not socially acceptable I remember being most dismayed at being less smart.

The third memory is also of Miss Wildin who tongue-lashed a group of us in the sixth form (including M Stanford) for taking the mickey out of Mr Vane, the biology teacher. She overheard us through the door between the biology annexe and the library room next to hers.

The Feeling of Tapton

P M Wildin - The Taptonian 1956

There is a general air of lack of orthodoxy at Tapton: we work in a house over two centuries old where corridors at twilight creak, so our headmaster, the least fanciful of men, tells us, under the ponderous tread of George Stephenson's ghostly feet: we are surrounded by beautifully kept grounds in which, in our strolls at break, we are likely to meet members of the general public; we paint our canteen red, black, mushroom, orange and purple and like it, and respectfully and affectionately address one of the cooks as Auntie Nellie. So it is perhaps not surprising that we have turned to the pinning up of editions of the Wall magazine, called *The Rocket*, rather than work on the production of the conventional type of annual school magazine.

This latter practice we must castigate as selfish. Children tend to be uncommunicative little animals; our conscience is smitten, whilst our imagination is titillated, by the thoughts of parents, whose interest in their offsprings' welfare has been stimulated by Parents' Evenings, gasping for news of the school, it activities and their children's part in them.

For this reason we are making a determined effort to produce at regular intervals - at least once, possibly twice a year, an edition of *The Rocket* puffing. To be successful in doing this we all, but particularly those of us who hold office as secretaries or committee members of the school societies, must rely on the influence of our school motto, 'Tenax Propositi', to inspire us to keep faithful records of events.

Time passes with astonishing rapidity and perhaps nothing more pointed may be said to suggest that in general we work hard and joy in the working. 'Plus ca change, plus c'est la meme chose'; for though staff come and go, and the amenities for science teaching steadily increase, and indisposed children may now be wooed to health by the tonic effect of the newly-decorated walls of the sickroom, and hale children may qualify for entrance into the sickness by too hearty indulgence in the goods now sold at the 'Shop'; though the silence notice in the Library is now a mere cypher and the sound of four different groups of sopranos vying against four different groups of manly basses intrigues the listening ear at House assembly Time on Friday mornings, yet nothing alters the particular 'feeling' of Tapton - the happy communal atmosphere - whether in the form rooms, in the staffrooms, in the prefects' rooms, in the Hall during morning assembly, in the Library during Staff meetings, or in the Park, snow covered or daisy strewn.

We are always pleasurably conscious of Mr Mellor's presence brooding near, and we use the term 'brooding' with intent after watching the ministrations to his offspring of the male blackbird in our garden. We remember his recently spoken plea for the composing of a School Song and make him promise that every effort will be made to produce one, though, remembering the standard he set by his own wording of the School Charter, we approach the task with considerable trepidation.

We face with joy the term at Tapton when 'the high midsummer pomps begin', and we hope sincerely that the high hopes of those examinees who have worked with purpose, will flower also.

Sweet Thousand

Helen Davidson 4R - The Taptonian 1956

When I die, I shall be sorry to leave these things; just one sweet thousand of earth's enchantments, ringing like little bells in a hall of memory. Here I can name but a few of those that crowd into my mind.
The crashing of waves upon the shifting shingle on the shore; upon the rocks, when the spray is flung miles high and falls to earth in a silver mist.
The wind in the tree-tops, in the chimneys, racing over hill and dale with clashing and roaring and whistling and hissing, like a rolling symphony.
The clean cutting wind of a cold morning, biting the skin, freezing the nostrils; when clouds of white breath float away and melt in the haze of morning mist.
Morning itself, with bird-song ringing clear, penetrating into rooms of still sleepy houses; the morning sun, weak yet, but rapidly gaining heat and colour; flowers heavily laden with sweet morning dew; the clanging of milk pans and the crow of the cock.
Laughter, the very essence of joy, which makes the hearer glad - reminding me of yet another picture: the ripple and the babble of the merry brook.
Mountains; inspiring one with the immensity of their volume; jagged rocks clothed in

a mantle of the purest snow wreathed in mists; and when this coverlet fades away to show the beauty and the exquisiteness of it all, then the very trees and flowers bow before this miracle of God.

Clouds, a world themselves, tier upon tier lined with gold so brilliant that one cannot behold this sight for long.

The butcher-boy's whistle.

Faces of so many dear ones

Why do I fear the departure of this sweet thousand? Is there ought I cannot find in the glades of memory?

The School That Was A House

Davena F Share - The Taptonian 1956

Modern architects succeed in constructing edifices of concrete and glass, standing aloof and superior, but without character. No doubt these schools serve their purpose in sending out efficient and qualified citizens into the world, but in Tapton House School we feel that a little tradition is valuable, if not necessary, as it is indeed found that the more advanced of the regiments in the British army are those who bear a long and honourable tradition.

Tapton House School, although perhaps not as convenient as these modern edifices, with their spacious rooms and barren corridors, is, however, enveloped by an atmosphere of warmth and friendliness. It is of stately Georgian architecture, its slender chimneys protruding from a roof under which several historical events may have taken place, the house once having been the home of George Stephenson, a railway engineer. Standing at the termination of the long meandering drive is the long, low coach-house, bearing on one of its outer walls the carved figurehead of a horse-the coach house probably once having sheltered the carriages of famous people.

The ivy-covered house is situated in a wooded park amidst public gardens which provide us 'residents' and the general community with an excellent view of the surrounding countryside. They provide the perfect setting for such a noble house.

We are fortunate in being situated in such a delightful setting for it is not only a valuable outlet for superfluous energy but is also a tranquil beauty spot in which to study, when our unfortunate friends in the schools with the so-called modern amenities are obliged to be content with bleak concrete yards. It has indeed been proved that pleasant surroundings are an inspiring aid to the imagination, and the House, though perhaps not literally haunted, has a 'lived-in' atmosphere which is specially sensed, not perhaps so much during the day when thronged with happy children, but in the evening when deserted by its lively occupants.

A one-time resident of Tapton House is Miss Violet Markham, whose knowledge that her home is now serving as a valuable establishment for the education of future citizens no doubt compensates for the nostalgic memories recollected for her childhood there, for although the artistically designed fireplaces and staircases, and decorated ceilings and walls, have been treated with due respect, they are now continually becoming more worn and effaced with the passage of time.

The beauty, both in and out of doors, stimulates inspiration and rouses respect within those who enter the building. Both teachers and children work in friendly harmony, which they feel is ample compensation for the lack of modern amenities and equipment.

We are proud of our reputation of friendliness and hospitality, but realise that we can ascribe it in the main to the influence of 'the noble men and gracious women who have lived in, and loved, this house'.

On Entering One's Last Term at School

Eileen D Sims - The Taptonian 1956

There have been times when the very thought of leaving the place which has so many happy associations for us was repugnant. We could not conceive of any existence other than our school life. But there have been other times when, physically weighed down by a dozen books and mentally exhausted at the thought of all the homework or examination swotting we had to do, we looked forward with anticipation to the day when we could leave it all behind. Now that the actual time for departure has come I cannot feel any emotion. Most probably the true realisation of what I have both gained and lost will come some time after I have left this noble house.

Leaving school brings to mind those words, 'Look thy last on all things lovely every hour'. We are extremely fortunate in having so gracious a house in which to work, but we shall not only recall the beauty of our surroundings. We recall the excitement of Christmas, our 'worthy carollers' who so delightfully and gallantly entertain the ladies of the kitchen, the kissing-ring wonderfully bright and colourful in the dusk of late afternoon. We hear once more the rustle of silks and satins, the giggles of white socked little girls for whom this is the first of many happy Christmases at Tapton House. Lest the picture appears too bright, we would remind ourselves of the agonies - yes, school life has its perils and stormy passages - of those lessons for which we had either no liking or aptitude. There were friendships true and long-lasting, friendships false and short-lived; there was Commemoration Day, there was the General Inspection; there were rounders in the park, and oral examinations on the second floor. Each little part of school life has its particular significance for us according to our individual personalities and interests.

The face of the school is continually undergoing alteration. There are those of us who can remember dining not in a fully equipped modern canteen, but in what is now known as the 'Chemi Lab'. This is one of the rooms of the school which has taken on a criminal complexion over the years. It was once, as I have said, a dining-room; it became Room 17, alias the music , alias the art Room, alias the 'Chemi-lab'. We have seen fireplaces and doors disappear. We have returned to find openings in solid walls and extra rooms manufactured almost overnight. But the essential atmosphere of the school will never change.

It is impossible, at the moment, to feel either sad or joyful at leaving such an establishment. Our fellows assure us that they, for the most part, have no desire to return. Our elders maintain that no days are so satisfactory as those spent at school but they fail to look at school life in perspective; they tend to remember only the happy days and think, wrongly, that the school-child has no burden of responsibility.

The school would not be complete without the staff and yet that does not remain entirely stable. Those who have come to make their home amongst us have settled down to become imbued with the Taptonian atmosphere, and even those who leave us take away with them a little of the spirit of this house. They are not constantly before our mind's eye but on reminiscent occasions we will talk of Mr ——— or Miss ——— ——— and our recollections are often intermingled with laughter and even tears. Some of us will eventually be known as 'the staff'. Shall we, I wonder, remembering our own errors, be able to look sympathetically at schoolchildren?

We of Tapton House would preserve our memory of its best if, to adapt the words of the School Charter, we would strive to carry its beauty and serenity to whatsoever part of the world we may chance to inhabit.

Privileged People

Barrie Birkin 1956 - 1962

I went to Tapton in 1956 from Holymoorside County School, the only one from that school. My eldest brother Roger was already at Tapton (52-57), so he helped break the ice.

I was in 1H (there were three classes of about 33 persons, 1T, 1H, 1S) and Jean Stokes was in the same class. I liked her then, but at that age boys didn't talk to girls much, so the friendship was casual!

Going through the school, I wasn't as clever as Jean, so we didn't meet at lessons. By that time she was friendly with an older Taptonian (bit older, played football and who subsequently married Carol Atkinson, also in our year) so I didn't get a look in!

Jean's father became seriously ill after year five, so she left to be an audio-typist with the NCB, while I stopped on to retake a lot of failed O levels (class was formed called Remove for us duffers!).

It was during this year, 1962, that I got in touch with Jean again, and the romance blossomed from there. I started work at Joseph Clayton and Sons Ltd, in Chesterfield where my father was MD (where I am general manager, and father deceased). I got engaged in 1965 and married Jean on 18 March 1967, and have been happily married ever since.
I think the grounds of Tapton were conducive to friendships, beside it being a mixed school which obviously brought several relationships together; Raymond Eagles, who was also in our class eventually married Barbara Raybould. Jean's younger sister Suzanne Stokes, married Bill Bailey, but most of these expupils have little involvement in the OTA.

My memories of Tapton are very happy. I messed about, but with the Peace Gardens, park, woodland and the beautiful buildings etc. we must have been the most privileged pupils ever to attend and be taught at such a wonderful place. Discipline was lax, but who cared at that age?

Mr Mellor - Obituary

Frank Silcock 1958

We were all shocked to hear of the death on Good Friday of Mr Mellor at the age of seventy-three. He had, we knew, been in failing health for a number of years but the end, when it came, stunned us and it was hard to believe that someone who had been so much a part of our lives and who had been held in so much affection was no longer with us. Only a little while before he had himself suffered a sad loss by the death of Mrs Mellor. His retirement indeed had not been as free from care and anxiety as he could have wished.

Mr Mellor was the first headmaster of Tapton House School, when it opened in April, 1931 as a senior Selective Central School. This new type of school was part of a great scheme of reorganisation of the Education system in Chesterfield which was being carried out under the guidance and genius of Dr H G Stead, then the Borough Education Officer. No better choice could have been made than that of Mr Mellor as first headmaster, who by his vision, temperament and burning belief in the value of education was most admirably qualified to start such a venture. And what a happy inspiration it was to make Tapton House a school! To build all the new schools needed was impossible, but Tapton House was standing empty and what could be better for a school than this dignified building set in its beautiful gardens and park, a house where, in a previous generation, children had lived happily, and where once again, many more children could grow up in gracious surroundings. The idea of a school in a house was always dear to Mr Mellor; the children were to be more than pupils, they were to be a part of a family and, as well as learning, they would receive sympathy, help, encouragement and guidance.

From the start Mr Mellor saw that many of the pupils could gain more benefit from an academic education and soon school certificate was being successfully taken by an ever increasing number of pupils. The demand grew for more advanced studies and in 1945 Tapton House became a Grammar school in all but name. From now on, the sixth form grew in strength, and the school reached full stature. It was not by accident that Mr Mellor chose for the school motto Tenax Propositi. From the beginning he had seen the possibilities in the school and that there was a need for another Grammar school in Chesterfield. He resolved that Tapton House should be that school and he never wavered in his aim.

For nineteen years he devoted his life to the good of the school and the welfare of its pupils and when he retired in 1950 Tapton House School and Mr Mellor himself stood high in the estimation of all. He had every reason to be proud of his achievements but, typically, he did not welcome retirement. He had so many more plans to put into operation, there was so much to do, so much that he could do. He had thrived on work, he had loved his teaching and being with young people.

How well we remember his neat, quietly dressed rotund figure, his face fresh and almost cherubic, his spectacles glinting, as he moved through the school with quick, short, resolute strides. Never a welcome sight to idlers and fools! In his lessons too, he was vital, brimming over with ideas; he was never so happy as when he was in front of a class, preferably a large one, and his only aids a blackboard and chalk. He was, by any standards, a very fine teacher and many have cause to be grateful to him for his insistence on hard work and high aims. He never abandoned the slowest and no trouble was too great for those who tried.

Many things spring to mind which were so much a part of him and of school life: his talks in assembly every Wednesday morning; Room 1 at one o'clock where the best work only was good enough and lame dogs were helped over many stiles. In the early days, who can forget those huge outings on Ascension Day?

But chiefly, when we think about him and Tapton we remember those Commemoration Days, the beautiful setting on the top lawn, the service, the prize distribution and then the play, this often written by Mr Mellor himself and often produced by him. The cast was always huge, the costume colourful; there were dances, fairies, knights and ladies, honest tradesmen, romance and farce. The whole never failed to captivate the audience and bring sheer joy to the players - worth all the troubles and tribulations of rehearsals. His love for the living theatre probably came next, after that for the school, and he began and inspired that long run of remarkable and successful productions which have been, and still are, such an outstanding feature of the school. This dictum - 'You get the standard you demand' - was never more fully proved.

And who will ever forget Mr Mellor in his most jovial mood at the Christmas parties. The school, in its variety of decorations, the Hall with its evergreens, streamers and balloons, the huge Christmas tree with its lights, the tea, the ageless games and Father Christmas. No wonder that 'happy' is the adjective most often applied to the school. Tapton was ever foremost in his mind. So closely was he bound up with the school that to former pupils it is impossible to think of Tapton without thinking of Mr Mellor, and not only to former pupils but to most people in Chesterfield and even beyond. All who came to Tapton will never cease to be proud of their connection with him and remember him with affection, admiration, gratitude and respect.

He was a man of wide reading and culture; a scholar of the highest order. He was by nature generous, kind-hearted and ever ready to help. He had a charm of manner and a sincerity that endeared him to all and an extraordinary gift for remembering not only

121

faces and names, but the persons themselves. He was honest, fearless and never afraid of supporting an unpopular cause; he never shirked a duty or a responsibility. Into all pupils he instilled a love of learning and a love for the highest ideals in the conduct of life. He himself had an unbelievable capacity for hard work and he never ceased to praise the value of work. To do anything less than one's best or to give in was shame - 'The full and strenuous exercise of all the powers of brain and body'. There in the School Charter he set out his ideals clearly and beautifully. He was a great headmaster; a noble example which indeed will be for ever a beacon set before us.

Train and Girl Spotting

Derek Hardy 1958-1964 Dorothy Munro 1963-1966

I started Tapton in 1958; it was quite a contrast to Hipper Street primary. After I had taken the 11-plus, my father was going to pick Chesterfield School as the number one preference, but I had different ideas. A neighbour who was two or three years my senior was at Tapton and took me there one Saturday during a trainspotting mission. (Most Tapton lads gained honours in trainspotting knowledge). So Tapton went down and there I went.

Dorothy came to Chesterfield from a small village between Wick and John O'Groats via Harrogate. Her father came to work at the AGD postal HQ. She started Tapton in 1963 along with her brother and sister, Jeanette and Donald, who are twins.

Chesterfield council built a large estate of houses for the AGD employees and families, 1,300 in all. When the first phase was completed, between Brockwell and Ashgate, a group of pals and myself went to assess the female-talent situation. It was then that I spotted Dorothy with her sisters and friends. I didn't know until the following week that she would be going to Tapton, and my next sighting was in the woods at school. It was initially very giggly and flirty and the first real conversation was to ask her if she would be going to the school dance at the Odeon ballroom.

At the dance she looked stunning in a kingfisher blue dress and permed black hair. We had three or four dances and the last waltz, and that's how it started. We were married on my 22nd birthday and it was our 30th anniversary last week. We have three sons, none of whom went to Tapton, poor devils, but to the new Chesterfield School at Brookside.

A Clanger

Andrea L Gaunt 1959 -1967

Tapton was a very special place and I enjoyed some very happy times there. I remember Slasher Haslam and the parents evening when my Mum, so used to hearing me call him Slasher, addressed him as Mr Slasher by mistake. He just laughed, fortunately.

I also remember the cross-country run. I have never been very athletic and because of this I used to opt to go on the cross-country run (or walk in my case) during games periods instead of playing hockey etc. A very select few of us used to walk round a short cut and then break into a trot when we were in view of the games mistress.

A Headmaster's Memories

Frank Chettle - Headmaster (THS 1959 - 1965)

I have very happy memories of my time as headmaster at Tapton House School and was sad to leave in 1965 when the School was supposed to be closing and the house was to become Chesterfield Museum. Closure was so near that the headship was not advertised and the deputy head was made acting headmaster. The senior mistress, Miss Wildin, was outstanding at producing drama, and the quality of her productions was the best I have known in any school. One of the outstanding achievements was a visit to Darmstadt in 1963 when thirty-three pupils presented T S Eliot's play *Murder in the Cathedral* (at the Germans request) at the Georg Buechner School and scored a dramatic triumph which filled the hall to capacity on three evenings and earned a magnificent review in the *Frankfurter Allgemeine Zeitung*. We were all very well received by our German hosts and friendships were formed in the early days of the links between Chesterfield and Darmstadt. One of my most difficult moments was speaking to the school assembly in German, but they seemed to understand what I said. When we were leaving I was asked if the school could do a play in German in Chesterfield and I had to say that the number of people speaking German would not produce the sort of audience we had enjoyed in Germany.

Following on the involvement of the school with drama, I introduced a House Drama competition in which Sixth form pupils produced plays which were judged by an outside adjudicator, initially Anthony Cornish from the Civic Theatre. Pupils would discuss the choice of play with staff, but once the choice had been made they were on their own. It went very well.

As you know George Stephenson had lived at Tapton House and there were stories of his ghost being seen. One Friday morning the caretaker told me that on the previous Saturday a workman was doing some decorating in the room in which George Stephenson had died and the caretaker went to see how things were going. The workman asked who the stuck-up old so-and-so who had walked through the room a little while ago was? He had not replied to his Good morning. When the Caretaker said there was just the two of them in the building, the workman said, I'm not staying here and walked out.

Dorothy Lowe, a member of staff, made the most of the George Stephenson connection. The door in the room where she usually taught often used to blow open, and when teaching a new intake, she would stop mid sentence and say 'Hello George, how nice to see you. Do sit down'. And to the boy nearest to the door, 'Close the door please boy'. After a few minutes she would say, 'Oh it's been very nice to see you again George. Must you really go?' 'Boy, open the door for George'.

Tapton House was a very special school. Being in a house gave it almost a family atmosphere and a feeling of togetherness and friendship not found very often.

Reminiscences of Tapton House

William Booker 1959 -1967

I have many memories of my time at Tapton, commencing in 1959 and through the school to my leaving in 1966 having achieved 9 O levels and 3 A levels along the way.

My memories of the school really start at my old school, Holmewood and Heath junior school, where I was one of 11 out of about 60, to pass the 11-plus entrance exam. I am the eldest of four sons; my father was an underground miner at Williamthorpe colliery and my mother was not in employment, being fully engaged in bringing us up. All except one of the other passed candidates were sons of miners. Of those 11, seven of us went to Tapton, the others to Chesterfield or Tupton Hall.

My parents were very proud that I had gained entrance, the first in the Booker clan to get to the Grammar. They did not have a lot of money and I do know that my uniform was obtained by way of a clothing grant; otherwise I doubt I would have been able to go. Throughout my time at Tapton they scrimped to ensure that I lacked for nothing for school, and later for my much younger brother, who obtained entrance to Tapton on his school record, the 11-plus by then having been scrapped.

First Impressions.

My first sight of the school was from the bottom of the drive, shortly after alighting from the Chesterfield Corporation bus, no. 37 I seem to remember. I had never visited the school or the park; my parents had been when a relative had played football against the school. We had been invited along to a Meet the staff and see the school afternoon on a Saturday close to the end of the summer term. Dad did not have a car and I believe that my first sight of Tapton was also my sudden realisation that here was something very special.

My choice of Tapton was based mainly on one thing, its proximity to the main railway north-south - I was a loco spotter and yet I had never visited this location for spotting.

We stood at the bottom of the drive looking up to the house - myself, Dad, Mum and my nine-year-old brother. I was in awe and admiration - how could this magnificent parkland and house be my future school? I spotted things for the future, horse chestnut trees (conkers), the slope down (ideal for winter sports), the shrubberies (games), the paths (peace and quiet for walks and reflection).

We walked up the drive and slowly the house presented itself to us, but the real magnificence was not seen until we walked through the gates at the front. We had been invited to enter via the main door, and we were met, to my surprise, by pupils who politely introduced themselves and led us to the hall, where the initial chat was to be given by the headmaster, Mr F E Chettle. The hall was a hive of activity, conversation and excitement. Teachers were walking around, chatting to parents and their children. These staff seemed strange, dressed in long black gowns and with different coloured 'scarves' made in material or fur. I had never seen them before. School pupils were busy bringing other groups of parents and students, seating them, making sure they were comfy, directing people to the toilets, bringing more chairs for late comers - a truly dedicated school.

My first sight of Mr Chettle was when suddenly there was a short buzz and several people appeared on the stage. These I later discovered were The head boy and girl, Miss Wildin, the senior mistress, Mr Pearson, the senior master, and central, Mr Chettle. He immediately struck me as a person who exuded authority and achieved respect. He spoke for about 30 minutes on the School, school life, the buildings, rules, uniform and sundry other matters. He invited all parents and future pupils to meet him either that afternoon, or at a future date before the end of term if there were any worries or queries. Mr Pearson then took over and invited the assembled horde to walk around the school with a member of school or staff. We were paired off with a very chatty young girl pupil leading a group of about 10 of us around and to my surprise, she led us out of the hall and on a very circuitous route via the games field, the woods, the Peace Gardens and back through the front door, explaining all along about the school, its history, location, and other amenities and varied gems of information. We were then led through the school, meeting other groups as we went, visiting all the rooms and, in some, seeing examples of work laid out for examination. After this tour we were led to the canteen, where refreshments were available, and a large number of the school staff were assembled and talking to parents and pupils. I had the privilege of being introduced to Mr Pearson and listening as he and my father chatted as old friends; they had been at school together. Mr Chettle was mingling and speaking to as many people as possible.

After a very enjoyable afternoon, and replete with the scones and biscuits forced on me by very attentive pupils, we decided to enjoy the evening by walking into town, via the railway and over the footbridge. A little bit of loco spotting was done on the way.

Then, to crown a magnificent day, I spotted the Indian touring cricket team bus parked outside the Railway Hotel. They were there to play a three-day match against Derbyshire at the Queen's Park, commencing the following day. Being a cricket fan I persuaded my dad to take us into the hotel to try to get a few autographs. We were met by the team manager who explained that the team was at dinner and he would do what he could and took our name and address. He also gave us a complimentary family ticket for the following day, first day of the match. We went to the match and several days later a letter arrived from the team, enclosing two sheets each filled with all the team autographs.

First Day

With great trepidation and a lot of butterflies I climbed the hill to school. I had on my new uniform, my lovely school tie - the first time I had worn a tie to school. Over my shoulder I hugged my new shiny leather satchel containing a kit of pen, pencil, ruler etc.

We had been requested to assemble in the courtyard in front of the hall, from where we were led into assembly. After this, we were asked to remain in the hall whilst school dispersed to their classes. We were then given our form master's Name and led by the form master to our form room. Ours was, I believe, Room 4, immediately opposite the Stephenson Room. Our form master was Mr Daddy Ashton.

The first day was a blur of paper, rules, timetable, and first lessons with our new teachers, finding out our classmates names etc. It was a very tired but very happy Bill Booker who caught the bus home that evening. I was met by parents and a couple of relatives, and had to tell them every morsel of the day.

After that day we soon settled down into a very hard-working routine and it was often mentioned to us that we were there because we were so bright and would therefore be able to work harder. I have never regretted the hard work or the rigid discipline of the first-year in the school. I do believe that it helped me on my way into a rewarding career and a very open view on life.

Memories of Staff

The school itself, by its very nature, had many staff who were highly trained and very individual. I will try to put down a few of my favourite memories, although I have too many to really write down every one. The ones I mention are the teachers I admired and who had a distinct impression on me.

Miss Phil Wildin. Many pupils held this senior mistress in great esteem, although there were others who did not like her at all. She had great presence and commanded respect. Woe betide anyone who incurred her wrath. She reigned in her book-filled inner sanctum and I thank her for introducing me to drama and the love of literature. She had a way of persuading even the most reluctant pupil to help at plays, special events, carol concerts and always had time to discuss anything with anyone. The girls may remember her for another of her duties - girls' uniform was under her watchful eye and she had frequent checks, with letters being sent to parents if uniform was not as detailed. Measuring length of skirt above knee with a ruler was not unheard of.

Miss Dot Lowe. A loveable lady whose daily accomplishment was climbing the stairs to the top floor where her room was situated. Miss Lowe freely admitted that she was over-weight and unfit but that did not spoil her. She taught me geography throughout the school and Economics in the sixth. I have reason to remember her affectionately for her patience and understanding. However, she could lose her temper and had a very loud voice when angry. It was this teacher who christened me Dormouse when I fell asleep in one of her geography lessons in the third year- the nickname stuck with me throughout and after school.

Mr Slasher Haslam - A great fan of cricket and I do remember several occasions when most of a lesson was abandoned in favour of a discussion about the current Test. Assisted at games and spent some time with me trying to perfect my cricket stroke. Unfortunately I did not have an eye for the ball and was invariably bowled out quickly with only one or two runs. This teacher had a very friendly, approachable nature but was also a person to respect. His favourite punishment was a piece of chalk tossed at a pupil who was not working, invariably striking at the back of the head, a punishment which would be illegal nowadays.

Mr Furber. Art master and a true eccentric. However he was expert at his job and inspired many pupils to efforts beyond their own perceived limits, including myself. He had a method of persuading pupils to assist at preparing special events such as plays and open days, without those pupils realising the amount of work they were actually volunteering for.

Mr Nobby Clarke - music master and a true gentleman. My main memories are of his method of greeting pupils entering his lessons in the hut. He played music, either on the piano or gramophone, of the type he was going to talk about or teach. Many pupils appreciated this and entrance to his room was usually very quiet, in respect for the occasion. On the odd occasion that there was noise this teacher just sat looking out of the window or facing the board until all sound had ceased. He then commenced his lesson. I have him to thank for introducing me to all classes of music. He could be very impassioned and I do remember one double lesson where he talked on Wagner and played snatches from his works. It was at that lesson where I began to appreciate that there were other types of music than pop, which could be enjoyed, and to this day I still enjoy most classes of music.

Mr Harry Routledge. Geography master and guardian of school stationary. A quiet spoken, but nevertheless tough disciplinarian. I do remember taking a full exercise book and being refused a new one because there were pages missing. I had to buy a new book and from that day I did not use exercise books for paper aeroplanes.

Miss Woodall. History mistress and a lovely lady. Tended to be strict on dates and facts and woe betide you if you got anything wrong in a homework. Insisted on reading round the subject and on one occasion took us to Chesterfield reference library specifically to show us the workings of study, this being during our first-year. Inspired me to take an interest in history and to this day my main interest is the area of industrial archaeology and history .

Mr Lean. A much younger history master, whose approach was more hands on. He was more interested in life in history and in the day to day workings, together with the history of campaigns and battles. Two memories stand out - my first is when he was describing the battle of Agincourt. The class was split into two with the French on one side and the English on the other. Mr Lean then produced two boxes of long wheat straws and gave them to the English. He then told them to throw them like spears into the air against the French. This was his way of showing the effect of the several thousand English archers at Agincourt. Each straw was an arrow and we really appreciated how devastating this was. Another memory is when we were discussing Napoleon and he took us on to the sunken lawn with a chair apiece and showed us how the Battle of Waterloo had progressed, using chairs and pupils as components of the battle. He himself took the part of Wellington, giving instructions from the top of the steps. I have never forgotten Mr Lean's animated lessons.

Mr Wilf Pearson. Assistant head, senior physics master, and my tutor throughout the school. Took a fatherly interest in my progress, I do believe because of his close relationship with my father. I never dared do anything wrong in his lessons or where he may find out, and thus get back to dad. I recall several special coaching lessons in his physics room when I was having difficulties before O level. I also recall many wide-ranging discussions with him on a myriad of subjects. He was a well-educated and well-read gentleman. In the sixth form it was not unusual for him to join us in our common room, by prior invitation, to discuss politics, the way of the world and a host of other items. I thank him for widening my horizons and helping my development as a well-balanced person.

Mr Frank Chettle. Headmaster and a gentleman who exuded authority and demanded respect, not just for himself but for everyone. My main memories of him relate to his presence at official functions, where it was quite apparent that he was a leader and doer. It was not unusual for him to walk around school, greeting and talking to pupils, staff and the cleaning and catering staff. He could quite often be seen, walking with a pupil or member of staff through the grounds in earnest discussion. I myself was one of his companions, when on one occasion I visited him in his study on a matter relating to my choice of options for O level. I was having great difficulty in making up my mind.. I wanted to pursue a career in the geography/geology/economics related field and was looking towards university entrance. I asked for a chat with him and this was granted. It was a lovely late spring afternoon and he suggested an amble through the gardens. On this walk, which included the Peace Garden where lower school were not allowed, he spoke to me of his own misgivings at his own early education. We chatted the matter through and discussed possibilities and after about 30 minutes repaired to the head's study. I left that room with my mind made up, feeling relaxed and with a renewed determination to succeed in my chosen subjects. I found out very much later, after leaving on completing my A levels, that several of my compatriots had similar sorts of experience with the head. He had a natural affinity to calming the worst fears and doubts. I had occasions to enjoy several similar ambles with Mr Chettle, sometimes with a small group, but usually alone. I believe that he purposely did it in this way firstly to get away from the 'official' office, and secondly to meet his pupils on neutral ground. It certainly worked with myself and a lot of others. It was with deep regret that I saw Mr Chettle leave, I believe at the end of my fourth year there.

Mr Hooper. Woodwork master and an expert at teaching pupils how to use tools correctly. He also had the knack of 'bullying' pupils into assisting at preparing bits and pieces for special events, plays etc. I was very cack-handed with tools and he spent a lot of time on my instruction. My pride was complete when I managed to complete a special fruit bowl by turning a large slice of elm. Mr Hooper afforded it pride of place at Commemoration Day display, and to this day I swear that this master printed my name larger than any of the others on the woodwork display. He taught me the principles of DIY and I still carry out a lot of my own new work and repairs at home.

Brian Denman. Sports master with a loud voice but a heart of gold. Recognised that I was not a sporty person, but still tried to teach me the principles and bring out my sporting character. I still have reports and on one his comment reads, 'Tries very hard but never really succeeds. However I have a goal and so does William. The goal is to make him an expert in at least one sport before he leaves school.' This master never gave up on even the most hopeless of cases. I took part in several sports days as a runner and javelin at which I was fairly proficient. When school started using outside sports such as golf, ten-pin bowling and I found I was pretty good at these as well. I still enjoy the occasional game. I also enjoy my membership of a gym, very similar to the circuit training which this master inflicted on us, and which I hated in school. How attitudes change.

School premises and grounds

I have already intimated on the unfolding of the glory of the main house, as we visited it for the first time. It was a truly magnificent sight to one who was used to an early 1900s building and asphalt playground with no shrubs and very little by way of sports area. The entrance hall was a delight and Room 1 a marvellous airy room spoilt by the clutter of desks. The main staircase was a wonder to behold, made even more so by the fact that lower school were not allowed to use it. I have not seen its like in many other buildings. It was impressed upon us from the start that this was a historic building because of its connections to George Stephenson. On the whole, pupils respected this and very little wanton damage or graffiti was inflicted while I was there. Respect for property was a watchword. It was very easy to imagine life as it had been in the old house and individual teachers reinforced this. Mr Furber taking us on a tour and pointing out unusual items of decoration, architecture, design or construction - then we had to draw or paint a copy. Miss Woodall with her descriptions of life upstairs and downstairs. The occasional visitors from historical clubs or overseas who were in raptures on seeing the house.

Library. A little crowded but still with a sense of history, with its excellent plaster mouldings and fireplace. A marvellous place to study especially on a summer's afternoon in the sixth.

The domestic science room. Mr Routledge's stationary den and the centre for the tuck shop which helped to support school events. A very light airy room ideally set out for its function. When I started school girls did cookery and boys did woodwork. I think I was in the fifth year before this regime changed and a choice was allowed.

Back stairs. Made of stone and lower school had to use these stairs. Invariably they were crammed at lesson change, lunch and hometime. A common excuse for lateness at lessons was 'stuck on the stairs'. I know - I used the excuse many times when in fact I had dawdled. I could never understand why so many were made to use these constricted stairs, while a few feet away was that magnificent wide circular but formal staircase. Art room. Mr Furber's den, which was also a centre of discovery, Mr Furber being a rather untidy teacher. He spent most of his time in there and quite often had pupils work on display in the room, and also in locations in the school.

Most of the rooms on the first floor did not have any really special features, except for their height and light airy feel, which I believe assisted in study.

The Stephenson room. Reputed to be George Stephenson's study or bedchamber, depending on who was telling the story. This room had a large door, which had an intriguing habit of opening on its own, when no one was near it or touching it. On these occasions, it was more or less a school tradition to bid 'Good morning, (or afternoon) George' as it was said to be Stephenson's ghost checking up on the house. Many former pupils will remember this room with affection.

The top floor rooms had low ceilings, having been the household staffrooms when the House was a magnificent home. Here we find:

Miss Lowe's room. A treasury for anyone interested in geography or geology as she had a wealth of books and magazines, rock and ore samples and artefacts from overseas. All the rooms on this floor were rather dark, given the small windows and cramped feel to the rooms. However they afforded magnificent views of the gardens and over towards Chesterfield and beyond.

The staffrooms. Den of all staff, and a room which no pupil wished to be invited to attend. If such an invitation was given it usually meant disciplinary action in some form. It was usual to see a small queue waiting at break, lunch, and end of school.

Biology lab. Dark and forbidding, containing many specimens of work, many preserved in bottles and jars.

Miss Wildin's room. A marvellous booklined room where this senior mistress spent a lot of her time, lecturing on drama and literature. An open invitation was held out to all interested pupils to visit her and discuss drama, as this was her main love. She allowed pupils to browse through her books and many found a love of drama and books through her coaxing and leadership.

Outside the main house there were the chemistry laboratory, hall, physics lab and woodwork lab. All had their own individual characteristics.

I believe every member of school will remember the tennis and netball courts, principally for the slight gradient down, which meant that matches were not altogether fair.

The modern buildings of the games' changing rooms and associated classrooms were at odds with the character of the house and stuck out as looking rather tacky when viewed from the bottom of the drive. I have no complaints about the space for sports. With a large area for football, hockey, cricket and ideal surroundings for cross-country running, the school excelled at most sports, with school teams competing strongly and doing well in a variety of leagues and friendlies. All sports were ably inspired by Brian Denman, Mr Haslam and others whose names sadly escape my memory. All sports staff and helpers always showed dedication to the sport they were teaching. Chesterfield Corporation staff looked after the park grounds and gardens, because the school gardens and grounds were classed as a public park. I well remember several exhortations to school to look after the surroundings because of this openness.

The park keeper had a cottage and nursery behind the hall and produced some marvellous results for school functions. From the fourth form upwards, pupils who were interested in horticulture were invited to join corporation staff on some days when they were working in the greenhouses. I attended several impromptu lectures on cultivation methods and plants, usually as an alternative to general studies or at lunchtime.

The grounds themselves were massive. There were the gardens, including the Peace Gardens which were out of bounds until the sixth form or by invitation from staff or a sixth former. During the sixth I spent a lot of time in that garden as I found it very peaceful and ably assisted study in such delightful surroundings. From the Peace Gardens there ran the Walk which had marvellous views over Chesterfield and an unequalled view of the spire, standing proud over the town.

The woods were filled with magnificent examples of several types of trees, most native to this country, and the younger pupils enjoyed many games in these woods. More senior pupils tended to use them more for walking and reflection, and in some cases for continuing courtship with the opposite sex.

The wilder part of the grounds ran down towards the railway, and many happy hours were spent in this area, principally because a large number of boys were trainspotters. I also recall at least two female spotters. We were all entranced by the mechanical beauty of the large steam engines which passed by, be they mundane engines working a coal train or a sleek express on the Master Cutler or some other mainline route.

Spring in the grounds brought out thousands of spring flowers, cultivated and wild.

Summer saw many small groups on the park grass, for we were encouraged to enjoy what lay around us. A lot of studying was done outside at these times. It was not uncommon for a teacher to surrender to entreaties to take the lesson outside. I well remember the summer in my third year, which appeared to be very hot. Several lessons

132

were held outside and it was not unusual to see several groups outside at the same time. It is sad that most schools are not able to enjoy this type of freedom.

Autumn meant sometimes draughty rooms but had its consolations. Horse chestnuts grew in several parts of the grounds and conkers was classed as a school sport at this time of year. I believe it was Mr Haslam who set up a school league and championship, with a small prize to the year's overall winner. I am not sure if this continued for any length of time after I left.

Winter could be a problem and sometimes resulted in school being closed for the odd day because of transport difficulties. However, being at the top of Tapton Hill, the school was ideally placed for winter sports. Sledging was positively encouraged, overseen by one or two teachers in case of any misadventure or misbehaviour. Snow fights and snowmen were allowed, as were skis and the first beginnings of snow boarding - pieces of plywood or plastic on which one sat or stood and progressed downhill. The drawback was the long hike back up at the end of the run. Many pupils obtained their first liking for winter sports at Tapton. I recall only one serious injury during my time there, when one pupil mistimed his stop at the bottom and hit the hedge, suffering injuries including a ruptured spleen, which meant a rather lengthy stay in hospital and recuperation. To the school's credit the sport was not stopped; we were just exhorted to take more care. I do believe that in today's nanny state, not only would this type of sport be banned, but a lot of the freedom we enjoyed also curtailed under the guise of pupil safety.

School Events.

Sports day at the Queen's Park track, was eagerly looked forward to by many pupils, not usually because of the sport and sense of occasion, but perhaps principally because it meant one or two days out of lessons. Day one was heats, when all participants were taken to the park in the afternoon and the heats completed with very little audience.

Day two was the big day, when after lunch all pupils made their own way to the park to enjoy the sports day which usually started at around 1.30 and continued until 5 or 6 pm. I took part in several, never winning anything, but thoroughly enjoying the occasion. A large gathering of pupils, parents, residents of Chesterfield and old boys and girls made it very memorable.

Carol Service. Held not at the parish church, but at Trinity Church where George Stephenson is buried. Although crowded the church had a great ambience and showed off Miss Woodall's and Miss Wildin's organisational skills to the full, as it was usually their task to organise this essential piece of school life.

Open days were held for new pupils and we were exhorted to produce special pieces of work for these days. Many pupils were given the honour of being chosen as guides, being given a briefing the previous day by Mr Pearson. I was chosen to be a guide on three separate occasions.

Commemoration Day. Perhaps the most important school event of the year. Most will remember the frenzied activity of the weeks leading up to the event with each year preparing a display of some type for the day. The day took place in the afternoon on the sunken lawn (in the hall if wet) and took the form of a service, school hymn and formal speech by the head followed by the display. There was the obligatory gym display undertaken by the finest of the pupils at gym. Perhaps a dance sequence overseen by one of the teachers interested in dance (I forget her name). Drama of some type was included, usually a short one act play, overseen by Miss Wildin, sometimes a monologue or dialogue given by talented pupils. School choir gave a rendering of a favourite work and sometimes teachers gave pieces. I do remember on one occasion that teachers gave a selection from Gilbert and Sullivan, including the Major General song, sung I believe by the chemistry teacher, Mr Jones.

After completion of the outdoor happenings, which were also attended by the mayor and mayoress, other civic dignitaries, school governors, parents and a sprinkling of visitors from outside, the whole assemblage were invited to tour school and view pupils' work set out for inspection and discussion. Teachers and pupils were on hand to explain and discuss anything and refreshments were made available in the domestic science room or canteen. The day usually finished with a play or concert in the hall, tickets having been purchased eagerly several weeks before.

School Play. An annual event, usually during the last four weeks of summer term and for which preparations and rehearsals had been going on for some weeks. Presided over usually by Miss Wildin and contributions from several parts of school. I appeared in what were cameo roles in two. Always a sell out and always eagerly looked forward to. School had a policy of encouraging as many pupils as possible to take part, whether that be in the play itself, lighting, sound, set preparation and movement, or simply as doers on the night.

As well as the official events there were many impromptu happenings, supported by the school and usually for the benefit of pupils' education. Many school trips took place, either as field trips, theatre trips, and overseas. My first field trip was to a weekend in north Wales to study geology. I do remember it was very wet and cold even though it was May. However I learnt a lot about rocks etc, principally from the outside lecturers who spoke to us not only in the hostel, but also on the specimen trails. My first trip overseas was by virtue of school, a trip to the Rhine in Germany and flight back from Strasbourg.

Community spirit was encouraged. Whilst in the fourth year and upwards, I helped to organise a lunchtime pop dance, very well patronised by school, which took place most Wednesday lunches. Teachers were not allowed and the aim was to raise funds for the Red Cross - I always think of these dances as the original Band-Aid as a lot of fun was had by all, and the funds were destined to help the less fortunate in the Third World.

In addition school assisted the community in a number of ways. I, myself, became a visitor and helper on a regular basis at the Mencap centre, which was not far from the old Chesterfield School. Others helped out at organisations such as Red Cross, St John's, hospitals and hospices. Many continued this type of voluntary work after leaving school.

Conclusion.

I have always remembered my time at Tapton House with affection, and I venture that the vast majority of former pupils have the same remembrance. I believe that school helped to turn me out as a well-balanced individual, knowledgeable and with an open mind. I cannot believe that many schools managed to have the same effect on their pupils - most nowadays seem to be more interested in figures than characters. Most pupils have no pride in their school and can hardly wait to finish their schooling.

It was with a great sense of loss that I discovered that my old school was to be closed, not only that but the two other bastions of grammar - Chesterfield and St Helena's - were being closed. The decision was made principally, I believe on political grounds and dogma by a Labour-controlled council, which hated to see any vestige of so called elitism. They failed to recognise that Tapton turned out very well-educated people who went far.

I was pleased however, when I discovered at a later date that it was to be used for further education purposes, but I still believe that a lot of pupils have missed out on the distinct advantages which I, and thousands like me, enjoyed and used.

I have visited the School on two or three occasions since leaving. The place has changed a lot, and there is no longer the happy buzz of pupils working. What still remains is the House in all its glory, and to stand at the gate and gaze upon it brings back many memories.

Here my story ends but the memories still return.

Guides Flamborough Camp1950

Back row: Judy Sutton, Margaret Mason, Noreen Carless, Mary ?, Miss Thomas, Miss Savage, Hazelwood, Audrey ?, Sheila Maycock, Joan Smith, Verna Twigg. Middle row: Pam Purdy, Barbara ?, ?, Barbara Turner, Doreen Sails, Mavis Webster, Doreen Hill, Sheila Fern, Carolyn ?, Barbara ?, Hilary Bateman. Front row includes Rusty Barnes.

Football team 1950s

School Photo 1951

School Photo 1951

School play 1951 A Midsummer Night's Dream -Bradbury Hall

Lysander (Tony Cable) - 'Demetrious, I'll avouch it to his head, Made love to Nedar's daughter, Helena, And won her soul; and, she, sweet lady, dotes, Devoutly dotes, dotes in idolatry, Upon this spotted and inconstant man.'

School play 1951 A Midsummer Night's Dream -Bradbury Hall

Lysander (Tony Cable) - 'Hang off, thou cat, thou burr: vile thing, let loose; Or I will shake thee from me like a serpent.' Pam Smith (Hermia) - 'Why are you grown so rude? what change is this, Sweet love?'

School play 1951 A Midsummer Night's Dream -Bradbury Hall

Back row: A Bradshaw (Demetrius), B Greaves (Hippolyta), P Pickerill (Theseus), Peter Wagstaffe (Philostrate), Tony Cable (Lysander). Front row: Pam Allen (Helena), Pam Smith (Hermia), Alan Orwin (Bottom).

School play 1952 St Joan

School Play 1952

Christmas in the Marketplace - The Adoration

School play 1953

Prunella - Pierrot (Peter Wagstaffe): 'Ah! I wish I had you in my nest!'

School Play 1954

Beauty and the Beast - Prince (N Watson): 'What's holding me?' Hodge the Wizard (Peter Wagstaffe): 'Magic, young man! The magic you've been laughing at all this time!'

6th form 1955 Outside the head's study

Back row:Alan Bellamy, Peter Laws, David Sims. Middle row: Stella Moulson, David Evans, Val Taylor, Joan Smith, Gill Ashley, Kath Forrester, Des Baker, Derek Mayfield. Front row: John Hutchinson, Iris Butler, Sheila Hickling.

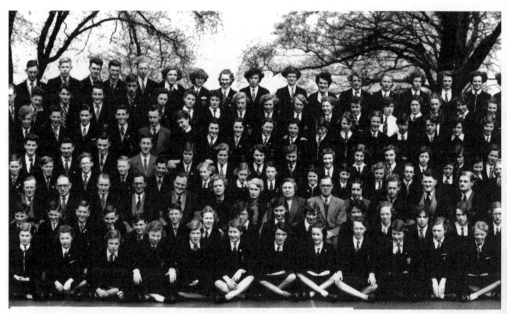

School Photo 1954

School Photo 1954

6th form boys 1955

In the Peace Gardens Alan Bellamy, David Evans, David Sims, John Hutchinson, Peter Laws, Stan Frost, Derek Mayfield, Des Baker.

6th form girls 1955

In the Peace Gardens Kath Forrester, Gill Ashley, Joan Smith, Stella Moulson, Sheila Hickling. Seated: June Ingleton, Pat Ford, Val Taylor, Iris Butler.

Pupils group 1956

Back row, left to right: Malcolm Handford, ? Metcalfe, David Gee, Michael Sunderland, Michael Grice, ?, Michael Barnes, Roy Hughes, Garth Rigby. Middle row: Judy Austin, Pat Dodd, Margaret Gould, Marion Yeldham, Ian Palmer, Mr Walkland, David Allen, Jim Symonds. Front row: Sylvia Cheetham, Christine Horsey, Eileen Heathcote, Jean Heliwell, Kath Hosey, Janette Cannon, Maureen Grady, Gill Cox, Mary Watson.

Form 2 Miss Maltby

Back row: Knight, Stamps, Martin, Jones. Middle row: Laine, Swain, Soresby, Staton, I Hoskin, L Taylor, M Martin, J Gardiner, F Thorneycroft, Grosvenor. Front row: M Wilding, D Coleman, J Stokes, Miss Maltby, J Richards, K Jagger, J Harris.

School Photo 1958

School Photo 1958

148

The Words Of Wisdom Of King Wilfred The Ready

Elizabeth Pearson 1960 - 1967

Thou shalt not take the name of thy masters in vain

Yea, though thou wilt walk through the Valley of the Shadow (especially up the main staircase) thou shalt carry before thee all thy baggage.

Verily thou shalt not 'cog' thy homework.

Thou shalt not whittle thy epitaphs upon the library tables.

I charge thee that thou shalt fast from thy 'jam butties' until the Holy Bell shall toll and shalt not covet thy Neighbour's fodder.

Thou shalt not scatter thy peanut papers around the Holy Cloisters.

If thou happenest to tread the path along which we ere and stray, and thou seest a morsel of litter, thou shalt not pass by on the other side.

Henceforth, thou shalt not tread underfoot conductors and smaller brethren of our order when mounting the corporation chariots.

Moreover I command thee that thou shalt honour thy pious prefects and have no other idols before thee.

(Translated from an old Taptonic Prunestone discovered in the cellars by the Chosen Few of the master)

Heroes and Villains

Jackie Green 1963 - 1968

I suppose we all have our own unique recollections of our time at Tapton House, whether they be pleasant ones or not. Mine are a mixture of both, and I would now like to share them with you in the order in which they popped up in my mind.

It has been interesting to me that most of the memories evoked here happened in the main hall. One of my earliest misadventures occurred during the first week of my first term in form 1N (Miss Nauman's form). I met with an accident in the PE lesson, which took place in the main hall. We had to do handstands off the end of a form and instead of balancing on the form I missed and hit the mat with full force. I never felt a thing, although everyone heard the mighty snap at the time! One girl screamed and pointed, 'Look at her arm!' I looked and saw what looked like a dog's hind leg rather than an arm. In horror, I nearly passed out. Anyway, I was comforted and borne away to the comfort of Mr Chettle's office by the PE teacher, Mrs Shail. Mr Chettle, a very large, kind and smiling man, bore me home in his car, going out of his way to pick up my Mother from home and taking us both to hospital, where he sat awhile, before returning to his duties. What an honour and a privilege to have ridden in his private car and to have been in such close proximity to this legend of a man, although at the time I was in so much pain, that I believe cried most of the time.

Another early recollection was being called to a special assembly in the hall and being told that one of the sixth formers called Graham Evans had died from liver failure. I dimly remember a pleasant smiling-faced, bespectacled boy who always looked a yellowy colour and I recall how shocked and sad we all felt, even though the majority didn't know him. What affected one touched us all in some way.

Another time, all the school was summoned to the hall by Phil Wildin. We knew there had to be a serious reason for this. Phil was known throughout the county for her support and work with Mencap, and ran all sorts of fundraisers without and within for this very worthwhile cause.

We all stood to attention waiting for her wrath to fall. I remember how controlled she was, how sad and sickened she was, to tell us that funds for Mencap had been stolen from her office. She finished by saying that if whoever had done this vile deed would return the money discreetly to her office within the next day or so, then nothing more would be said about it. In the end, this is, in fact, what happened. The incident was then forgotten. But I remember distinctly how she gave the performance of her life up on that stage. She made us all feel that we ourselves had stolen this money, by making us feel wretched and ashamed and totally repulsed by this action. Of all the teachers at Tapton, I loved and respected Miss Wildin and she has had the most impact on me through my life.

I remember her command of the English language and her love of theatre and literature, which she passed on to me in no small measure. The slash of red lipstick with a pronounced cupid's bow as a reminder of past theatrical days and her relationship with and admiration of us and admiration of Dylan Thomas, who she would reminisce about after playing records to us of his varied works. This admiration of him also passed on to me. She was, every inch, an actress, in her every move and stance, her teaching was exciting and she thoroughly loved teaching her great love to us mere mortals. I have a lot to thank her for indeed!

Yet another minor mishap occurred in the hall. After assembly each Thursday morning, the headmaster would somberly read out in alphabetical order a list of names of the poor unfortunates who would be placed in detention after school for the week ahead. At one point in the school year, my friend Julie Oldfield and I always seemed to be in detention for some misdemeanour or another. Our names were read out so much that eventually they began to be read out together as a couple, 'Green and Oldfield', thereby omitting the seven letters H-N and grouping us together.

Assembly was always a very austere and impressive occasion. Usually, the school would line up in rows with teachers at both ends of every row, respectfully awaiting the arrival of the headmaster, followed by heads of departments, who would then stand patiently, not taking their seats until the headteacher was seated. On one occasion I remember, after the hymn, Mr Wilfred Pearson taking several steps backwards to take his place on the very regal looking chair. Unfortunately, he misjudged the space and ended up in a heap on the floor, legs upright and kicking! You could have heard a pin drop! No one dared to laugh or even snigger. Mr Pearson was a very strict disciplinarian and no one wished to suffer the consequences of such a disrespectful action. (A good man, God rest his soul.)

Two other teachers hold a permanent place in my memory. The first one being Miss Dot Lowe (Ma Lowe to us all), a rather loveable, eccentric character. One day, whilst teaching geography to us, I remember a bee buzzing around my head and, panicking, wildly trying to get rid of it. Ma Lowe was extremely agitated and shouted at me, 'Don't move, the bee is more frightened of you than you are of it. Stay still and it will go away.' Good advice! I froze and eventually the bee left me and began to seek out the fleshier bones of Ma Lowe. Did she follow her own advice one might ask. No. She waved her hand frantically, the same as me, which caused the entire class to erupt into uncontrolled laughter. The bee was eventually squashed by a brave student and needless to say, the whole class had to sit through a detention session after school.

Another teacher who is imprinted in my mind forever is Mr Denman, the games master at that time, and acting headmaster at a later stage. He did not like me and he seemed to dog my every move at one time. I remember in my third year, practising for the gymnastic display for Commemoration Day, on the sunken lawn one afternoon. I was larking about in the ranks while waiting my turn, when suddenly a loud voice boomed out summoning myself and Phil Johnson to come forward. We made our way into the middle of the lawn with fearful hearts and trembling knees, surrounded by large number of students. Mr Denman then gave us the biggest dressing down that I certainly have ever experienced in my life. He set about to demolish and humiliate us. His opening words to us were 'You- with hair like a woman!' and then set about us with such a verbal tongue lashing, that we both felt about two inches high. We were then given 1,000 lines each, to complete in a week's time, OR ELSE!

Each lunchtime, I slaved and sweated to complete my 1,000 lines. In the end, I pleaded the help of my colleagues in contributing a few hundred lines. My lines were then complete. I took them along and handed them to Mr Denman, who was on sandwich duty that day, praying he would not look too deeply at the pages near the back. However, he made a great deliberation of slowly tearing each page up in front of the sandwich eaters. All that hard work destroyed in a matter of seconds! The funny thing is, I can't even remember now the form which the lines took, although I recall that it mentioned somewhere in the text that I had a mouth just like a man. What a guy. Thirty-three years on and thoughts of him can still make my blood boil. Talk about creating a lasting impression on someone.

Wonderful, Colourful Memories

Susan Bradshaw 1963 - 1969

Tapton was more than just a school. It was a way of life. Some of my happiest moments were experienced during those special years, culminating in the honour of becoming head girl in 1969. It was with great pride that I stood before all on Speech Day and represented the school I so loved. The wonderful, colourful memories are bountiful. Words cannot capture or effectively reproduce them, and time will never release them from my heart.

Other Titbits:
The deadly hush descended over school assembly every morning as Miss Wildin walked on to the stage, turned and glowered. No words were needed, not even one.

The frequent smell of sulphur dioxide exuding from Mr Walker's experiments in the chemistry lab!

(Winter 1963-64)
The park became a sheet of ice - impossible to walk up to school in the normal way. One boy took the initiative of bringing a pair of spikes to school. He rescued many who had ventured too far. Many black stocking tops and suspenders were to be seen (much to the delight of the boys of course!)

Falling in love for the first time during Miss Lowe's double geography lesson on a Thursday afternoon (1966). I used to tuck my feet under my chair and place them on top of Brian's. This was the start of a relationship that lasted for seven years.

During geography homework I spelt the word separate wrongly on seven different occasions. As punishment I was ordered by Miss Lowe to write out the word 700 times before the next day. I thought she was somewhat harsh. However, never since then has separate been modified to seperate.

The first time I read in morning assembly: I recall the vast sea of faces (about 660) looking my way; the magnificence and size of the Bible, how tiny I felt at the age of 12 and how ecstatic afterwards as I skipped down the corridor to return the Bible.

Mr Chettle

He was a leader with a special touch
Kind, compassionate, firm and just.
A man in whom we could place our trust.

We were a little in awe of him
And greatly respected him.
The head that wore his robes so well
As with purposeful stride he walked through the school.

How few true leaders of our time
Can acclaim such success through being resolute and kind.
If there were more with 'Mr Chettle' qualities
The world would suffer fewer tragedies.

Additional comment: No pupil of that time could ever forget how we cheered until throats were dry when he donned his 'rugby stripes' to take part in the staff versus school hockey match.

All Was Beauty - Part 2

Peter Wagstaffe - The Taptonian 1965

The same green stillness among the trees beyond the lawn; the same silent wilderness of nettles by a broken border wall and fencing near the links; the same expanse of grassland dipping towards the town roofs in the warm distance of a July afternoon. Voices of children in the Peace Garden: shouts as they ran into a fine spray from the gardener's hose snaking across glistening turf. It was their first entry - unwittingly out of breaktime bounds one early September morning - and their first week of wonder at the House on the Hill, where so many assemblies were to be attended, so many mornings were to be worked through, and lunch-hours to be leaped through in crazy zig-zags down the woodland path, afternoons to be passed, more calmly, as the nights drew in towards small lighted windows on an upper floor, or remained far away for long leisurely hours of talk or chess or play rehearsals in the friendly end-of-term summers.

The same footsteps rustled along shaded walks now, and over the same pathways, whose promise used to be infinite, past a man remembering.

This tree, mysteriously, was once protected by bars: the square of iron had been Pickerell's Jail for one terrorising week. Over in the sheltered corner where the wilderness began was Dentith's Prison, but its secret path had not kept its secret, and other hands had bared the branches: even the smallest first-former could escape now. The central shrubberies were sparser too; clearings took the place of laurel bush dens where hearts had pounded as prefects prowled by, badges glinting.

The man remembered hot-necked shame when the head stood calling their names and two daffodils lay irredeemably crushed in evidence at their feet. Mercifully, the cane had remained unmoved. They had been thoughtless in a wild time of war-hoops and hunting across the swinging stretch of parkland: an adult intrusion into a self-centred world was needed.

Now the native had returned. He saw that things had not remained as memory would have them: change had come as gradually as a season sees the shaping of her trees.

There were other voices now in the Garden. Under cover of Christmas dark at party time, figures glided across the lawn into a shrubbery of shadows for their lust: Killer stabbed her whimpering to silence on soft leaves, while music vibrated scratchily in a hot and happy hall, its wallbars hung with evergreen.

The same smooth lawn - how wide it once seemed! - and the same bushes backing it. This place had seen the setting of social gatherings and plays in uncertain summers. Pierrot had twirled there with his Columbine; nymphs had danced to music relayed by Roy Smith from grey speaking boughs; Paris had found the apple of his eye; the flags of all nations had flapped on parade, and Titania had met her Oberon in the dangerous moonlight of a gathering midsummer storm.

In the Garden, the watcher was moving away to the House and out-buildings, to a re-union which was sadly slender, for the faces, seen dimly in the dusk, belong to young, flushed teenagers, the new Taptonians. To move among them was to feel a stranger. Voices pounding out Pop amply filled the colour-filtered air: on the stage, their times' image, a Group. The other, more enduring, group to which he had belonged had long since been disbanded. But some of them somewhere may perhaps remember the companionship of the House, the times of freedom on sunlit slopes, and the constant trees whose repose was only the more enhanced by those other voices chasing each other among the leaves, their pockets bulging beechnuts and their hearts in a flutter when summer brought out skirts of blue and glances blushing to be won.

Tapton As I See It

Margaret Martin U6A - The Taptonian 1966

Tapton evokes many different sentiments in me, depending on whether I consider Tapton to be merely a building, situated in glorious surroundings, or a school where I spent seven years of my life. These different aspects must be dealt with individually in order to present a complete picture of 'Tapton as I see it'.

Before I saw Tapton for the first time, I had subconsciously formed an opinion of what I expected a secondary school to be like. Because Tapton is so individual, my first feelings on visiting the school were disappointment mingled with surprise and admiration. I was disappointed as I had imagined all secondary schools to be rather forbidding, formal buildings, in which, owing to few distractions, one did very little apart from work. Tapton lacked the atmosphere which tended to associate with a school. I, on my first visit, could not help but notice the air of warmth and friendliness which pervaded the building. This was partly due to the architectural design, which is, of course, that of a large manor, not of a school.

The wooded park and beautiful gardens impressed me greatly, for they possess an almost unrivalled splendour and serenity. Even though I am, by now, used to the

155

surroundings at Tapton, I cannot fail to appreciate the beauty of them for they are equally impressive when they are covered with a blanket of snow in winter, as when they are filled with a glorious display of multi-coloured, sweet-scented roses and other flowers in summer. During my first-year at Tapton, I soon discovered that the park and gardens were not merely ornamental, but useful also, for the sloping park provides an excellent sledge-run during the winter months and the sunken-lawn proves an excellent setting for the annual Commemoration Day service.

When I have left Tapton, I shall often re-visit the school and I shall realise, as I look at the house, that it was during my seven years of education there that my character was moulded in many ways, as is perhaps natural when one spends so long in such influential surroundings. The atmosphere in and around Tapton cannot fail to affect each individual, and it is the duty of every Taptonian 'to carry its serenity into whatsoever part of the world they may chance to inhabit.'

During school holidays, I occasionally visit Tapton, and I am struck by the fact that, despite many modern additions, the school still retains much of its old-world charm. It is so easy to imagine it as a stately home, and as several 'noble men and gracious women have dwelt in and loved this House', it seems an ideal place for a 'Son et Lumiere'.

Tapton is not merely a brick building which stands sedately on a wooded hill, but a school comprised of separate members (i.e. staff and pupils), all of whom are an essential part of one, and although one is not constantly aware of this, it is true to say of a person who has ever spent any length of time in the school: 'Once a Taptonian, always a Taptonian.'

Tapton As They See It

Sheila Gaunt, Christine Thompson, Philip Rooke, Susan Bradshaw, Lynn Annetts, Maureen Holmes, Margaret Martin, Joyce Needham, Michael Johnson, Peter Trickett, Christine Bombroffe, Jane Pygall, Robert Taylor and Elizabeth Pearson - The Taptonian 1966

Despite the wide variety of treatments and the great range of feeling evoked, the majority speak with one voice of the beauty of our surroundings and of the incalculable but real effect upon our minds of such beauty.

———::———

First Impressions

Little do we realise that the first steps we take into the school gates at Tapton House lead us to signing a pledge of dedicating our lives to the happiness of the English people.

Tapton House, standing regally on the top of a wooded mound, may conjure up for those unfortunate enough to know it, impressions of a draughty mansion, a store house, or at best a block of offices.

My first impression of the school, as I wandered up the drive and approached the main entrance, was that of a fine mansion, but as I strode round the side of the house and past the headmaster's study, my impression changed. Two satchels were hurled out of the window and landed at my feet. I was at Tapton, the School.

As I look at the house now, I do not know what to think. One minute all is quiet and peaceful, the birds sing in the Peace Gardens and the flowers blow in the cool breeze; and then the bell goes, teachers and pupils rush to the doors, and Tapton erupts once more into everyday routine.

Twilight

Now, the school, especially in the twilight, looks old, romantic and deserted. This, to me, is a really enchanting sight. On the park, the occasional dog may appear, accompanied by his master who is enjoying his nightly stroll. In the woods, the tall majestic oak trees sway gently in the cool breeze. Homely sparrows harbour in their bold inviting boughs, while other members of their species hop around in the courtyard searching for odd scraps of food. The classrooms stand bleak and empty. The floors are swept clean and all the chairs sit upside down on top of the desks, waiting for further use. The only signs of recent occupation are the chalk marks on the blackboards. All doors are locked, the school barred to intruders. These sights are both pleasant and peaceful.

Through The Seasons

In the Spring, when the daffodils are in full bloom, the school surroundings certainly do look inviting, but with the flowers come the wasps and bees. Nothing caused more irritation in a lesson than a wasp. As it buzzes round the class, pupils dodge out of its way. The teacher tells his pupils that it is better to sit still, then it will go away. He soon contradicts his advice, however, when the wasp bombards him and he is inclined to race for the blackboard duster to extinguish the flame of excitement in the class.

When walking through the grounds, it is not difficult to imagine young ladies dressed in crinoline gowns of silk and expensive lace, being courted by young gentlemen clothed in suits made in Saville Row, and golden carriages with red velvet seat covers and decorated with horses' heads, being pulled by a team of snow-white horses equally well-attired. Now, in their places, are pupils studying, laughing, playing and talking, but just as happy in the environs of Tapton and enjoying the specialities of the grounds, which always provide an interesting walk, no matter how well one keeps to the paths.

Friends

To me it seems natural that if one's surroundings are dull and dingy, one's work is also non-descript and utterly depressing. Perhaps this is why Tapton is so successful at enlivening characters and stimulating friendships.

————::————

Many others extol, some in exaggerated terms, the friendliness of the school, the readiness to befriend newcomers, innumerable acts of kindness from seniors to juniors, the trouble members of staff take to help their pupils, particularly those whom they tutor. The large majority find this a friendly school and derive more benefits from this feature than from any other aspect of Tapton. Not everyone's spectacles, I am glad to say, are tinted.

Commemoration Day

Commemoration Day is not a reality; we all loathe it. We are all quite polite and say the right thing, at the right time. But we are really acting. As in a play, the characters are made to look real, but underneath, they are entirely different people. Foreigners looking at our work, people who are not really interested at all; they come to wear their new hat, or speak to Mr Brown about their holidays abroad. Is this Tapton House?

The real Tapton House is the every-day happenings: Mr Pearson losing his temper, everybody losing their temper, even pupils; the little crowds that gather to relay the local news; the smile on Mrs Lean's face when someone throws a paper aeroplane; the smile that turns into a shout. In the real school, everyone knows each other's weaknesses, their faults, and their eccentricities. We all fight one another, with words, yet let anyone speak against Tapton and a uniformed army turns against them. As the head Boy (I think Miss Wildin told him to) very cleverly remarked, 'Not so much a school, more a way of life'

————::————

Naturally, the fiercest opposition turns against the proposal to absorb the School in a re-organisation that would overwhelm its identity and remove it from Tapton Hill. Some, indeed, waxed militant and rhetorical. Would they agree with the following picture?

————::————

I have heard Tapton described as a holiday camp and I think this can be applied to the school as a whole. The school stands in well-kept spacious grounds with free amusements and a miniature zoo. The place swarms with 'black coats' who make sure everyone is where they should be. Finally, all those who are caught breaking out of 'camp' are rewarded with an extra length of time in it, with plenty to do during this period.

————::————

Few of the critics are whimsical. Most seriously point to difficulties of running a large school with too few large rooms and most therefore overcrowded. They marvel at the success attained despite material handicaps.

————::————

Sport

Even with the constant threat of becoming part of the comprehensive system we can still provide a six-cup winning team on sports day; we can, although by far the smallest school, still provide excellent competition against tough opposition in the North-East Derbyshire sports, and although our tennis team is not, as yet, at Wimbledon standard, our cross-country team is second to none. This, the unfailing and dauntless spirit of Tapton, never ceases to astound me and truly lives up to its motto.

The football pitch at School is ideally situated and perfectly flat but the drainage is terrible. This is not because there is a lack of drains under the pitch but because above the drains is a layer of clay, which does not allow water to pass through it. On the other hand, the football pitch at Lockoford Lane has excellent drainage, because, unfortunately, the pitch is on a slope.

Because the cricket pitch is also uneven it is unsafe to play on without fear of being struck by the ball.

The lack of proper games facilities does not finish there, for the hall, which is used as a gymnasium, is far too small for the number of boys who sometimes have to use it. This is not only inconvenient, but also very dangerous.

A Summary:

We pupils have much to be thankful for at Tapton. The huge park, the education, the peace and quiet, the lenient rules and yet the strict discipline, the right of each pupil to speak for himself and to become an individual are a few advantages among the many. Why should anyone wish to destroy this unity and the advantages given to Tapton pupils?

Traditions at Tapton

Gaye Hadfield 1967 - 1974

Buildings often seem to influence the culture of an organisation. Tapton House was built as a home, and even as a large school there was always that family feeling to the place; teachers took on the role of parents and the students never grew up but that's what made the place special. That together with the location, standing on a large hill overlooking the surrounding area. The hill brought lots of differences: if you were late everyone in the school could see you legging it up the hill; when it snowed tobogganing was an official sport for games afternoons and the canteen became depleted of trays which were used as makeshift sledges; we were all fitter for the exercise but many compensated for this by smoking in the numerous hideaways the environment provided.

It was a great shame the school didn't play rugby, we all had so much scrummaging practise. Firstly there was getting in and out of the school building. Being a very grand house in its day, Tapton had both the beautiful, wide, wooden front staircase and the functional, narrow, steep, stone, back staircase, the latter presumably used originally only by servants. For the first four years of school life one was destined to use the back stairs which had clearly not been built to accommodate large numbers of raucous students. The teachers mostly seemed to hide in the staffroom during the great exits from and returns to the school, and who can blame them? Although there were exceptions and I remember the usually softly spoken Mr Routledge always tried to restore order if he was in the vicinity. Staff, fifth and sixth formers had the luxury of using the front stairs; a more equal distribution of numbers between the two staircases would have improved safety, but our early years gave us all a good training in negotiating large crowds.

Secondly there was the fight to get on one of the three double-decker buses that waited at the bottom of the hill each day to take pupils into town on their journey home. I suppose that the total capacity of the buses was less than two hundred so when school finished at 3.45 and over five hundred of us charged down the hill to secure a seat on one of the buses it was a case of survival of the fittest.

Finally there were the tuck shop queues. The tuck shop operated from a window in the domestic science room; boys and girls had separate queues, the boys' queue was always shorter, and streetwise girls got the boys to make purchases for them. Order in the queues frequently broke down as the time to return to lessons approached and would-be customers realised they were unlikely to get served. Again, it was frequently

Mr Routledge who stepped in to the breech to restore order, or when all else failed slammed the sash-window shut and declared the shop shut. However rowdy the queues it was the resultant litter that finally caused the tuck shop to be closed for the final time. Being located in a public park, litter was always a cause for concern and in the end Mr Pearson, the headmaster, decided the root cause of the litter problem would have to go. I don't think any of us really thought of the school grounds as a public park; we never saw a member of the public, probably because we were all so tough and threatening no one would choose to visit when the pupils were out.

Generally the school had a bad press, but never more so than after our production of *She Stoops to Conquer* in 1972 (or 1973) when the Derbyshire Times published a slating report of the performance. I was in the play and even my parents struggled to say anything good about it, so it must have been awful. Nevertheless no one approved of the press criticising children and the Derbyshire Times decided not to review school plays in future, which was a shame, because the following year we put on an excellent performance (the cast's opinion) of Peter Ustinov's *Photofinish* and it would have been nice to see a press review.

Although the school didn't play rugby, sport had a significant influence on school life; if you were good at games, gymnastics or athletics you were valued. The same is true of so many educational establishments, and the house system at Tapton increased the profile of these activities. I wasn't good at any of them but I realised it would improve my standing in the school if I was involved, so I tried hard and represented the school at hockey, tennis and athletics. But no amount of effort could conceal the fact that I couldn't catch, so I was never in the running for the netball or rounders teams. One of the great joys of playing for the tennis team was to see the expressions on the faces of the opposition when they saw our sloping tennis courts; they could truly not believe that they were expected to play on such a steep gradient. Just one of the many interesting quirks that being positioned on the top of a hill brought.

Mr Denman, the games master, tried to improve our social skills and his Friday lunchtime discos were the envy of every school in the borough. Dancing, he believed was a key skill in life, so on the winter days when poor weather prevented games taking place, but there was no snow for sledging, it was into the hall for ballroom dancing. It began with the girls lining up on one side of the hall and the boys on the other and was followed by the most mortifying experience; one by one the boys selected their partners. Oh the agony of waiting to be chosen. All the practising culminated in the Christmas school parties, one for each year, held in the evenings just before the holidays and they were great fun. We talked of nothing other than our planned outfits for weeks before. Along with his influence on the physical activities of the school Mr Denman made every effort to maintain standards within the school; if your behaviour or appearance didn't meet his requirements he let you know in no uncertain terms, and usually in public. He was a respected and influential member of the family and helped to maintain discipline.

I could not talk about influential teachers without mentioning Miss Wildin. She retired while I was at Tapton and was greatly missed. She always appeared to be an ogre, but no one who had contact with her had anything but good to say about her. She combined those wonderful attributes of fairness, firmness and caring but we were all terrified of her because we knew there would never be any fooling her; she knew your thoughts before you did. I remember being reported by fellow students for cheating in an exam. I lied to the member of staff who subsequently interrogated me over this and I got away with it but you can be sure there would have been no deceiving Miss Wildin. She made sure everyone realised the consequences of their actions without ever devaluing them as individuals and took on the really difficult tasks, like dealing with hysterical girls who had been playing with a Ouija-board in one of the haunted classrooms. Most of the classrooms were in the original house so there were lots of rumours of ghosts of past occupants, particularly in the Stephenson Room, though I'm not sure George actually died there.

There was only one death at the school that I remember during my stay - Tony Grafton, a dear friend whose life was brought to a tragic end as the result of a road traffic accident. He was a talented footballer and full of humour; I'm sure everyone who knew him would wish him to be remembered in this book.

Finally, I would like to take this opportunity to thank all the staff and friends who educated, influenced and advised me during those critical years. A true tutorial system operated whilst I was at the school, a rarity then and virtually extinct in state schools now, and I'm sure many of us benefited from it. I'm sorry the building is no longer a school. Many young people are missing the chance of having an education in beautiful, historic surroundings and furtive fun in the gardens, woods and air-raid shelters that make up the grounds of Tapton House.

Ghosts and After Reorganisation

Merv Lambert 1967 - 1991

The following account was related to me by Mr Pearson, who was headmaster at Tapton House School for fifteen of my twenty-six years there as a member of staff. I understand it took place in the 1930s.

Early one morning the caretaker's wife was at the bottom of the stone (or servants') staircase, when she was confronted by a man in old fashioned dress on the stairs. He demanded, 'Where is my shaving water?' Frightened, she ran to find her husband, and told him what had happened. He immediately went with her to the stone stairs, but there was nothing unusual there, no ghost to be seen. They reported the incident to the headmaster of the time, and he invited them both into his study. Taking a book from a shelf or cupboard, he opened it at a certain page and pointed to a print. He asked the caretaker's wife if that was the man she had seen. She replied that it was. The headmaster then informed the couple that it was a print of George Stephenson.

Nearly everyone connected with the school knows that the great railway pioneer lived for the last six years of his life at Tapton House, and that he died there in his bedroom on the first floor, a room on the middle corridor. When my wife went to teach there in 1964, she was in the middle of a lesson in that very room (then known as the Stephenson Room), when the solid wood door swung open of its own accord. Nobody came in. My wife said, 'Who's there?' The class chorused, 'It's George!' She, being new to the place, asked, 'George who?' to be answered with 'George Stephenson!' The door had mysteriously swung to again. I myself experienced the same phenomenon in later years, although I did not need to ask who was there. I think that George probably did not care much for French and departed quickly.

Towards the end of Tapton House's time as a school, in the academic year 1988-89 I came to hear via a colleague another story, which, unbeknown to me, involved myself. He was taking a class in Year 11. The class discussion happened to lead to the following story. A rather quiet girl, bright but not particularly imaginative, related that one morning she had been waiting outside Room 4 in the middle corridor (the rooms had been renumbered some years before). Room 4 was directly opposite the Stephenson Room, and, as mentioned before, the doors of the rooms on the middle corridor were of solid wood and had no glass panes in them. At that time she was the only pupil in that particular German class. She said that she did not know whether I had arrived and was perhaps already in the classroom. Therefore she opened the door and looked in. Sitting at a table at the back of the room was a girl with long blond hair and wearing a high-necked, long white dress. She was writing. 'Oh! Sorry', said my pupil, and closed the door. Shortly afterwards I arrived, greeted her, opened the door, and we went in. There was nobody else in the room. The windows were closed, and the only access to that first floor room was through the single door. However, the girl said nothing to me about all this at the time. It was some days or maybe even weeks later that I was able to ask her about this other ghost. In fact, whether you believe her story or not (and I am quite certain she had not foreseen this) I was able to discuss this ghost story with her as part of her recorded German oral exam later in the year. It provided an unusual topic for the examiner to listen to, certainly more interesting than most.
It is a well-known fact that Tapton House was for as period of about 6 years a girls' private boarding school in the latter part of the nineteenth century. Could this other ghost have been catching up on some work from that time?

163

These are but a few of my own very happy memories of a very happy school. The high regard and affection felt by former members of the school were evident on the occasion of the school's 60th anniversary held in 1991. The car parks at the top of the hill were full, and there were cars parked on the grass on both sides of the road leading up the hill. The house itself was crowded, and I was delighted to meet Sally Johnson, whom I had taught in the sixth form in 1976. She had driven up from London just to be there.

When Tapton lost its sixth form in the early 1980s due to reorganisation, for a year the students who would have been in the next sixth form, but who had had to go elsewhere for their A level studies, kept coming back to see us. They really wanted to stay at Tapton. It was rather like a haunting. They were constantly in the background, attending school functions, and keeping friendships going. Perhaps, if it is not too romantic a notion, there was almost a feeling of some kind of paradise lost. I too believe that Tapton House School was rather special.

Lost - Miss Lowe (THS 1941 - 1968)

Miss Pennington - The Taptonian 1968

There is no doubt about it: something has disappeared from the women's staffroom - something of bulk. The desk near the window has been stripped of its normal gear; the room is empty, silent, undisturbed by gusts or irrepressible mirth seeping through from Room 9. And it is no use sending out an appeal for its return. We know where it is - comfortably stretched out at length on a settee in front of a warm fire avidly reading every newspaper she can get her hands on, or watching *Schools Programmes* and *Watch with Mother*, or acquiring all the background information she needs for her visit to Greece in the Spring, a follow-up to a visit to Rome in September which she enjoyed with the enjoyment of one who can at last satisfy to the full her insatiable curiosity about people and places.

For the school the loss is irreplaceable because Miss Lowe was what is commonly called a character. (During the forty years I have known her, in the holiday-new-acquaintances-guessing-game of 'What is your occupation?' no one ever guessed that she was a teacher.) The secret of her popularity with both children and staff lay in her being always herself, and so you knew exactly where you were with her. As a result, every relationship she formed was anchored in a feeling of security. That self was full of vitality: she not only loved the school, she enjoyed every moment of her 27 years teaching here. Every child she dealt with was an individual; every lesson she taught - geography, Economics or Current Affairs - was an adventure in personal communication. She was a mine of information on all sorts of topics, information acquired as a result of assiduous reading. She herself irreverently said of her self that she was a rag-bag of scraps, an unjust assessment because it was the ability to dip into the bran-tub for the right illustration at the right moment which helped to stimulate the children's interest and cause them to make the right 'connection'.

She believed in the therapeutic value of work for work's sake. Woe betide the child who did not hand in his homework at the right time, or who did not report before school started to be trained to read a passage of scripture in assembly. Yet the back-sliders held her in the highest respect for they knew that she exercised justice without fear or favour; justice, to her, was even-handed (though I do believe that you had a greater chance of a larger slice of mercy if you were a boy with long eye-lashes and a charming smile).

Most of all perhaps we miss the leaven of her sense of humour which penetrated every phase of school life. Many is the time that a whole class has been helpless with mirth; many the time that we have not heard a knock on the staff-room door so loud have been the howls of laughter within; many is the time that an awkward contre-temps has been averted by the humorous aside from Miss Lowe.

She was large in every way, large in size, large in personality, large in mirth, large in kindness. An old student, Des Baker, will remember coming to the staff-room, having retrieved a personal belonging of hers which she was in the habit of leaving behind, for she was an untidy creature, and saying to the assembled staff, 'Aunty Dorothy's handbag!' She was in fact the large universal aunty of the whole school.

Long may she enjoy her retirement, happy in the knowledge that thousands of young people will remember her with deep affection and have a more balanced sense of perspective as a result of her influence.

Miss M Pennington (THS 1942 - 1968)

Jean Davey - The Taptonian 1968

A formidable player of hockey and tennis, a beautiful, exhibition-standard dancer (particularly of the tango), and an inexhaustible hill-walker. Few people who have known Miss Pennington in the latter part of her career only would associate these activities with her, but in a way they illustrate the varied and contradictory side of her personality which have been carefully concealed by her during her years at Tapton. Self-effacing to a fault, she had an intense loathing of publicity and the icy winds of disapproval will undoubtedly play around Tapton when she realises she is the subject of this article.

The apparent contradictions are many. Not everyone realises that under that seemingly frail physique lies a spirit of tempered steel and an indomitable courage which brought her back to Tapton within a term of a disastrous accident in which her skull was fractured.

Likewise, no one enviously regarding that incredibly slim figure would suspect her consuming passion for chocolate and cream cakes. Though she has a strong aesthetic sense, and an intense love of painting (provided it is not too modern), her own artistic ability - or lack of it - resulted in her being thrown out of art class at school - but did not prevent her teaching art at Tapton during a period of acute staff shortage. Her knowledge of English and French grammar is phenomenal, as generations of Taptonians know, but she still maintains that she cannot understand the simplest Latin construction. She has a profound love for and knowledge of music, but she insists that she can neither sing - nor play a note - except for the combs! She must be one of the few people in Chesterfield who have a permanent booking at the Civic Theatre from the day it opened, but wild horses would not drag her on to a stage.

Outwardly calm and unruffled (except when the famous temper flashes out) and often apparently detached from her surroundings, she actually has a most keen perception, a penetrating understanding and an astringent wit, which is the more devastating for being so unexpected. She has a completely analytical and unsentimental approach to life, but that does not prevent her from having a very deep affection for all young things - human as well as animal, including the many generations of Taptonians into whom she has most diligently endeavoured to hammer the rudiments of the French language.

She has served Tapton faithfully for over twenty years - in the early days playing a considerable part in the social life of the school. She has been an indefatigable collector of 'props' for school plays, and the silver house plays trophy bears witness to her keen interest in drama at Tapton. She has been an assiduous - if reluctant - organiser of French exhibitions for past Commemoration Days. She has taken part in several school journeys abroad in the days when they were full of unexpected incidents and excitement, and has always shown a keen appreciation of their funnier moments, intentional or otherwise. Someone should persuade her to write her memoirs of some of the richer moments in Tapton's history, including a most memorable and hilarious visit to Bavaria.

Most conscientious and punctilious (her stock-books and registers have always been kept with awe-inspiring efficiency), she has a real devotion to Tapton's interests and has at times been deeply distressed at what she has felt to be a falling off of standards in some directions.

Last year's difficulties in the French department caused by Mr Ashton's long illness were a great strain on her health and spirits, and undoubtedly influenced her decision to retire, but no one need doubt that her courage and resilience will soon bring her back to the top of her form.

A rare bird - not easy to get to know or appreciate, but the long procession of pupils past and present who have knocked on the door of her new house, either bringing flowers for her birthday, or offering to hammer nails, change fuses or lay carpets, shows that as usual, Taptonians recognise quality when they see it, and that their affection for her can outlast their school-days.

To her friends her departure has been a sad blow - but at least we can derive comfort from the fact that she has decided to settle in Chesterfield, so that we shall not lack her very individual presence at Tapton's public occasions.

Miss P Wildin (THS 1936 - 1968)

Jacqueline Sanderson - The Taptonian 1969

Paying tribute, like testimonials, can be a difficult task, ranging from having to say something about practically nothing, to having to select from sufficient material to fill a book. To write about Miss Wildin is to give one the latter exercise, so where does one start? At the beginning? No! - there isn't space for that and it isn't necessary. Miss Wildin has never been out of date or, really, any different, and all who know her, whether aged fifteen or fifty, recognise the same person - a strong character and personality, with considerable drive and enthusiasm. No task has ever seemed too much for her or beyond her capabilities and one still wonders just what form of 'immovable object' could match this 'irresistible force'. No one could have brought William Shakespeare and his characters more vividly to life than Miss Wildin. Can't you hear her speak these lines of Nick Bottom in *A Midsummer Night's Dream* - these lines, representative of her own spirit and range of ability?

'Let me play Thisbe too; I'll speak in a monstrous little voice'...'let me play the lion too. I will roar, that it will do any man's heart good to hear me'

In the daily round we've heard the 'roaring lion' shake the rafters, but we've also experienced the 'monstrous little voice' and the quiet words of advice and understanding. In Miss Wildin was to be found the versatility and variety of approach so necessary in the successful teacher. Not only were her lessons, whether grammar or Shakespeare, pleasurable and rewarding to attend, but each pupil, whether 'backward' or 'forward' enjoyed being a person to her. Her prime interest was in the lives of her pupils, who she always appreciated could be so different and so illogical as to require the individual treatment she was patient to give. One always found her firm yet friendly. She could act ruthlessly or sympathetically as occasion demanded. She could command and hold the crowd as well as the individual, she could 'get on' with the 'character' without condoning his behaviour. She had a variety of weapons in her armoury, used effectively and correctly in defence or attack.

In her earlier years, Miss Wildin did much successful pioneer work with backward children and she always championed the cause of those who found life difficult for whatever reason. One was ever conscious of her delight at the ultimate success of an apparent 'failure' and equally conscious of her self-criticism and disappointment when her efforts seemed fruitless. Miss Wildin was a teacher in the fullest sense, working 'with' her students, who in her opinion should be given every opportunity to prove themselves. She would bristle at the suggestion that anyone, however poor, was a 'write-off' and she deplored public criticism of an individual's failure or shortcomings. One need not here dilate on Miss Wildin's countless activities in school and outside, and one has only to mention her name in this district to realise that it is synonymous with 'excellence' in the field of drama.

In her latter years at school Miss Wildin experienced difficulties domestically and physically, but despite these she continued undeterred. Her demanding work as senior mistress, her excellent play productions, her lively 'tonic' teaching and numerous other tasks lost none of their original and usual effectiveness and vitality. Despite rheumatism in her knee and neck, she climbed the stairs and walked out to the satellite rooms, expecting no special consideration.

Many of us here, whether staff or student, are among countless numbers who are indebted to Miss Wildin, for her help, advice and encouragement spread over many years. We salute a worthy Taptonian, thank her for her unique efforts and wish her a happy and healthy retirement.

Miss Wildin - As I Knew Her

Michael Kerry, U6 - The Taptonian 1969

Don't say 'Learn 'em', Toad,' said the Rat, greatly shocked. 'It's not good English.'

'What are you always nagging at Toad for?' inquired the Badger rather peevishly. 'What's the matter with his English? It's the same what I use myself, and if it's not good enough for me, it ought to be good enough for you!'

'I'm very sorry, said the Rat humbly. 'Only I think it ought to be 'teach 'em,' not 'learn 'em'.'

But we don't want to teach 'em!' replied the Badger. 'We want to learn 'em - learn 'em! And what's more, we're going to do it, too!'

There I was, poor child, in the middle of a first form class, my primary school innocence untarnished, sitting in absolute horror and astonishment at this senior English mistress leaping about frantically behind the teacher's desk, glasses on end of nose and arms dancing like an octopus!

...And that was the first time that I had met Miss Wildin, cum Rat, cum Toad, cum Badger.

Mr Grahame's above conversation might well have been a dialogue between the inseparable dynamic duo of Wildin and Lowe, for they too cared and 'teachin' 'em' and 'learnin' 'em'. And like Miss Lowe, Miss Wildin had her own inimitable way of 'learnin' 'em'.

Throughout the seven years I have known her, Miss Wildin has been a pillar of strength to Tapton. Her indomitable spirit, in the most hum-drum of daily routine, has been an example that many pupils have respected and sought to emulate. It was this driving force within her that, at times, made her seem as hard as a nail. Her unwavering determination to succeed might have been mistaken for an unsympathetic nature, by someone who did not recognise the 'Wildin bark' which summoned everyone to attention.

Yet the silence that has prevailed whilst she spoke in school assembly was not just the result of her disciplinary command of the school, it was an acknowledgment of respect for her by every child in the school. Many people speak of the younger generation having no respect for their elders, yet it has respect for those who earn it.

Miss Wildin believed that every child should have dignity. She once nearly lost her job for refusing to make pupils march into town in army formation. She had special beliefs about the nature of a Taptonian - courage and strength, steadfastness in thought and deed, purity and honour in intent and act - 'that these should be the distinguishing virtues of a true child of this house'. To these she added one more virtue, the generosity of the Taptonian. Time after time, her own charitable nature has influenced pupils into opening up their hearts, in kindness for the mentally handicapped children, who, as she was quick to point out, are so less fortunate than ourselves.

Occasionally, in school life, 'something happens', and when it does the result is usually detention or more homework. But, when that 'something' is a 'big something', then the ultimate deterrent must be used - a 'talk' with Miss Wildin. There are two sides to justice, and Miss Wildin knew them both. Any unfairness to a pupil brought the Counsel for Defence into the headmaster's study, where it prosecuted.

Acting as an unpaid Marjorie Proops for both boys and girls was one of her side-lines. With the deep sincerity and understanding she possessed, Miss Wildin was able to help many people in mental torment to solve their problems. She took a personal involvement in the lives of her pupils that induced a relationship of mutual trust. She was able to communicate with young people, and that means more than just 'teach 'em' or 'learn 'em'.

Besides having a grin like a Cheshire cat, she had a full repertoire of facial expressions that could 'take the mickey' out of any person or situation whenever she wanted - and usually she wanted. Staff and pupils alike often felt that they were being 'got at', but could not prove it because she never actually said anything - hers was a subtle humour.

Apart from being the effervescent character she was, the contribution Miss Wildin made to school life at Tapton was immeasurable. Her unselfish devotion to the school meant hours of work outside the normal timetable. Sometimes the strain must have been almost overwhelming, but to show weakness or give up was something alien to her nature.

You will notice that I refer to Miss Wildin in the past tense. This is really inexcusable, for although she is no longer a member of the teaching staff, her spirit of 'tenacity in all things' still prevails at Tapton, and will do, I am sure, for many more years, such were the unlimited bounds of Miss Wildin's influence.

As I Remember Her

Elaine Brazell, L6 - The Taptonian 1969

How could one possibly forget her? I can see her now taking off her glasses with a slow exaggerated movement of the arm, slamming them on the desk, pushing her smoky-grey hair from her forehead with the same hand, in a movement which portrayed deep frustration at our stupidity, with the result that we became rooted to our seats, in expectation of the storm, after the thunder and lightning. And what did we get? Certainly no storm, but only the now cool, calm, collected, explanatory voice of Miss Wildin.

She has the most piercing crystal-blue eyes I have ever seen. I often fancied she saw more than met the average person's eye - perhaps this was because her experience of life gave her extra insight into other people's lives.

There radiated from her grace and nobility, too. I remember her personality as being fair and honest. She believed in the capabilities of us young folk. She believed that our ideas - although often way out - were practicable and often better then those set down by our elders. She believed in us and we in her. Often when we were floundering on the beach of trouble she would rescue us, reprimand us, explain why, and then place us back into the flow of life again, with her watchful eye upon us, ever-ready.

I often think I spent most of my time in her lessons taking note of her rather than taking note of what she was trying to teach me. Her full mouth and beautiful white teeth fascinated me; the movement of her hands soothed me; the glare in her eyes scared me.

Wherever she goes she will have an effect upon people. They will find themselves thinking of her and of the things she did - little things like smoking a cigarette, laughing at making a joke. A fantastically interesting person! Someone I would almost wish to model myself upon if I believed in that sort of thing. As it is, I do not wish to be like her, but only to have people remember her - the way I remember her; for as a teacher, I admired her; as an authority, I bent the knee to her; and as a person, I liked her, and like her still!

David Ashton (THS 1946 - 1969)

Paul Webster - The Taptonian 1969

Many readers of this magazine will remember David Ashton as a man waging constant battle against ill health, a battle which severely limited his activity and participation in the life of the school. Knowing him in his latter years, one may find it difficult to imagine him as an active man, though of course the young find this difficult in any case when assessing the older generation. David played for the staff at cricket and he enjoyed walking. He was quite an expert in folk dancing and was devoted to the arts, finding intense pleasure in the theatre and in music. He was a prolific reader and was well informed and up-to-date in most topics of modern thinking. His mental ability was exceptional. He was a 'memory man' and had something of a photographic mind, able to reproduce, almost word perfect, anything he had heard or read. David Ashton was undoubtedly in the Brain of Britain class.

Mrs Ashton was a regular visitor to our school functions and it was fitting that we should entertain her and her husband to lunch at Christmas and afterwards to coffee in the Library, where the presentation of a retirement gift was made and we expressed our appreciation of Mr Ashton's services.

Relieved of the pressure of the daily round which had become very exhausting for him, we hoped that Mr and Mrs Ashton would enjoy some years of happy retirement together, but that was not to be and shortly after Christmas, 1969, following another spell in hospital, David Ashton died.

A struggle against odds had come to an end and we admired the courage and tenacity of the man who had been involved in it and we were not unaware too of the strain imposed upon his family, and whilst they were relieved of this strain and David of further suffering, the final parting was no easier and we offer our sincerest sympathy to Mrs Ashton and her family in their sad loss.

Robert D Furber (THS 1948 - 1969)

Peter Wheatcroft - The Taptonian 1969

Robert D Furber was a first-class craftsman who never really found scope for his ability in the confines of a school art room. Taptonians generally associated him with his specialist subject and only those who succeeded in really getting to know him realised the extent of his technical skill. Refer him to the expense of having a car overhauled, a watch repaired, new tiles put on the roof, and you at once got the answer 'do it yourself' and he meant it. An unobtainable spare part for an obsolete machine? Buy a lathe and make it yourself! Visit the house and workshop at Chandler Hill and you realised that R D Furber was able to practise what he preached. He was a modest man, never regarded his craftsmanship as exceptional and sincerely considered his advice as being within the capabilities of anybody with common sense. Engineering problems absorbed him and filled him with wonderment that left us behind. To him, the movement or method of operation of some part of a machine was a thing of beauty; a polished cam-shaft adorned with its bearings, big ends and other appendages would merit a place of honour in any lounge - Beautiful? Of course!

Plants, greenhouses, trees, shrubs, flowers and wild life equally absorbed him, and as he lifted his glasses to take a closer look at the inside of a 'stopped' wristlet watch or the blemished petal of a flower one was conscious of his intense interest in the technical and natural worlds. It was significant that he should choose the latest in automatic food mixers as a retirement gift. At his presentation, his first action was to take it apart and explain how it worked, not failing to mention its aesthetic and technical shortcomings.

Of the 'old school' upbringing, R D Furber had an intense dislike for waste of material. He will be remembered for counting the brushes with gradually shortening bristles, for checking the paint, the plasticine, the paper, the pencils and other paraphernalia, - not always appreciated by those in the process of being trained or those craving the gay abandon of free expression, but certainly appreciated by those who hold the purse strings and those who advocate temperance in all things.

As many know it became increasingly difficult for Mr Furber to get about and a period of indifferent health over the past few years curtailed his activities and brought about his early retirement. Mrs Furber, herself an artist and sharing her husband's love of the natural world, was often to be seen at our functions. We appreciated her interest and along with our thanks to Mr Furber for his long service to the school we would wish them both many happy, healthy years of retirement together.

Phil Wildin

Ann Wheatcroft, niece of Phil Wildin

You have asked me to talk about Phil Wildin, my aunt. This is rather sad for me because

Phil Wildin

174

I was very close to her and she meant a great deal to me.

One of the things that I owe to her more than anything, as I believe most students at Tapton did, was the fact that she gave to me an appreciation of English literature - particularly of Shakespeare.

I was taken by her at the age of seven, to London, to see John Gielgud and Gwen Frangcon-Davies in *Macbeth*. Now everybody said, in those days, that a child of seven was much too young to appreciate such a play. When I tell you that I can still almost remember the entire cast word perfect, that I can quote that Scottish play almost entirely, all the way through, you will know what an effect it had on me. I think, in fact I know, that it shocked both Phil and Dorothy that I had taken it on board in the way I had. Now, if that experience affected me the way it did, I can only imagine what it must have been like to be taught by her to appreciate those plays and English in general because somehow she could enthuse you with the essence of what you were learning at the time.

Another great high, as far as plays and literature and Phil went, was her production of *Murder in the Cathedral*. Now I didn't know T S Eliot by the time Phil did it in the hall. I had a very poor education, I hated school, we had an English mistress who, if you didn't get anything right in poetry made you write the poem out over and over again. She would, without Phil's help, have ruined any appreciation of English literature whatsoever.

My entire appreciation of literature is from Phil. That play is now part of my life. The whole appreciation of T S Eliot has come because I enjoyed that production. I have seen *Murder in the Cathedral* about three times since, with professionals, and none has had the same effect as that production had that Phil produced, and although the children acted absolutely brilliantly it was the way it was produced. I shall never forget one of the knights turning round, the way he said, 'And you, and you, and you are responsible.' And he said it, first of all with his back to the audience and then turns and points to the rest of the audience and says 'And you'. I have never seen that in a pro performance and it was riveting. I know that when Phil took the play to Darmstadt; she often said that it worried her how the Germans would take to it. Because it was not long after the end of the war and Germany was still a ruin in many ways and the way that play gets at people who are evil and do evil things, and the accusation in the word, 'And you'. And it worried her but she needn't have done so, because they made her very welcome and I am sure the German children would remember the play just as well as people remembered it in this country.

All her plays she did at Tapton were unbelievable. She seemed to bring out the very best in the children that acted for her and the influence of that literature shows you how important literature is to people today if only they could learn how to do it.

You asked me to tell you what it was in essence how she controlled a class or why she managed to do it. That I don't know; she just did. I think that sort of thing is a mystery in personality just as the plainest person in the world like Edith Piaf can get on to the stage and hold an audience. What makes a personality have that charisma that can make and teach people, I don't know? I think you have got to answer that question for yourself.

I can tell you a little more about her philosophy. We often had long discussions about philosophy, not religion - because religion was something Phil didn't really believe in. God was in the mind, the core of the personality. God existed most certainly for Phil. She liked Dr Jenkins (the Bishop of Durham) and his views, which upset so many churchgoers. She also, like me, read the book *Honest to God*, when it first came out, which also shocked the religious sector. Phil believed God was in all people and I think that is why she had such compassion for other people. We also had long arguments and discussions about things like chameleon personalities. We both agreed that and we both thought that we were chameleon personalities, we were all things to all people. Was it kinder to be yourself through thick and thin which in a way was to be like Dorothy or was it better still to be something different to each person?

Now coming back to Tapton there were one or two quite nice stories about Tapton House. One I remember was during the war. She used to go firewatching on the roof and used to do a stint with whoever else was on it at the same time. She had a dog at that time, called Sammy, who was an Airedale. Sammy would go with them to keep them company on the roof. One night they were up there, and as you know Tapton is supposed to be haunted. Phil never thought anything about things like that; ghosts never worried her at all until this one particular night. All of a sudden they heard footsteps and there was this tap, tap, tap of feet going down the stairs and the noise went down one floor and they went down the next. They peered down the well of that wonderful staircase and there wasn't a sign of anyone but they could still hear the noise going down the stairs. They were so frightened in the morning that they had hardly got the courage to go down. It may have been different if they had got the dog with them but they hadn't.

Anyway, in the morning, when they finally plucked up enough courage, and went down the stairs. It was broad daylight, they got almost to the bottom of the flight of stairs and there lying on one of the steps, was one of those huge dog biscuits that dogs used to have in those days. A rat had found this thing at the top of the stairs and had pulled it all the way down and left it outside a hole in the wall; these were the footsteps.

I remember, when I was very young, the amount of marking that Phil used to have to bring home. Night after night, I hardly ever saw anything of her when I used to go to stay with my Grandmother because she would be marking, long into the night. She read every essay, everything with the greatest of care; her marking meant such a great deal to her because she was well aware that those marks could damn a child, or not. So wherever she could, she would put encouraging remarks. If she had to cross a sentence out, rather than just leave it with a line through it, she would write what she thought was a better sentence or a better word underneath. If she had to correct a spelling, the same way, she did not just cross it out but she would write the correct spelling underneath - anything that would help a child wanting to learn.

She had, of course, in her very early days, taught at a school in Chesterfield, I think it was at Brambling House, but I might be wrong. She used to teach a class of seriously backward children. And so she had learned in her very early days of being a student, how to get across to these backward and difficult children. It was from there that Mr Mellor saw her and took her to Tapton. He realised that somehow she was getting through to these children and I think that had she not had that class of children like that, she might not have learnt how to teach so well.

I remember another incident. As a small child she was always very keen on literature; it was something that was born in her. She wanted to go to Sheffield to see a play but I can't remember which play; it was something that she has told me about.
In those days my Grandma was not very well off at all, my Grandfather had died and the tickets for the theatre were quite expensive and they couldn't afford the bus fare so they walked to Sheffield and they walked back. And granny went with her. They were great walkers, the whole family was. We always enjoyed walking over the Derbyshire Peak and thought nothing of walking twenty miles at the weekend. So they walked to Sheffield, they saw the play and they walked back again. Such was her dedication and that is again I think why it meant so much to her. If something does mean as much as that to you, you can usually get it across.

It wasn't just literature; art and architecture had a great influence on her. She always thought that Tapton, because it was such a beautiful place, was very important in the education of the children who went there. It had that beautiful staircase; the proportion of the rooms and the building itself left pupils with a feeling for design and beauty. She was very worried in later years that the architecture of schools became so hideous - functional, square lines, glass. There was nothing to give the children any idea of beauty and this upset her very much. She also felt that in this present day and age she couldn't have taught the way that she did; but I just wonder, there are still good teachers who get through to children however difficult they are.

She had a very great friend in Chloe Gibson, who ran Telefis Eirean in Ireland and who was a great producer of plays. Phil would go up to London or across to Ireland and would meet a great many of the actors at the theatres in Dublin and also in London. I don't think she would have minded me saying but quite a number of times things that she suggested for some of the TV productions and theatre productions were actually put into practice by Chloe Gibson.

Phil's love of the theatre was very, very great and several times people tried to persuade her to actually go on the stage. In the early days she used to go up to Hucklow to the theatre there in the days of L du Garde Peach. She played a very fine Lady Macbeth and many other parts and she did think quite seriously about leaving teaching. I think it was because she could project her personality that she could teach so well. She was very autocratic; she could be a very grand lady and I say that a little unkindly because she knew she was doing it. She could put on quite an air and pull herself up to her full height and be extremely autocratic and very frightening to me as a child to begin with. But as a member of the family, as I got older, we sometimes saw the funny side of it. She could take a joke against herself.

I will finish with one little picture of her of laughter that we all had. We were one day in Matlock, walking along the main street, there with all of the ice cream shops and cafes. There was Chloe Gibson, Dorothy Lowe, myself and Phil. Phil was wearing a very expensive, very beautifully cut, white summer frock, of which she was very proud. She had told us many times how much it had cost and we were all getting a little fed up of hearing about it. Anyway we went into a café, to get an ice cream. We sat at a table and while we were sitting there, Phil got up to go to the counter. A young man with his lady friend on his arm; I think he had been cycling, he was very pink, in shorts and was very shy. He said to Phil, could he have two large cones. The beautiful frock had been mistaken for an overall. I have never seen Phil so disconcerted - ever! You can imagine the effect it had on the three of us seated at the table. We staggered out into the street completely convulsed with laughter, unable to speak, and unable to even see - 'Corpsed' as Dorothy said, and can you hear Dorothy's infectious laugh!

We left Phil to her fate. She eventually reappeared, absolutely furious, saw us in the state we were in and of course started to laugh herself. It was typical of Phil that one of the reasons she was angry and cross was because the poor young man was so shy and it was so embarrassing to him in front of his ladyfriend. I don't know how Phil got out of the situation but I know that she would have left him very much more at his ease.

TAPTON HOUSE SCHOOL, CHESTERFIELD

ERFIELD.

School Photo 1960

180

School Governors 1960s

Back row, left to right: Lyn Harrison (head girl), Miss Wildin (deputy head), head boy, Mr Pearson deputy head, governor. Middle row: governor, Mr and Mrs Hancock (governors), Mrs Thorneycroft (governor). Front row: governor, Mr F Chettle (head), Rev Dr R Mosley Canada, Mr and Mrs Hadfield (mayor and mayoress), Mrs Mosley, Mrs Chettle.

Presentation Day 1960s V Graham, F Chettle, Dr A Stewart, W Pearson.

Commemoration Day 1960s

Girls Hockey 1961

Back row: J Broughton, K Woodroffe, S Davies, ?, ?, ? Front row: ?, J Hardwick, M Jones, ?, ?, J May.

Boys Hockey 1962

M Pucci, B Mitchell, ?, R Greatorex, R Culpin, R Wallmie, J Vintres, R Butt, Mr K Bates
Front row: Jennings, G Dell, J Mitchell, J Kerslake, ?

Athletes 1962

Back row: Mr Haslam, ?, S Huckerby, J Ellis, Mr Denman
Front row: J Kerslake, ?,?,?, Mr Chettle

Pupils and Staff 1964

including Mr L Bibbings, R Oldman, Gallagher, Mr W Pearson.

Staff 1965

Camping Holiday 1965

Back row: Mr A Hooper, ?, ?, K Pollard, ?, J Vintner, B Bailey, Mr and Mrs K Bates + child. Front row: D Burton, ?, M Fisher, ?, S Foster, ?, A Ortor, ?, J Prescott.

Athletes 1965

Includes Mr Haslam, Mr Denman, Mr Pearson, B Mitchell.

Pupils and staff 1965

Back row: Mr D Mee, R Wallace, S Beresford, J Parsons. Front row: V Graham, P Collins, J Babister, M McKelvey, Mr K Bates.

Girls hockey 1966

Back row: Mrs Clipstone, P Denman, M Beresford, A Gent, K Bingham, J Babister, F Smith. Front row: L Annetts, S Mills, E Pearson, S Gaunt, J Needham, Mr Pearson.

Athletics team which won no fewer than four trophies in the Secondary Schools Athletics Championships, held in the Queen's Park annexe, in 1966.

Left to right (boys) Walter Ellis (Boys 15-17 years Championship Trophy), John Smith and Kenneth Wilde (Robinson Trophy for the Boys Under 15 Championship), Philip Carnall and Martin Pates (Grammar School Trophy for Boys under 15 Relay). Jill Babister and Lynn Annetts (Girls 15-17 years Championship Shield), Angela Gosney (Derbyshire Times Trophy for the Under 15 Mixed Championship), Janice Platts and Felicity Smith (Senior Girls 15-17 Relay Cup, The Wragg Trophy).

Speech Day 1967

Boys trip to Germany 1967

Pupils and staff 1967

School Photo 1968

School Photo 1968

Cricket 1967/8

Back row: ?, C Parks. Middle row: J Raynes, A Poe, ?, R Walker, ?, ?, ?, ?, J Coleman. Front row: K Scoffham, K Pollard, Allison, ?, ?

Netball 1968

Lower 6th 1972

Back row: Pendleton, Carpenter, Mahoney, Bates, Stenton, Horton, Hardwick, Webster, Beeson, Baker, Watts, Hill, Brown, Patton, Robinson, Gambles, Moore, Smith, ? Middle row: Langham, Margaret #, Lizzy #, Sandra S?, Helen F?, Karen K?, Janet W?, Sandra H?, Ann J?, Janet M?, Sandra White, Enca H?, Gina L?, Helen Coe, Wendy Clark, Diane P?, Gaye Hadfield, Gillian Conway, P Ford. Front row: A Norns, J Lander, Hazel Tomlinson, A Miekle, Andrea G?, Mr Pearson, Lynne S?, Hugh Lomas, Mr Denman, Jason Styles, Zena B?, Richard Novak, Julie Wheatcroft, P Taylor.

Under 18 girls hockey 1973

Pupils and staff 1975

Pupils and staff 1976

Artroom 1991

Room 1 1991

Stairs Bottom 1991

Side Window 1991

Stairs Top 1991

Inside Entrance Hall 1991

Headmaster's Study 1991

Sunken Lawn 1991

197

Drive Window 1991

View from Entrance Hall 1991

Old Taptonians

Norman Hoddle 1936 - 1937

We OTs would not have existed without the foresight and vision of one man, Dr Stead, The Director of Education for the Borough of Chesterfield in 1929. One man's vision, that was at least seventy years ahead of his time, placed Chesterfield along with Southampton as the two leading education authorities in England at that time. They maintained and kept alive that spirit and intention of Education as envisaged by Dr Stead. He was supported by the education committee of the day which included Alderman H Cropper as its chairman, Violet Markham, Florence Robinson, Miss B Eastwood, Dr Stirling, P M Robinson and Edwin Swale among its enlightened members. Harry Mellor was a teacher representative on the Joint Advisory Committee and became the first headmaster of Tapton House School. The basic principle of the four year reconstruction of Chesterfield Education Service was one of universal education, freely provided according to aptitude, ability and need. It was positive: no artificial obstacles: assessment of pupils at 11-plus was not seen as an end but a beginning. The reconstruction covered all the schools in the Borough in every respect including buildings, educational features etc., but the main impact was on the implementation of an integrated and overall strategy for secondary education. In brief, a common core curriculum but each secondary school had a specific and designated role e.g. Violet Markham (Girls) Nursing - Domestic Science .....William Rhodes (Boys) Engineering - Building - Sciences..... Tapton House (Co-ed) Selective Central (Academic - Professional) and freedom of transfer between all the secondary (including local grammar schools) according to educational need and irrespective of geographical residence.

For many years, the system worked well and with great success under the leadership of the Borough Education Officer, Mr A Greenough and various local headmasters - Miss Weniger at Violet Markham - Mr W Stevens at William Rhodes - Mr H Mellor at Tapton House - Mr C Lowe at Hasland - Mr F Crofts at Manor School - Mr F Silcock at Newbold Green and others.

Sadly, the 1960s saw a period of reappraisal and change. Political influences became more apparent in many respects. Earlier understanding and appreciation of the basic educational values inherent in the *Stead* philosophy appear to have been overlooked, lost, mislaid or even ignored. The received impression at the time was that individual school success in its own particular allocated sphere of activity was no longer an acceptable criterion. This factor and the introduction of The Doncaster Plan along with other schemes marked a period of attrition until finally Tapton House was closed in

1991. But, today, with the memoirs included in this book, those of us who were privileged to attend can remember with affection, pride and heartfelt thanks our time spent at Tapton with Tubby Mellor, his staff and those who followed in their steps.

A far-sighted educational concept; Tapton House a purposeful school set in a glorious natural, healthy setting and with a dedicated and caring staff.

A Letter to Barbara

Helen Davidson -The Taptonian 1958

Dear Barbara,

Yesterday I died, or nearly did, and I wanted to tell you all about it. I lay in a white hospital bed with a black rail. When I realised I was going to die I was suddenly frightened and clung on the bed-rail, but it broke and I stumbled into a passage of darkness, yellow-brown and foul as smog. In front of me I saw a light and ran towards it as hard as I could. Soon I came to a beautiful garden which contained everything beautiful I have ever seen - heavy red roses like velvet queens and Chinese laburnums with yellow candles and the grass was wet with rain. I stood on tiptoe and gazed at the garden through the bars of the golden gate.

'It's beautiful, beautiful, as beautiful as heaven', I cried.
'It is heaven', said God who was sitting under a tree.
'But I have seen all these things before!'
'That is why they are here', said God smiling.
'And the wrinkled olives and the blackbirds and the Avon freckled with shadows and laughing with leaves, and Vesuvius, rising from the mist serene, reflected in the satin sea, all mauve and white, and the rain; O please is the rain there too?'
'They are all here', said God. 'The rainbow sweetens the April showers. Tears and smiles are one. Come in. Come in. The garden is yours, you made it'.
'And may I stay here for ever and ever and ever?'
'For ever and ever', said God nodding and smiling.

I pulled open the gate towards me and just as I was going to enter the garden I looked up at the acorns and oak leaves on the gilded carving above me and I thought how much it reminded me of the wrought-iron gates in the garden at Tapton. Then I turned and looked behind me to take a last glimpse of the world below. I saw a great battle on the plain and the earth was strewn with broken chariots and hands and arms and legs everywhere, rank and vile. I heard a hubbub of discordant voices and the strife of steel and the moan of stricken women. They lifted up their eyes to me and wept. And the ships sailed away, over the ocean, full of wailing captive women. And the men who were groaning and wounded were suddenly stiff and cold and their eyes blind and bleeding.

And I thought of my quiet room full of Spring and the blackbirds outside my window.

'Please God, my brothers are unhappy, and their voices are harsh. I too have heard harsh voices and have wept. I do not want to weep again. I would like to remain in the garden for ever, but please God I would like still more to strew the flowers on the earth, and make the world as sweet as music, and see my brothers smile and scent the holy roses'.

'And what if your brothers are blind? Perhaps they will not see the flowers?'
'Do you then give them eyes, father my God, and I will strew their way with roses and make the world as sweet as lilac'.

So saying, I ran into the garden, heaped my arms with flowers, kissed God and promised to return in a little while, and ran out into the pain.

So I came back. But now my flowers seem few and paltry specimens and I keep losing my way and wondering if I shall be able to find my way back to the garden. Sometimes I wonder if the pain was worth while.

But perhaps if I give the world my flowers, unworthy though they are, God will open men's eyes, and they will make gardens of their own far lovelier than mine. And there will be no wailing, there will be no weeping: none of us will ever weep again.

TENAX PROPOSITI

Tapton House Gardens

Gate entrance to forbidden kitchen gardens, now destroyed.

Contributors

Gill Ashley   1949 - 1956

After leaving school she attended Derby Training College until 1958 and taught in Clay Cross, Derby Road and Hasland. Left Derbyshire in 1961 to teach in London and then on to Devon where she taught until 1993. Gill and her husband Danny, formerly of the Civic Theatre, are kept on their toes by an ever-growing McCormack family and also by building their dacha on their mountainside in west Cork, Ireland.

Peter Ashley   1940 - 1945

Leaving school in June 1945, he eventually honoured a family tradition by entering the coal mining industry. After he had worked at several collieries in the Chesterfield area, the mid-fifties found him at the Bolsover headquarters where he strenuously hewed in a rich and inexhaustible seam of paper until 1985. Having helped to raise a family of five, he now devotes his time to exploring the remoter byways of Britain.

Kathleen Barber   1938 - 1941

Started work in 1942 as a junior clerk with Chesterfield Corporation gas department, progressing to shorthand typist, secretary, and senior typist and remained there until 1973. In July of that year transferred to local government as clerk-typist in the parks and cemeteries department where she worked up to senior clerical officer until retirement in 1992.

Barrie Birkin   1956 - 1962 and Jean Stokes   1956 - 1961

Jean worked for the NCB as an audio typist until they had the children in 1969 and she became a full-time mother. Barrie joined his present company of Joseph Clayton & Sons Ltd. in Chesterfield in 1963. This is a tannery making specialised industrial types of leather, but now making more leathers for saddlery, cricket balls, and various hydraulic and polishing leathers.

Pamela Birks   1939 - 1943

Clerical work after Tapton, then a wages supervisor in Worksop. She moved to Worksop with her husband, who was an accountant. They have two children, one is a journalist in Suffolk and their daughter is a language teacher. Unfortunately her husband had to retire through ill health in his early fifties and she cared for him until he died three years ago. She is a member of the WRVS and was invited to meet the Queen last year at a garden party at the WRVS headquarters in Abingdon for which she felt very honoured.

Bill Booker   1959 - 1966

Joined and progressed through Barclays, working in many locations and positions with the most enjoyable being in Organisation and Methods based in south Manchester. Spent the last eight years with them in Credit Control. He took voluntary redundancy in 1995 and spent a year out of work enjoying himself. Now works with British Midland Airways as a Customer Services specialist. He is married to Shirley and has a daughter, Emma.

Susan Bradshaw   1963 - 1969

Trained at Bedford college of PE and became a teacher in Nottingham. Took a year out to see the world. The first and last stop was Spain where the 'one year out' stretched into twelve. A Viking crossed her path in Tenerife, she fell in love (storybook fashion) and moved to Sweden in 1988. She now lives out in the country, south of Stockholm with Janr Olov and their two children (8 and 5 yrs). She has taught English and currently leads fitness/aerobics groups.

Jean Briddon   1936 - 1940

After leaving Tapton, attended Chesterfield Technical College for a secretarial course. She was employed by H White Builders for two years and then went to Shrewsbury as secretary to a group of army officers during the war. Worked for government departments until she moved to Hove, East Sussex, where she ran a business for 10 years. Finally returned to work at Scarsdale Hospital before running the post office at Loundsley Green.

Sheila Burgess   1940 - 1944

On leaving Tapton returned to her family home in Seaford, East Sussex. Met her husband in 1943 and they were married in 1949, but after a brief honeymoon in the Isle of Wight he went to Hong Kong with the RAF, where she later joined him. Returned to the UK in 1952 with two daughters and two sons but travelled widely with the RAF until they left the service in 1970. Retired 1989 after working as a nurse, librarian and medical receptionist.

Tony Cable   1946 - 1951

Worked as a YMCA secretary from 1957 - 1982, beginning his career at Chesterfield with Charles Nunn. He pursued his interests and gifts in music, drama and involvement with young people and worked several Holiday Centres. From 1982 to 1998 he and his wife, Margaret, opened their own guesthouse in Eastbourne where he continued to be involved in drama, writing and producing musicals.

Frank Chettle   1959 - 1965

After graduating in 1939 with BSc (Hons) (London) first class in mathematics, spent the war years weather forecasting for the RAF. After demobilisation taught mathematics in Norwich and Nottingham, where he was head of mathematics dept of the High School. His first headship was at Tapton in 1959 and he was very happy there, but when the school was due to be closed so that it could become Chesterfield Museum (so he was informed), he moved to Redditch County High School in 1965. When he retired in 1979, he and his wife moved back to Chesterfield.

Pamela Clark   1945 - 1949

After leaving Tapton, attended Chesterfield Technical College for a one-year secretarial course. She was then employed in the typing pool at Sheepbridge Company for seven years and Trebor Accounts for four years. Married in 1957 and produced three daughters (one attended Tapton). She organised and supervised Boythorpe pre-school playgroup for 20 years. She is now retired and enjoying gardening, caravanning and Frank Sinatra.

Joan Clarke   1943 - 1947

Joined the BTH after leaving Tapton reluctantly, eventually to become the production manager's secretary, gaining qualifications by attending Chesterfield Technical College. In the late 1960s moved to New Zealand with her husband's job. Worked at the University of Auckland. In the late 1970s moved back to UK. Now lives in rural Wiltshire where she worked as secretary at Lackham College of Agriculture. Has retired except for teaching word processing at Lackham one day/week.

Douglas A Cox   1948 - 1956

On leaving Tapton, he held several senior appointments in comprehensive education before becoming headmaster of a comprehensive school in Staffordshire, where he stayed for seventeen years, retiring in 1982. In retirement his time is taken up with extensive travel, the theatre, concerts, bowling, dancing, Sale Rugby Club, Probus Club, gardening and infrequent household chores.

Bob Doughty   1954 - 1961

Went to Nottingham University to read zoology and gained 2.2 honours degree. Worked for 33.3 years for the Blood Transfusion Service (Sheffield - PhD and Newcastle), finishing as acting chief executive before retiring. Many hobbies including rambling which first started going into the Peak District with Mr Woolhouse, his biology teacher who also had a profound influence on his life.

Sam Dunkerley   1947 - 1955

Spent five and half years in Training Command in the RAF before reaching Tapton in 1947 and was dreadfully sorry to leave in 1955. Appointed to a large department in a technical grammar school in Nuneaton responsible for craft but also art, PE?, music? and domestic science?? Retired to Burton upon Trent in 1955 and with his wife May celebrated their diamond wedding in 1999 - and they are still talking.

D. Durward   1935 - 1938

Worked for private industry until he joined the Royal Navy in 1941 and was demobbed in 1946. Eventually worked in the Post Office as a postal and telegraph officer and had the pleasure of serving Tubby Mellor, on the counter at Chesterfield who always addressed him by name (surname!). He then worked in the Civil Service until his retirement in 1985. He lists his hobbies as 1. Avid reader, 2. Very gentle 'keep fitter', 3. Busy Granddad.

Douglas Gillam   1948 - 1953

Left Tapton to be head of maths at a technical school in Smethwick. Finally settled in Grays, Essex, (15 years as a headmaster). The first head of Grays Comprehensive School built in the 1960s. Continued his interest in drama. Churchwarden at St Boniface Church, Birmingham for several years. Retired from school in 1980 and later moved to Peterborough. Has begun writing his memoirs, covering his life as a prisoner of war in 1943-45.

Fred Goodwin   1931

Joined the glassworks to train as a glass technologist. Continued his education at Sheffield Univ (Saturday's) and Chesterfield Technical College (evenings). Continued to play cricket for the works team and both he and his wife (Eileen Boyce) were keen tennis players. Moved to the North East in 1964 to manage the sister glass factory at Benington on Tyneside. Retired in 1985 and is still a Newcastle United season ticket holder.

Cliff Greaves   1943 - 1946

Started work as a fitter at Summitt Works followed by indentured apprenticeship at BTH. HNC in mechanical engineering in 1953, National Service in RAF to 1955. Renewed engineering work at Bryan Donkins as draughtsman, project engineering and, finally, in buying department. Took voluntary redundancy in 1991 and started degree studies with OU. Graduated in December 1995 with BA (Upper 2nd Class Hons). Married Marion Elizabeth Rankin (Brimington) and they have two sons.

Jackie Green   1968 - 1973

Worked in a bank, which although well paid was incredibly tedious. Married husband at 18. Have two children, Rachael and Joshua, and two grandchildren, Rebekah and Charlotte. Became a Christian in 1979. Trained and worked as a secretary. Now work at a ladies fitness centre in Chesterfield, which I love, as I am very much a 'people' person. I have a lot to be thankful for indeed!

Gaye Hadfield   1967 - 1974

London University honours degree in chemistry in July 1978. MSc in microbiology at Newcastle University and PhD in microbiology at St Mary's Hospital Medical School in 1985. Ten years in the pharmaceutical industry before retiring (?) to have children. Two boys (three and five). Now works part-time as a consultant to the healthcare industries. Married and, apart from the year in Newcastle, has lived in London since she left school.

Roy Hartley   1933 - 1937

Distinction in National Certificate of Commerce. Held positions at Firbeck, Worksop and Clay Cross Co. before emigrating to Australia. Worked with a large motor spares group and retired at 55 with a golden handshake. His present wife shares his love for music and literature, which was fostered during his too-short time at Tapton. Jimmy Routledge, led him to an appreciation of Beethoven, Mozart and many other composers.

Mavis Hill   1940 - 1944

Worked in an office, latterly for the NCB. Married Harry Clough in 1950 and had three sons. She followed her interest in theatre by becoming a founder member of Hasland Theatre Company. She is a past president of Walton Women's Institute and has been involved with the Old Taptonians' Association for many years. She worships at St John's Church Walton where she is a Church Warden.

Norman Hoddle   1936

Joined police service. In 1945 became a student of St Johns College York. Taught in Derby and then William Rhodes School in 1949. Part time lecturer at Chesterfield Technical College and College of Art. Became a student again in wood, pottery and finally history of architecture in Sheffield. Supported various local organisations: Civic Society, Round Table, Derbyshire Historic Building Trust, Eyre Chapel Restoration etc. Ran his own business from 1980 until retirement in 1996.

Roy Houghton   1942 - 1947

Started work as an apprentice mining surveyor but became a fully fledged coal-face worker at Holmewood and Grassmoor Collieries in 1952. Fulfilled first short-term ambition of buying a new car in 1954. Attended Dudley Teachers Training College 1957 - 1959 and taught handicraft locally and in the County. Retired from Violet Markham School in 1991 after 16 years at that establishment.

Doreen M Housley   1940 - 1943

Left school at the age of 14 and worked in various retail shops in town, then at the Royal Hospital as a wages clerk. Married in 1950 and after having two children, obtained a job as a school secretary.   The Headmistress encouraged her to become a teacher so she obtained five O levels and one A level at Chesterfield Technical College, trained at Totley Training College and qualified in 1971. Taught until retirement at the age of 60. Interests are tapestry, cross-stitch embroidery, reading, gardening and crosswords.

Rita Jackson   1944 - 1949

After leaving school she worked in Chesterfield Royal Hospital pharmacy until she married in 1959 and moved to Stafford. Her first son was born there and after moving to Norwich they had two more children, a girl and a boy. Ten years later they moved to Northampton where she spent 24 years in Northamptonshire Library Service. She retired in 1998 and now has seven grandchildren.

Barbara Johnson   1947 - 1954

Started work at Hollingwood County Girls' School in 1956 after two years in a teacher training college. Married in 1959 and moved to Rochdale where she worked for two years until son Simon was born. In 1963 moved to Lincoln and returned to Chesterfield in 1965 to teach at Edmond Street Junior School until 1970. Taught drama and English at Newbold Green School for 20 years to 1990. After spending one year teaching at Brookfield Community School she has been warding off senility with a variety of pursuits, especially theatre.

Tom Jones   1936 - 1940

From school he went to work in a laboratory as an industrial chemist. He then began to supplement his income by writing for magazines. 'Rather foolishly,' at the age of 26, he quit his job and took up writing as a full-time occupation, which didn't work out too well. Gave up the struggle and went into teaching. He enjoyed the life, although it was exhausting. Early retirement enabled him to take pleasure in computer studies.

Merv Lambert   1966 - 1991

Started teaching at Tapton in 1966, finishing as the head of modern languages department. With reorganisation of the schools in Chesterfield in 1991 and the closure of Tapton House School he went to Newbold Community School and took early retirement after two years. Did a final year at Tapton School in Sheffield.

Joyce Marsden   1938 - 1942

Left school hesitantly for banking, it being the best job available at the time; not a good idea. Married Peter Fox (who still feels underprivileged because he didn't go to Tapton). Did some accountancy, then both made a big career move to the canals, converting a pair of traditional narrow boats and running them as a floating hotel. Loved the life despite the incredibly hard work and felt they had found their niche. After 22 years reluctantly sold the boats because of ill health. Now live in Lymington, Hampshire.

Sheila Maycock   1945 - 1949

Left Tapton to start work in the family grocery shop and small bakery due to family pressures. Her father died, so she automatically continued with the shop and taking care of her mother until her death in 1980. She married David Barber (ex-William Rhodes) in 1981. They have since retired and now spend time on their narrow boat exploring the canal system - full stop.

Doug Morris   1937 - 1941

Worked for a short time at Scarsdale Brewery before being apprenticed as a fitter at Bryan Donkins on Derby Road. He was called up in October 1945 and went to India with RAF Maintenance Command and was a sergeant at the handing-back ceremony in September 1947. He carried on working in engineering since then at Rolls-Royce on jet engines and coal preparation plants for Birtley Engineering, and finally retired in 1987.

Malcolm Nicholas   1950 - 1955

After an introduction by Mr Jennings he was articled to a Chesterfield chartered accountant. He qualified in 1963 and commenced practice in 1965, having several Taptonians as clients. He sold the partnership in 1994 and in semi-retirement now enjoys, amongst other things, holidays, walking and watching cricket. He married in 1968 and has a son and daughter.

Robert B Nightingale 1932 - 1935

Left Tapton to work in the building trade from 1935 until 1938 when he joined His Majesty's Forces and fought for king and country until demobilisation in 1946. After the war he continued in the building industry as a builder and decorator and finally retired in 1981. He left for the Isle of Wight in 1997 and now lives in a lovely spot called Freshwater.

Joan Norman   1937 - 1941

Worked at Grassmoor colliery in the wages department. Joined the GTC and took part in firewatching activities during the rest of the war. In 1946 she got engaged to Ray Newton and they were married in 1948, after his return from the army. They celebrated their golden wedding anniversary last year. They have one son, David Paul born in 1951. She has been a member of the Hasland Mothers Union for over 40 years and still meets friends from Tapton days.

Elizabeth Pearson   1960 - 1967

Continued her studies at Chesterfield College of Art where she met her husband John. Then in 1971 graduated from Ravensbourne College of Art and Design at Bromley, south London, and took up her first job as a junior designer with Ladybird. Spent the next 20 years designing for rag trade companies, including Courtaulds and Viyella, and setting up Hawk Racewear with her husband, and bringing up their two sons Jonathan and Simon. Started teaching just like her Dad after completing a Post Graduate Certificate of Education in 1992.

Brian Quartermain   1943 - 1952 and Joan Lancaster 1944 - 1951

Brian did national service in the RAF on leaving Tapton, then studied physics at Leeds University. The next thirty years encompassed a series of teaching posts (school, college and polytechnic including Chesterfield Technical College) interspersed with ones involving engineering research and consultancy. Married Joan in 1957 and have a son Alan. After attending Avery Hill Training College, London, in 1951, Joan taught in several local schools until she retired in 1989.

Harry Routledge   1932 - 1972 (except for war years)

He retired with Hazel, his wife, to Bakewell in 1972. They were very comfortable in their home with 1/3 of an acre of garden to keep them busy. Due primarily to asthma problems they had to leave Bakewell and now reside in a bungalow in Darley Dale. He says he is extremely fortunate in having Hazel to look after him, and they celebrated 48 years of married bliss last March. At the age of 90 Harry is doing remarkably well and putting a lot of Old Taptonians to shame with his writing for our benefit.

Smudger Smith   1932 - 1935

Worked at Chesterfield Golf Club. Signed up for 12 years during the war and came through it practically unscathed after service in India, Assam, Burma, Singapore, French Indo-China and returned to Southampton in June 1946. Posted to Palestine followed by Cyprus and finally demobbed at May 1948. Married at Christmas 1948 but had to return to war in Korea until Christmas 1951. Worked at De Havilland Aircraft until retirement. Never a dull moment with his second wife, two daughters, nine grandchildren and one great-grandchild.

George Tagg   1936 - 1940

Started work as an apprentice fitter at Sheepbridge in June 1940, a few days after sitting his final exam. Joined both the Home Guard and the ATC. In 1941 he was accepted as a junior engineer in the Merchant Navy and started a four-year series of voyages around the world. Returned to a variety of engineering jobs until retirement in 1989. Enjoys photography and playing cricket.

Peter Wagstaffe   1947 - 1954

He left Tapton in 1954 and after graduating from Cardiff University, where he continued his interest in drama, taught English in various London schools (producing the plays, naturally!) until retirement in 1990. He lives in Wimbledon with his French wife - and a number of screenplays (as yet unsold!)

Roger Webb   1949 - 1955

Planning department at the Tube Works, then Royal Air Force for five years as a photographer and later, as a lithographer. Accounts of his adventures in the RAF are detailed in his book entitled As You Were, published in 1997. Over 24 years working as a histologist (chief technician), retiring at 50 as part of a plan devised by a well known Prime Minister. He fells trees, restores machinery, makes video films; keen gardener and walker (finished the coast to coast last year). Lives in Holmesfield.

Ann Wheatcroft

Born in Chesterfield, now lives in Hay-on-Wye, but still regards Chesterfield as home. Mother and Ann built up their interests in horses and ponies with much help and encouragement from Aunt Phil Wildin and Dorothy Lowe. Has a successful farm, breeding ponies, exports them world-wide and is an international senior judge. Council member and past president of the Welsh Pony & Cob Society. She has had two stallions, the property of HM The Queen, standing at her stud. Opera is her other great love along with singing, music and theatre.

Marion Yeldham   1951 - 1956

Worked in the accounts department from 1953 - 1963 at what is now Trebor Bassett in Chesterfield. In 1963, joined the Post Office, working in various sections of their finance headquarters in Chesterfield. From 1972 to 1995 specialised in pension administration for the Post Office. Took early retirement in 1995 to pursue interests of walking, family history and botanical illustration.